The Preamble *and* Mission *of the* Constitution

This book is part of the Peter Lang Humanities list.
Every volume is peer reviewed and meets
the highest quality standards for content and production.

PETER LANG
New York • Bern • Berlin
Brussels • Vienna • Oxford • Warsaw

Michael J C Taylor

The Preamble *and* Mission *of the* Constitution

PETER LANG
New York • Bern • Berlin
Brussels • Vienna • Oxford • Warsaw

Library of Congress Cataloging-in-Publication Data

Names: Taylor, Michael J. C. (Michael Julian Christopher), author.
Title: The preamble and the mission of the Constitution / Michael J C Taylor.
Description: New York: Peter Lang, 2019.
Includes bibliographical references and index.
Identifiers: LCCN 2018034709 | ISBN 978-1-4331-5835-3 (hardcover: alk. paper)
ISBN 978-1-4331-5836-0 (ebook pdf) | ISBN 978-1-4331-5837-7 (epub)
ISBN 978-1-4331-5838-4 (mobi)
Subjects: LCSH: Constitutional law—United States—Philosophy.
Constitutional history—United States. | Constitutions—United States.
Federal government—United States. | United States—Politics and government.
Classification: LCC KF4550.T39 2019 | DDC 342.73—dc23
LC record available at https://lccn.loc.gov/2018034709
DOI 10.3726/b14294

Bibliographic information published by **Die Deutsche Nationalbibliothek.**
Die Deutsche Nationalbibliothek lists this publication in the "Deutsche Nationalbibliografie"; detailed bibliographic data are available on the Internet at http://dnb.d-nb.de/.

29 Broadway, 18th floor, New York, NY 10006
www.peterlang.com

This work is dedicated with love
to my beloved wife Bonnie Sue Taylor (1964–2016)
who gave to me love and encouragement for 29 wonderful years.

Contents

Permissions

This work contains material from the following published works:

1984 by George Orwell. Copyright © 1983 by Houghton-Mifflin-Harcourt, Inc. Used by permission of the publisher.

A Machine That Would Go of Itself: the Constitution in American Culture by Michael Kammen. Copyright © 1986 by St. Martin's Press. Used by permission of the publisher.

Active Liberty Interpreting Our Democratic Constitution by Stephen Breyer. Copyright © 2005 by Alfred A. Knopf. Used by permission of the publisher.

Cato's Letters, or Essays on Liberty, Civil and Religious, and Other Important Subjects (Two volumes) by John Trenchard and Thomas Gordon, edited by Ronald Hamowy. Copyright © 1995 by The Liberty Fund. Used by permission of the publisher.

Commentaries on the Laws of England (4 volumes) by William Blackstone, edited by William Draper Lewis. Copyright © 2004 by the Lawbook Exchange. Reprint of 1922 edition. Used by permission of the publisher.

Democracy in America (Two volumes) by Alexis de Tocqueville, edited by Phillips Bradley. Copyright © 1990 by Vintage Books. Used by permission of the publisher.

Discourses Concerning Government by Algernon Sidney, edited by Thomas G. West. Copyright © 1996 by The Liberty Fund. Used by permission of the publisher.

Feudal Society (2 volumes) by Marc Bloch, edited by L. A. Manyon. Copyright © 1961 by Phoenix Books/University of Chicago Press. Used by permission of the publisher.

Founding Fathers: Brief Lives of the Framers of the United States Constitution by M. E. Bradford. Copyright © 1981 by the University of Kansas Press. 1994 Reprint. Used by permission of the publisher.

Friends of the Constitution: Writings of the "Other" Federalists edited by Colleen A. Sheehan and Gary L. MacDowell. Copyright © 1998 by The Liberty Fund. Used by permission of the publisher.

George Washington: A Collection edited by W. B. Allen. Copyright © 1988 by The Liberty Fund. Used by permission of the publisher.

History of the Peloponnesian War by Thucydides, translated by Rex Warner. Copyright © 1972 by Penguin Books. Used by permission of the publisher.

Leviathan by Thomas Hobbes, edited by Richard Tuck. Copyright © 1996 by Cambridge University Press. Used by permission of the publisher.

Lincoln: Speeches and Writings 1859–1865 by Abraham Lincoln, edited by Don E. Fahrenbacher. Copyright © 1989 by the Literary Classics of the United States, Inc. Used by permission of the publisher.

Man and the State by Jacques Maritan. Copyright © 1951 by The Catholic University of America Press. Used by permission of the publisher.

Nations and Nationalism by Ernest Gellner. Copyright © 1983 by Cornell University Press. Used by permission of the publisher.

Notes of Debates in the Federal Constitution of 1787 by James Madison. Copyright © 1966 by Ohio University Press. 1985 reprint. Used by permission of the publisher.

On Duties by Cicero, edited by M. T. Griffin and E. M. Atkings. Copyright © 1991 by the Cambridge University Press. Used by permission of the publisher.

On the Good Life by Cicero, edited by Michael Grant. Copyright © 1971 by Penguin Books. Used by permission of the publisher.

Original Meanings: Politics and Ideas in the Making of the Constitution by Jack N. Rakove. Copyright © 1997 by Vintage Books. Used by permission of the publisher.

Political Writings by Voltaire, edited by David Williams. Copyright © 1994 by Cambridge University Press. Used by permission of the publisher.

Rome and the Mediterranean by Livy, translated by Henry Bettenson. Copyright © 1976 by Penguin Books. Used by permission of the publisher.

Social Contract edited by Ernest Barker. Copyright © 1960 by Oxford University Press. Used by permission of the publisher.

Speeches and Writings 1832–1858 by Abraham Lincoln, edited by Roy P. Basler. Copyright © 1989 by the Literary Classics of the United States, Inc. Used by permission of the publisher.

The Agricola and The Germania by Tacitus, edited by Harold Mattingly. Copyright © 1970 by Penguin Books. Used by permission of the publisher.

The Anti-Federalist: Writings by the Opponents of the Constitution edited by Herbert Storing. Copyright © 1981 by the University of Chicago Press. Used by permission of the publisher.

The Canterbury Tales by Geoffrey Chaucer, edited by R. M. Lumiansky. Copyright © 1971 by the Washington Square Press. Used by permission of the publisher.

The Creation of the American Republic, 1776–1787 by Gordon S. Wood. Published for the Omohundro Institute of Early American History and Culture. Copyright © 1970 by the University of North Carolina Press; new preface copyright © 1998 by the University of North Carolina Press. Used by permission of the publisher.

The Early History of Rome by Livy. Translated by Aubrey De Sélincourt. Copyright © 1960 by Penguin Books. Used by permission of the publisher.

The Federalist (The Gideon Edition) by James Madison, Alexander Hamilton, and John Jay, edited by George W. Carey and James McClellan. Copyright © 2001 by The Liberty Fund. Used by permission of the publisher.

The Founders' Constitution (5 volumes) edited by Philip B. Kurland and Ralph Lerner. Copyright © 1987 by The Liberty Fund. 2000 reprint. Used by permission of the publisher.

The Golden Bough by James Gregory Frazier. Copyright © 1922 by Collier Books, 1922. Used by permission of the publisher.

The Growth of the Law by Benjamin Nathan Cardozo. Copyright © 1924 by Yale University Press. Used by permission of the publisher.

The Histories by Herodotus, edited by John M. Marincola. Copyright © 1972 by The Penguin Group. Used by permission of the publisher.

The History of English Law Before the Time of Edward I (2 Volumes) by Frederick Pollard and Frederic William Maitland. Copyright © 1923 by Cambridge University Press. Used by permission of the publisher.

The History of the Kings of Britain by Geoffrey of Monmouth, edited by Lewis Thorpe. Copyright © 1966 by Penguin Books. Used by permission of the publisher.

The Nature of the Universe by Lucretius, edited by Ronald Latham. Copyright © 1951 by Penguin Books. Used by permission of the publisher.

The Papers of Benjamin Franklin (Volume IV) edited by Leonard B. Larabee. Copyright © 1961 by Yale University Press. Used by permission of the publisher.

The Papers of George Mason (3 volumes) edited by Robert A. Rutland. Copyright © 1970 by University of North Carolina Press. Used by permission of the publisher.

The Politics by Aristotle, edited by T. A. Sinclair. Copyright © 1962 by Penguin Books, 1992 reprint. Used by permission of the publisher.

The Republic by Plato, translated by Francis Cornford. Copyright © 1941 by Oxford University Press. Used by permission of the publisher.

The Revolutionary Writings of John Adams edited by C. Bradley Thompson. Copyright © 2000 by The Liberty Fund. Used by permission of the publisher.

The Rights of Man by Thomas Paine. Copyright © 1995 by Oxford University Press. Used by permission of the publisher.

The Rights of War and Peace (3 volumes) by Hugo Grotius, edited by Richard Tuck. Copyright © 2005 by The Liberty Fund. Used by permission of the publisher.

The Social Contract and Other Later Political Writings by Jean-Jacques Rousseau, edited by C. D. H. Cole. Copyright © 1973 by Charles E. Tuttle Co., Inc. Used by permission of the publisher.

The Social Contract and Other Later Political Writings by Jean-Jacques Rousseau, edited by Victor Gourevitch. Copyright © 1996 by Cambridge University Press. Used by permission of the publisher.

The Spirit of the Laws by Baron de Montesquieu, edited by Anne Cohler, Basia Miller, and Harold Stone. Copyright © 1989 by Cambridge University Press. Used by permission of the publisher.

The Twelve Caesars by Suetonius, translated by Robert Graves. Copyright © 1957 by Penguin Books. 1989 reprint. Used by permission of the publisher.

Thomas Jefferson: Writings edited by Merrill D. Peterson. Copyright © 1984 by Literary Classics of the United States, Inc. Used by permission of the publisher.

Two Treatises on Government by John Locke, edited by Peter Laslett. Copyright © 1960 by Cambridge University Press. Used by permission of the publisher.

View of the Constitution of the United States, with Selected Writings by St. George Tucker, edited by Clyde N. Wilson. Copyright © 1999 by The Liberty Fund. Used by permission of the publisher.

We the People: Foundations by Bruce Ackerman. Copyright © 1991 by The Belknap Press of Harvard University Press. Used by permission of the publisher.

Witness at the Creation: Hamilton, Madison, Jay, and the Constitution by Richard B. Morris. Copyright © 1985 by Henry Holt and Company, Inc. Used by permission of the publisher.

Preface

This book is not a chronology of the Constitution's construction: It is an exegesis upon the abstract ideas the Framers studied, and which were later incorporated into the governing document of the American nation. The methodology is clearly evident: the evolution of historical, legal and philosophical concepts into concrete expression. Its purpose is to discern the original intent of those who constructed it by utilizing their own words, along with a careful examination of the works they cited as inspiration. For more than two decades the Framers' path of knowledge has been traversed by this historian to contemplate with accuracy the lessons they gleaned from the past; to ruminate upon the Enlightenment philosophies they often quoted; and, to reflect upon their expressions within the context of the purpose of government. This was done to conclude their essential objective for the charter at the heart of the American republic.

The Constitution of the United States is a social contract, a legal instrument which constructed a specific system of governance. As in all legally binding contracts, the Preamble is the mission statement of the document. It portrays in clear terms its goals, as well as its aspirations. Therefore, it is crucial that all parties to the agreement—in this case the citizens and the government of the United States—to comprehend the intellectual depth of the clauses presented, as they demarcate the contract's perimeters and limitations. Rather than being a collection of legal statutes, the Constitution is a structure of government: A construct of the branches and a delineation of their powers. With allegiance to this contract, the citizen is guaranteed specific political privileges, which are termed 'rights'.

But what exactly are 'rights' and the people's responsibilities to them?

Within the Greek model with citizenship came responsibilities. The Athenians adopted popular democracy as their form of government to free themselves from a wealthy oligarchy. Under Solon's constitution every citizen played a role in the city's essential business. In turn, anyone who conspired against the state, or who made the effort to gain political power for themselves alone, to benefit themselves at the cost of everyone else, lost their citizenship rights. Thus, a citizen's freedom of action was placed within the strict perimeters of what was best for the wellbeing of the state, as dictated by its laws.

The Romans viewed liberty as the outgrowth of the civil law. Adopting the same ideology as the Greeks, they believed government was the sole institution capable of guarding against intrusions upon their essential rights as Roman citizens. What Americans today regard as 'rights', the Romans termed as 'virtue', which to them meant the liberty of action which ran concurrent with the wellbeing of society. Thus the focus of Roman law and politics was the stability of the state, rather than the freedom of the individual, for if the former declined and fell the latter would be of little consequence.

Within the purview of British law, according to Sir William Blackstone, the concept of liberty had a specific definition: It consisted of acting in tandem with what the laws of the realm permitted. As such, rights were meant to guarantee citizens security, for while the law stood staid and obdurate, human nature was controlled by the fear of ostracism and punishment under the laws. Thus, in each scenario the citizen's individual rights went concurrent with their responsibility towards the realm.

Each of these paradigms the Framers knew well and revered, and used them as the model of the federal constitution they constructed during that hot summer in Philadelphia.

This work was also meant to dissuade the popular notion the Constitution was the product of ordinary men who sought to govern themselves. They were children of the Enlightenment, among the most perceptive and well-educated men of their time. Nearly all of the books they read were deemed unfit by the British government, as they questioned accepted paradigms of sovereignty and governance. They also held the firm belief government was to serve the public good, and the proper distribution of power between separate branches provided protection from corruption.

During the 1787 constitutional convention, the Framers voiced their concerns for the very issues which afflict our country over 230 years later. It was not that they possessed a crystal ball, it was that they had seriously contemplated history and, thus, understood those who did not learn from it would inevitably repeat it. They also discussed political philosophy and law; confronted one another both in person and in a series of newspaper editorials; and, in the end, came to a compromise which forged a charter of government that remains the essential law of the land. Though they themselves were products of eighteenth century social norms and mores—and would not have personally agreed with specific tenets of our modern culture—they nonetheless accepted the innovations of an ever-evolving civilization, for the document they designed allowed it to flow and change with the progression of American society.

Whereas the Framers envisioned America as an enlightened society of continued learning and innovation, over time it has devolved into one which has all but rejected books and ideas. Rather than growing together into a nation one and indivisible, Americans have become divided and suspect of compromise. We afford respect based upon the quantity of possessions rather than the quality of character. Thus, we are a country which has forgotten the vital principles upon which it was founded.

For the United States of America to regain the Framers' dream we, the people must prove ourselves worthy of it. We must embrace the lessons of history, the visions of philosophical thought, while shedding the delusion of partisan dogma. The Constitution was the gift of our ancestors who saw more in us than we now see in ourselves. We in our time are the keepers of this vision. This book is a journey to reclaim that national legacy, in which we must be engaged if this country is to be what the Framers envisioned for us.

Michael J C Taylor, PhD
30 June 2018

Acknowledgments

I would like to take this opportunity to thank everyone who has contributed to the completion of this book: the culmination of over two decades of research, reflection, and composition:

The members of my doctoral committee at the University of Missouri Kansas City. Dr. Patrick Peebles' for his diligence in the consistency of methodology. For his insistence on detail, I thank Dr. Dale Neumann for instilling within me the penchant to never follow the path of least resistance in research. To Dr. Curtis Hancock for his expert instruction in modern political philosophy that broadened my understanding and interest in the abstract ideas which have motivated politics—especially of those within the Constitution.

To Dr. Ed Beasley, a storyteller whose tales were unforgettable, I am a historian due to his extraordinary example.

Fr. Ed Burger, S.J. of Rockhurst University, for his colloquium course on the great historians that fostered a love for the practitioners of my chosen craft. And to Dr. Monte Piliawsky, Dr. John Gazda, Dr. Fred O'Grady, Prof. Hugh Owens, Dr. Charles Moran, and Dr. Max Skidmore, all of whom unselfishly offered their expertise, advice and friendship.

To my colleagues from Dickinson State University, Dr. Stephen Doherty and Dr. Frank Varney; from Bemidji State University, Dr. Tom Murphy and

Dr. Brendan McManus; and, from Paine College, Robert Jones and Dr. André Key.

To my friends Sylvia Pryor Nicol, Stephen Barncard, Keith Keller, Bill Pryor, Michael McQuary, Samuel Tanner, Rod Merkel, Karol Heim, John Cancilla and Gregory Wilson, I am grateful for your thoughtful contributions to this work and for your ever-loyal camaraderie.

Also my gratitude to two important scholars who had a profound impact upon my work and intellectual development: David Atkinson and Gary Bedell. There were few people whose company I enjoyed more than Dr. Atkinson. His extensive knowledge of the U.S. Supreme Court, coupled with his understanding of the political environment in which it operated, made for intriguing and lengthy conversations. What he taught me as to constitutional interpretation is evident within this work. Dr. Bedell's insights into the connection between philosophy and humanity contributed tremendously to my own philosophical underpinnings. Your presence and inventive intellect are sorely missed!

To Mrs. Arlene Porter, the elementary school teacher who introduced me to history and fostered my affinity for it. I hope I have made her proud.

To Mrs. Rebecca Wood, Mr. Nick Beardshear and Mr. Max Putz, three of my high school teachers, for it was they who opened the door to my passion for lifelong learning.

To Dr. Louis Potts whose contributions to my comprehension of constitutional history has made me a better historian. It was his penchant for detail and immersion in the primary sources which have justly influenced this work. Also, through his excellent example I learned how to be an effective classroom professor.

To Dr. Herman Hattaway, my sincere thanks for being the finest demonstration of all a scholar and mentor should be. Despite his own often hectic schedule, he was always generous with his time and constructive with his advice. Following the completion of my doctoral studies in May 2001, he became among of my most cherished friends. It is my goal in life to write history as fluid as he.

To my son Christopher, a young man of intelligence and integrity who has borne a tremendous burden with grace and dignity. I am proud of him and grateful for our close friendship. His troubles despite his innocence made vital the need for this work.

Finally, my sincere gratitude and respect for the two amazing women without whom this work would have neither been undertaken, nor had reached fruition. For my beloved wife of 29 years Bonnie who at the deepest ebb of my despair urged me to seek solace in undertaking this project. As my Bon-Bon sadly passed away on 13 July 2016, it saddens me she did not live to see this work in its completed form, as it would have made her smile.

To Mary Ellen Brooks who shone her loving light into my grieving heart and insisted I complete this book. Mary has blessed my life in more ways than I can count, and for which she has garnered both my sincere esteem and permanent affection. She is my inspiration, best friend and my future. It is clear without these two extraordinary women this moment would not have been possible, and for which I shall always be grateful.

Prologue: "We, the People of the United States"

Political Sovereignty and Its Influence on American Constitutionalism

The moral legitimacy of governing has been a concern since human beings first gathered together in groups. With the initial confrontation between a tribal head and his challenger this conduit of dominance emerged as the essential utility of social politics. Whether a commune of nomads or a complex interrelation of regions, political leadership cannot exist without the undisputed mantle of appropriate jurisdiction. Sovereignty is the source of personal deference, and at its lowest ebb a willful challenge to its authority will result in tyranny. Using an artistic analogy, the elements of the decision-making process are as pigments in an artist's portrait: Each triumph being the depth of blue in the heavens, while the degree of tribulation are the darkened hues within the tempest, all created by deliberate brushstrokes.

It is reasonable, therefore, to conclude any proper definition of government encompasses more than mere political administration. It must focus upon the enigma of authority amongst those chosen to rule along with the rightful means of ascent. Ethicists Daniel C. Maguire and A. Nicholas Fargnoli argued though people with social commonalties gather together in communities for their mutual protection, the legitimate placement of sovereignty is at the heart of the civil religion which binds societies together.[1] Nearly five centuries ago a transition began with the undisputed rule of a sovereign derived from either force or divine command, and evolved into a sovereignty of political equals derived from their consent.

As a product of Enlightenment, the United States of America has been a nation with an identity crisis. Its governing charter established a republic in which representatives made decisions for their constituents, yet they insist their government is a democracy in which they themselves governed.[2] While constituents expect their central government be fully empowered to protect national interests and provide unity for the several separate states, this same electorate preferred the preponderance of political power be placed at state and local levels. Americans also demanded efficacy and efficiency based upon the will of a fragmented people with differing precepts of public policy. A nation constructed upon constituent consensus is one whose existence is precarious. Rather than pursuing policies beneficial to its entire population, a democracy often seeks advantage for a few carefully selected sectors within it. Instead of forgoing a unified national agenda, democracy is gagged by the dictates of partisan political maneuver. All the while citizens display a pride in a government document they know precious little of.

There are problems inherent between political parties whose agendas represent specifically defined ideologies who claim legitimacy by mobilizing citizens to their cause through exaggeration and patriotic fervor. During his travels throughout the United States during the 1830s, French diplomat Alexis de Tocqueville concluded American nationalism was a consequence of democracy, its citizens playing a "spirited part in the government of society."[3] Rather than a government based upon class and privilege, it was founded upon the mandate of its constituents, as registered by their votes cast in a free election. Thus the key element of American democracy was legitimacy. Tocqueville also observed such loyalty was not the by-product of popular participation; rather, that Americans looked upon "the fortune of the public as his own, and he labors for the good of the state, not merely from a sense of pride or duty, but from what I venture to term cupidity."[4] If a group shared a common descent, language, culture, and history, and inhabit a fixed territory under one government, can a democracy cultivate and buttress these attributes within a fragmented society?

In his book *Nations and Nationalism* social anthropologist Ernest Gellner theorized citizens could, as Tocqueville recognized in the 1830s, concurrently identify with their nation-state and be capable of envisioning a condition in which government was not present.[5] Gellner argued nationalism was defined by the "striving to make culture and polity congruent, to endow a culture with its own political roof."[6] The reason for this was a nationalism based upon similitude by design.[7] Such conditions were established when a community standardized its traditions in a manner which ensured self-perpetuation.[8] When such circumstances were met the identification with the nation-state was natural, "the conditions of life are such as to make the idea seem compelling, rather than, as it is in most other situations, absurd."[9] Concurrently, the foremost danger to the nation-state was the incremental absorbing of power by the military, its politicians and special interests who seek it for their own advantage.[10] Gellner concluded a nation cannot long survive without the state, for it was government which executed the laws that reinforced its mores, traditions, and values.

The question of who should rule and the source of such authority has vexed the soul of Western civilization since its inception. Pondering the nature of government has occupied the most fertile minds without having either penetrated its unyielding mystery, or conquered its intellectual depths. It has inspired philosophical treatises, sparked innumerable debates, and has been at the heart of political parties and the laws they pushed to establish. Four centuries before the advent of Christianity the philosopher Plato and his student Aristotle argued over which political system was the most efficient and just, and provided western civilization with its foundational political concepts.

The divine right of monarchs has its base in the premise a God or gods had predestined specific human beings to wield supreme executive authority over the masses, with a display of supernatural strength or wisdom as demonstrated by Greek and Roman mythology. According to mythologist Sir James George Frazier, "so long as men look at their gods as being akin to themselves and not raised to an unapproachable height above them, they believe it to be possible for those of their own number who surpass their fellows to attain to the divine rank after death or even in life."[11] This adage was illustrated by the tale of Perseus who, to obtain his position as the rightful heir to the throne of Argos, had to claim superiority in every task set before him by the deities of Mount Olympus.[12] The hero's task was to obtain the head of the gorgon Medusa and defeat the sea monster released by the god Poseidon. Once he had accomplished these challenges, Perseus attained his kingdom, married his queen Andromeda, and forged a legend to be passed down through the generations.[13]

A further example was King Arthur, who captured the interest and imagination of historians and writers from Geoffrey of Monmouth in the twelfth century to Robin Collingwood in contemporary times. As for Arthur's importance as a leader, historian Geoffrey Ashe surmised he assumed the throne at a time when the country had endured usurpation and pillage, and the populace divided against itself, afterwards he united the people and came to embody all that was understood to be 'British'.[14] Arthur was born of the Countess Ygerna and King Uther

Pendragon, and at age 15 he was chosen King after he had drawn his father's sword which was embedded in an anvil.[15] Through a combination of bravery and generosity he emerged as a powerful, but respected leader of men. Geoffrey of Monmouth wrote Arthur became so influential "even the men of noblest birth, once he was roused to rivalry, thought nothing at all of himself unless he wore his arms and dressed in the same way as Arthur's knights."[16] Frazier contended in the stories of Perseus and Arthur there was a common maxim: They were leaders who were envisioned by their countrymen to be a mixture of both king and god.[17]

In the era of the Roman Empire the divine right of monarchs was pivotal to the political cohesion of an ever-sprawling collection of conquered territories. Because the conquered inevitably challenged the sovereign authority of the conqueror, an ancient ruler had to assume a mantle of divinity for practical political reasons: A conquered people would not so readily take up arms against a king who would bring about divine retribution. In his introduction to Tacitus' *The Agricola*, historian Harold Mattingly detailed the interrelationship of theology and power politics within the figure of the Roman emperor:

> As pontifex maximus (chief priest) he was head of the state religion. While he lived Rome sacrificed only to his genius (spirit); but in the provinces he was actually worshipped as a god. After death, unless memory was condemned, he was consecrated, became Divus (the divine), and received full religious honors.[18]

The Roman historian Suetonius testified to the validity of this axiom in the tale of the praetor who, at the cremation of the Emperor Augustus, attested to the Caesar's spirit ascending into the heavens out of the flames.[19] Nearly three centuries later Emperor Constantine was eulogized by his biographer Eusebius as being comparable to Christ.[20]

Roman history is filled with potent examples which demonstrate the political necessity of a sovereignty based upon divine right. In his introduction to the second volume of Livy's *History of Rome*, historian R. M. Oglivie contended during its peak the political power of the Roman Republic was monopolized by patricians who had descended from those who had been members of the Senate during the time of the Etruscan rulers.[21] In *The Histories*, Tacitus revealed in his account of the Emperor Galba, in offering a political confidante a commission as principate, the ruler justified his status as being a divine calling to power.[22] Tacitus revealed Governor Mucianus of Syria implored the Emperor Vaspasian to accept the position as the will of the gods.[23] Historian Norman Cantor asserted sovereignty of this category had potent benefits: If there be but one god to rule the heavens, there should be but one king under his wise providence to rule the earth.[24] Cantor explained this notion as a form of monotheism within the realm of politics.[25]

This was the vital point of Saint Augustine of Hippo's treatise *The City of God*, in which government was premised upon realistic necessity rather than moral obligation.[26] In contrast with the classical Greek thinkers who viewed human society as a necessary purgatory where spiritual purification was achieved, St. Augustine asserted the goals of civilization were noble, though the means were often the opposite.[27] He insisted political perfection was hopeless due to human nature based upon avarice and greed.[28] Democratic regimes were an integral element of this discord, for such a government was nothing more than rule by self-aggrandizing thieves who sought to plunder the people they govern under the guise of political principle.[29] St. Augustine asserted the best form of government that could be achieved on Earth was a rule by Christian emperors, for it would be they who would administrate the law with justice without being prone to fall under the influence of the toadyism of minions.[30]

St. Thomas Aquinas agreed with St. Augustine's reasoning.[31] His view was based upon the Aristotelian philosophy of natural law, in which morality and society was normal to the human condition and an objective and universal moral code based upon human nature exists.[32] Aquinas contended practical politics was an interrelationship between heavenly and earthly authorities, and though he acceded to Augustine's concept of the Christian emperor, and contended so long as such a ruler never deviated from biblical principles, as well as the law, the likelihood of tyranny was removed.[33] Though Aquinas had based his theology upon the philosophy of Aristotle, his philosophy of politics was similar to Plato. Democracy was untrustworthy for it fostered dissent which ran counter to the social good.[34] St. Augustine and St. Thomas Aquinas represented the philosophical underpinnings of the divine right of monarchs in the transition from the Roman to medieval society. The success or failure of a ruler was prefaced by his ability to create the perception of a divine hand guiding his actions. Historian Norman Cantor theorized Medieval monarchs themselves played a large part in preserving these philosophical traditions by their adaptation of the old Roman codes of law which influenced governments in medieval times to act accordingly.[35]

A potent example of its successful use was the British monarch Henry II. The first Plantagenet ruled, as per his biographer Richard Barber, with an air about which suggested a king of divine origin who often sacrificed himself to the public good.[36] Barber theorized the bulk of Henry's success as a king was in his ability not only to effectively utilize his political power, but also through his application of both the divine prestige of his office along with the popular resurrection of the

Arthurian legends of which he himself laid claim to.[37] Later examples of the successful use of divine prestige within the British monarchy were the reigns of King Edward I, King Edward III, and Queen Elizabeth I.

An illustration of its unsuccessful use was the English monarch Edward II, of which historical opinions are unanimous his reign was a failure.[38] Throughout his rule Edward II was disinterested in the conduct of government, prone to favoritism in his choice of ministers, and ineffective in the defense of his country. However the most damaging to him as the ruler of the nation was the popular image Edward possessed amongst his subjects as being a coward.[39] His reign ended with an uprising led by a triumvirate consisting of his queen, her lover and the king's own son. Later examples of the unsuccessful use of divine prestige within the British monarchy were the reigns of King Richard II, Queen Mary I, and King Charles I.

The fourteenth century English author and poet Geoffrey Chaucer reflected upon the nature of sovereignty in *The Canterbury Tales*. Though a literary work focused on a pilgrimage to the shrine of St. Thomas Becket at Canterbury, the author revealed his attitudes regarding medieval English politics, and specifically the divine right of monarchs. In both "The Knight's Tale" and "The Man of Law's Tale," Chaucer conveyed the reciprocal nature of sovereignty in which he claimed kings gained their moral and political ascendancy from God, for "he can make of an individual in his own way whatever he desires."[40] To clarify this point, in his initial tale the Knight told of a "worthy Duke" who, because of his wise and unselfish rule, was "crowned with laurels as a conqueror" and "lived all his life in joy and honor."[41] Chaucer imbued his Knight with a second tale in which he passed judgment on an ignoble lord who ruled by his own vanity.[42] The moral of "The Knight's Tale" was rather than the means justifying the ends, the means *dictated* the ends. Though God had given a ruler a sacred trust, it did not decree a ruler to govern with providence. For reasons the will of the monarch preordained the fate of a nation, in "The Man of Law's Tale" Chaucer concluded it was "only right that a man himself follows the rules he sets for other people's behavior."[43]

What Chaucer alluded to was the basic premise of *Magna Carta*. In June 1215, following two years of restive negotiations with his barons, King John issued a royal charter which guaranteed specific rights to the nobility. The document limited the fiscal powers of the king, as well as his ability to punish any subject beyond what was prescribed by law. In return the barons did not challenge the authority of the courts whose judges were appointed by the monarch. With this document the absolute power of a monarch was replaced by the rule of law, for though a monarch may rule by divine right, he must adhere to the authority and permanence of law. Whether Chaucer, writing over a century-and-a-half later, had studied the document is unclear, but his writings reflect a popular sentiment in favor of this most basic assumption.

The rights and privileges embodied within *Magna Carta* were a transfer of power from its apex downwards rather than emanating from its base upwards. This instance demonstrated the most inherent flaw of the divine right of monarchs: In the contractual obligation of a monarch to rule it was inevitable the ruler becomes separated from the people he governs. Philosopher Jacques Maritan, in his book *Man and the State*, argued such aloofness was "truly and genuinely required only as an *existential* status or condition for the *exercise* of the right to govern."[44] Because the genus of political sovereignty carried with it the threat of tyranny, historians, political scientists and philosophers have reasoned the transition from the divine right of monarchs to popular sovereignty was an obvious attempt to rectify this problem. If power was checked by a popular mechanism, the threat of tyranny was lessened or eliminated.

In a further example historian Michael Grant argued the Emperor Augustus attained his position through the realization that following a century of political strife and civil war, Roman citizens would welcome the stability of one-man rule so long as it was cloaked in the visage of republicanism and tradition.[45] During this period the Senate had become dysfunctional due to personal agendas and the infighting among its members which had run rife for over a century. It had weakened the body to impotency and necessitated a central source of sovereign authority. The Roman poet Lucretius bemoaned this ineffectual state. He educed the gods were representatives of the complexity of human existence, and to secure their personal wealth and prestige, earthly kings sought to embody divine attributes, which was absent from the popular representatives.[46] But the more power a king exercised the more he was corrupted by it, the danger being "[t]he man of greater riches finds no lack of stalwart frames and comely faces to follow in his train."[47] To Lucretius, the ascension of Augustus to absolute power was an omen for a divinely empowered monarchy which would lead to the destruction of civilized man.[48]

The primary issue to the sixteenth and seventeenth century political philosophers was a legitimate popular sovereignty which was both efficient and equitable. Their disparate propositions caused as much quarrel as consensus. Should democracy's foundation be placed upon individual liberty or communal sovereignty? How can one be protected without undermining the other? In what way could self-interest be utilized to achieve a genuine popular sovereignty? The first modern political philosophers to elaborate upon the means and ends of political power in two controversial but influential works were Niccolo Machiavelli and Thomas Hobbes. Though their lives were separated by both a century in time and diametrically opposed cultures, these two men came to similar conclusions regarding sovereignty and its source of power.

The first was Niccolo Machiavelli, who viewed the prime aim of power as the preservation of the hierarchy which exercised it. Though his major work *The Prince* was a catalog of the political skills of his benefactors and their rivals, it was also a study of the life cycles of republican politics. Virtue was not of any intrinsic value for it was the preservation of the state that was justified by any means at the disposal of the ruler.[49] Order was based upon political centrality and rested with one absolute ruler. This sovereign walked a fine line between admiration and terror, for one inspired the populace toward communal achievement, while the other was a mechanism to thwart dissent. Should the occasion arise in which a ruler must choose between the two, fear was preferable due to the anxiety associated with retribution.[50] These assertions challenged the notion of a civil society based upon legal rights and embodied in documents such as England's *Magna Carta*, yet they were accepted by both the rulers and the politicians of that time.[51]

It was at the culmination of both Europe's Thirty Years War and the English Civil War that Thomas Hobbes wrote *Leviathan*, the progenitor of modern social contract philosophy. Hobbes expounded upon Machiavelli's theorem of sovereignty and argued a ruler and his constituency entered into a social contract freely in which both were governed by an established code of law.[52] Within this construct government was morally culpable for the welfare of its constituents.[53] Citizens submitted to the common bearer of the governing power, the sovereign.[54] The ruler was the embodiment of both political and moral authority of the state and served to ensure the stability of society against all forces which threatened it. To meet this charge once sovereignty had been placed with a monarch, the ruler's power was absolute. To maintain political equilibrium civil disobedience was not tolerated.

A ruler's duty was not to be virtuous, but to preserve the society.[55] The edicts of the sovereign were at the center of his explanation of liberty, defined by Hobbes as freedom impeded by the laws of the state through its ruler.[56] Fear and liberty were consistent, Hobbes example being that one rectifies debt in fear of retribution inflicted under the law if left unresolved.[57] Constituent freedom was consistent with the unlimited power of the sovereign, while the greatest liberty for a constituency was the silence of the law.[58] Within this context a citizen must practice freedom to validate its existence; thus, freedom as an inherent gift of birth was nonsense.[59]

In his work *Six Books on the Commonwealth* political philosopher Jean Bodin defined sovereignty within the existence of government.[60] Bodin contended sovereign authority could not be dissevered from its original source, but it could be delegated to a representative as both ruler and citizen were equal under the civil law.[61] The exercise of sovereign power by a prince was the embodiment of the law and was bound to uphold not only his own edicts, but those of his predecessors.[62] If the sovereign entered into an agreement with a subject or subjects by the passage of a law or issue of a decree, the choice was either uphold the edict, or the ruler's jurisdiction was illegitimate. It was Bodin's conclusion if sovereignty implied absolute rule, then the only sovereign power was possessed by God; thus, absolute sovereignty was unobtainable on earth and could only be approximated by an earth-bound ruler. If all of mankind were subject to the absolute natural law of God, then both ruler and subjects were bound by its derivative, the civil law.[63]

In his *Second Treatise on Government* John Locke claimed civil government consisted of a social contract forged between a constituency and the sovereign chosen by them to rule. Its principles were composed of two primary ideas: 1) the State was based upon a contract between ruler and subjects; and, 2) both ruler and the constituents agreed and adhered to a common social will as exemplified in that contract, while the sovereign chosen by the constituency assumed the burden of government in agreement with their will.[64] Such an accord was necessary for the stability of society, for without there would be disunity, and with it the dissolution of the community.[65] The chaotic state of nature and the unstable unity of society itself made political stability precarious, therefore an agreed-upon legal code was a vital prerequisite and its enforcement necessary to guarantee both the solidity of the community and the sovereignty of its laws.[66]

Locke asserted rather than loyalty to a ruler, the primary element of sovereignty was property. Man had bested the state of nature through a combination of labor and self-mastery, not through the coronation of a ruler—a parallel to the strong work ethic prevalent within Calvinist theology.[67] The state of nature not as a condition of evil and ignorance from which humans escaped to progress, but a stepping-stone from which rights originated. In the state of nature all human beings were equal belonging to the same biological species, and endowed with the faculty of rationality and abundant resources from which to draw from. Thus, it was the conquest of the state of nature that was the beginning of civilization, and which bestowed upon a human being dominion over himself and his property.[68] Refuting Hobbes' tenet of absolute power, an inept sovereign placed a society in worse predicaments than the state of nature, and a tyrant exercised power beyond what was moral. Thus, the only legitimate sovereignty was that to which the constituency had consented and was best expressed in a popularly elected legislature designed to counterbalance the powers of the sovereign.[69]

In his tract *Of the Original Contract* philosopher and historian David Hume questioned the validity of social contract philosophy. He concurred with Hobbes and Locke human existence within the state of nature was cruel. Hume traced the development of society and its governmental systems from the ancient Greeks to modern Britain based upon what he viewed as a consistent pattern of social politics, and concluded all governments had been forged either through conquest or usurpation, which eliminated any consent from the inhabitants involved.[70] It was normal for the people to be dissatisfied with their government regardless of whether it was established by a monarch or a constituent majority.[71] Thus, the idea people had willingly submitted themselves to a compact with a ruler was ridiculous.

Hume queried if this social contract existed, who then held the right to the title of sovereign? The problem was that human instinct was such as to influence them to indulge their whims, seek conquest of another polity, or both; therefore, a clash would inevitably arise between allegiance to the sovereign and the fidelity of each individual to the original contract.[72] It is this conflict between government and private property interests which led to the usurpation of power in which either monarch claimed total sovereign power, or the constituency overthrew the sovereign. No social contract ever existed for reasons neither side could ever agree to the terms of such a political relationship. Hume concluded all current monarchs lacked the legitimacy to claim their throne, as it belonged solely to the first person to occupy the position.[73]

Throughout the seventeenth century, the debate over the nature of sovereignty led parliamentarians to question the jurisdiction of the monarchy. In England this transition began with civil war and the execution of an anointed ruler, and ended with the abdication of another, along with the institution of a constitutional monarchy. Historically there had been an intimate association between social contract and natural law philosophies. Social contract theory had been around since the fourth century BCE and possessed a clerical tinge used to vindicate the cardinal rights of religious liberty. In his 1581 treatise *Vindicivoe, Contra Tyrannos* French diplomat Hubert Languet, writing under the pseudonym "Stephanus Junius Brutus", developed a scheme based upon liberty of conscience and the rights of citizens against their rulers in defense of the French Huguenots.[74] Eighteen years later the Spanish historian Father Juan de Mariana, S.J., in his book *De Rege et Regis Institutione*, put forward a theory of social contract rooted in Catholicism in which the authority to establish civil law originated from God and was passed down to the citizens.[75] Father Francisco Suarez, S.J. simply stated the monarch received his power at the behest of the people.[76]

In the seventeenth century Sir Edward Coke voiced his assessment sovereignty was the outgrowth of a natural law. Laws apparent within nature were self-evident first principles of natural rights, and if there were any limitations imposed on them they were due to a voluntary contract made of the possessors of such rights. Coke trusted neither the king nor the people alone to mediate any agreement between them. Only an independent court system guaranteed both obedience to and justice under the civil law through an interpretation rendered by trained and impartial representatives.[77]

The Reverend William Goodwin was one of the foremost champions of this notion. In his *A Sermon Preached Before the Kings Most Excellent Majestie* published in 1614 as a political tract, he stated those who challenged the divine right of kings were the vilest elements of society.[78] The Reverend Roger Maynwarning in his 1627 tract *Religion and Allegiance* cited the book of Ecclesiastes as the basis for his argument in favor of the divine right of kings, and warned that diluted sovereignty was a dangerous doctrine in which the sole result was chaos.[79] In his 1636 tract *A Briefe and Moderate Answer* clergyman Peter Heylyn argued a peaceful coexistence of divinely ordained monarchs and popular sovereignty was impractical. Just as Goodwin and Maynwaring, Heylyn cited the ordination of God as represented in the anointing of a monarch during coronation as the basis of the sovereign power of the king.[80]

British politician and philosopher Algernon Sidney condemned both the divine right of monarchs and the definition of liberty proposed by Hobbes. He was a forceful advocate of a government which combined the rule of law with the popular sovereignty of political equals. The prime tenet of his republican theory was that sovereignty rested with the citizens and ascended upward until it rested with the monarch or ruling body. Because the arbitrary use of political power as practiced by monarchs was not in the best interests of the citizens, its use was illegitimate. Both bodies must rule concurrently, each restricting the other's power. To guarantee this balance of governing, a compact, or constitution mutually agreed upon assured the rights of the constituency.[81]

It was these ideas which provided the intellectual foundations of the political upheaval in Great Britain that culminated with the Glorious Revolution of 1688. The influence of their ideas were demonstrated in the actions of parliamentary leaders who ousted a tyrannical monarch without initiating the tide of bloodshed. It was a struggle over sovereignty itself: individual rule or collective right? In the process the notion of a divine right to reign was discredited, and the right to rule under popularly constructed restrictions was instituted.

British Whig historian Thomas Lord Macaulay reasoned the Glorious Revolution was a battle over sovereignty. On the one side were supporters of King James II who firmly believed in the monarch's divine right to rule.[82] Supporters of William, the Duke of Orange contended the usurpation of the throne would secure political goals more conductive to a popular sovereignty.[83] Though the British Tory historian David Hume agreed with the basic tenets of Macaulay's thesis, he maintained James II had asserted there should be a more energetic government, but was unwilling to either appoint or maintain ministers who did not accede to his political will.[84]

With the death of King Charles II in 1685, there was no living heir and, thus, the throne passed to the monarch's younger brother James, the Duke of York. At first the transition was smooth: a Parliament was elected friendlier to the Crown than any since the early years of the Restoration. It was King James II who initiated opposition by continued friendship with Catholic France. Later, the king ordered Parliament to grant his request for substantial funds for the operation of the court and government, the authorization for a standing army, and the authority to appoint Roman Catholics to posts within the government. When Parliament refused consent, King James dissolved it. After the birth of an heir the king's position seemed solid, yet a challenge by his son-in-law William of Orange at the behest of several of his closest advisors and former members of Parliament was mounted.

William of Orange led the largest disciplined force to invade England—11,000 foot soldiers. Crucially, the officers and crew of the King's forces held deep disaffection for the monarch and purposefully missed its chance at intercepting the advancing force. Though the king's army was large its morale was patchy. At the crucial moment, the king's commanders deserted and his forces never saw action. By Christmas 1688 James II and his infant prince were exiled in France and Duke William was provisionally in charge of the government. This 'glorious revolution', unlike the English Civil War two generations before, was nearly bloodless. Not only did this event open a debate on the terms of the social contract, but also of its structure and beneficence.

Following the Glorious Revolution there were divergences in the sovereignty arguments. Whereas the Communitarians focused on the needs of the constituency, the Civil Humanists concentrated upon the rights of individuals. Two British political parties emerged from this ideological struggle which later defined the first party system of the United States in the late 1780s. The Tories asserted sovereignty was indivisible and should be left entirely to the representative body, which was bound by the will of its constituents.[85] On the other hand, the Whigs argued for a shared sovereignty between the monarch and parliament, for conflicts forced them to compromise and produce balanced public policy.[86] Though each group had embraced the notion of a popular-based sovereignty, it was there the similarities ended. The Whigs sought controversial reforms which diminished governmental power, such as the redistribution of representative seats and limiting the duration of sessions, as well as strict regulations which maintained an equality of jurisdiction between the king and the parliament. Throughout early eighteenth century the rivalry between these two political parties was bitter. The Whigs dominated parliament during the years of the Stuart monarchs. So when the Tories gained power with the ascension of King George I several outspoken Whigs—which included the future Prime Minister Robert Walpole—were arrested and jailed.

When the Whigs regained power in 1721 an ideological war developed that persuaded writers to comment on what they viewed as Britain's political dysfunctions. John Trenchard and Thomas Gordon published weekly discourses supporting Lockean-based libertarian ideas, the most important being *Cato's Letters*. In their minds, the leaders of the Whig party had abandoned the philosophical principles of Algernon Sidney and John Locke, and the corruption and usurpation of power had resulted.[87] It was the prime contention of *Cato's Letters* that by embracing government as embodied by chief ministers such as Robert Walpole or Henry Pelham, British politics had lost its legitimacy and only a radical restructuring based upon individual liberty and political equity could redeem it. More importantly, Trenchard and Gordon targeted the colonial audience, advising them not to adopt such iniquitous political practices, to the point where they openly advocated their eventual independence.[88]

Political thinkers over time had used the contract concept as a convenient premise in which to develop an argument and then support it. In doing so, rather than offering a solution to the inherent problem of majority rule—rationality in collective decisions is impossible due to preferences in society are centered upon the needs and wants of the individual—they have established the basis for political debate and dissension. Akin to the post-revolutionary period in England, arguments over the basis and beneficence of popular sovereignty provided the foundation of America's first political parties.

The American poet John Godfrey Saxe wrote: "Laws, like sausages, cease to inspire respect in proportion as we know how they are made."[89] This remark, often misattributed to German chancellor Otto von Bismarck, exemplifies the reason people hold a general interest in politics and government, but not an ardent fascination for it. Making laws is a tedious and messy affair wrought through compromise rarely pleasing to all factions, the end result being vague legal language left to others to interpret. It is only when there is a legal challenge mounted the true meaning of a statute is defined. This paradigm is no less true with the Constitution of the United States, which was created out of the ideological clashes between the Federalists and Anti-Federalists.

Throughout Europe in the seventeenth and early eighteenth centuries the idea of political power originating from a constituency was the source of heated arguments. As demonstrated by the English Civil War of the 1640s, the temper of these debates led to violence, mayhem, and the public execution of an anointed monarch. Concurrently, the best philosophical minds of the time attempted to specify both the framework and the function of popular sovereignty. Though these thinkers had put forward powerful abstract ideas regarding the nature of sovereignty, they had offered but mere morsels as to a structure of operation for efficient government. Their works had focused upon the benefits to either the group dynamic or the individual citizen. They left the task of fashioning their abstract ideas into a functioning system of government to the next generation. According to historian Jack Rakove, the challenge of the 1787 constitutional convention was to find a median "between the clouded heights of principle and the familiar terrain of specific interests."[90]

Historian Jack Greene asserted that at the conclusion of the Glorious Revolution sovereign power had frayed rather than shifted. The experimental nature of a constitutional government based upon popular sovereignty had intriguing repercussions within the British political system.[91] Greene argued the struggle in pre-Revolutionary America between *virtual* representation in the House of Commons in London and *actual* representation created a barrier between mother country and her colonies. It culminated with a struggle in which the unquestioned authority of the English parliament upon the colonies was seen as unacceptable and, thus, be resisted.[92]

Writing at the cusp of American Independence, Thomas Paine confirmed Greene's analysis.[93] Paine's pamphlet *Common Sense* defined the justifications for American independence. A substantial portion of this treatise was dedicated to the spurious rule by divine right, echoing Sidney's arguments.[94] Historian John C. Miller argued Paine's pamphlet was crucial, for not only did it dare to criticize both the king and his parliament, it put forward easily understood terms a rationale for American independence.[95] But Paine gave only vague hints at the structure of government to be established following the overthrow of British rule: Legislatures which met annually presided over by a president.[96]

Perhaps the most conspicuous omission of the political philosophers was that they failed to recognize the potential of social disorder inherent within the overthrow of an established government system. It is a circular relationship: Social stability was dependent upon the legitimacy of the political authority which maintains it, but the validity of such a political entity is dependent upon its ability to establish and maintain social stability. Therefore, the success of any political revolt was more contingent upon the adept substitution of a new lawful government infrastructure than on battlefield victories.[97] Following the overthrow of British rule, achieving a stable peace after a long period of turmoil was the most important challenge for the newly independent American states.

Once the thirteen English colonies had declared their independence from Great Britain in 1776, there rose the task of uniting these separate, sovereign states under a single political entity. Due to their fear of centralized political power, the representatives wanted written assurances they were not merely replacing a foreign tyrant with a native-born version of their own design. They sought a union in which political administration was localized. America's first governing charter, the *Articles of Confederation* took nearly five years to ratify. The Reverend John Witherspoon of New Jersey conveyed his confidence in the *Articles* as an example of "the present enlightened state of men's minds we might expect a lasting confederacy".[98]

Yet the *Articles* failed as a catalyst for national unity to the point where, as Alexander Hamilton asserted, the burgeoning republic was in a state of continuous degradation.[99] By placing the bulk of political power in the state governments it had enfeebled all efforts to bind the thirteen separate states into one fully functioning whole. Congress rarely attained a quorum and was unable to conduct business. Economic stability crumbled. By spring 1786, state currencies had destabilized and devalued, and the national government was impotent to halt the severity of the post-Revolution economic depression. Alarmed by the political disintegration of their new nation disgruntled citizens openly displayed their hostility.

The most prominent was in Massachusetts where a centralized commonwealth government was implemented under a charter written by John Adams. Representatives of fifty New England townships, an area hit hard by economic downturn, met in Hatfield, Massachusetts to protest everything from lawyers' fees to commonwealth taxes. On 31 August 1786 insurgents, war veterans with little means, shut down the operations of the Massachusetts Supreme Court in

Northampton. Governor James Bowdoin called for the state militia to end the stand-off and allow the government to conduct business.[100] Within weeks similar incidences occurred in Worcester and Springfield. The national Congress authorized Secretary of War Henry Knox to raise a militia, yet by the time he had built the force the insurgency had disintegrated and had broken up by itself.

On 26 December 1786 a new band of dissidents under the leadership of Daniel Shays, an army captain during the Revolution, marched toward Springfield, Massachusetts. When word reached Congress, Secretary Knox again raised a ragtag militia force and placed it under the command of Benjamin Lincoln. Though troops under General William Shepherd routed and arrested the rebels, these events sent shock waves throughout the nation. By its incompetence to quell a threat to the internal sovereignty of one its states, it was obvious that confederation government was impotent to suppress any serious menace from a hostile external force.[101]

Throughout the early- to mid-1780s Alexander Hamilton reiterated his view government power must be concentrated with a sovereign head, for power diluted was power diminished. The beneficence of government should rest with the constituency rather than each individual member.[102] Hamilton's opinion was that States should pay for a central government, and then allow it full authority to preserve the country from its own internal destructive forces.[103] But as dysfunctional as Confederation government was any effort to amend the *Articles* or frame a new constitution were bleak. Supporters of a strong central government viewed the continuance under the *Articles* as a danger to the nation's existence. The Federalists sought to construct a government in the mode of John Adams' *Thoughts on Government* which had proven effective when instituted in Virginia and Massachusetts. It consisted of a multi-tiered political authority based upon what Locke had delineated as a balance of power and interests.[104] Its foundations, according to James Wilson, were states independent of one another, yet united in a common national cause.[105] The country had been born out of a calamity which had given rise to the *Declaration of Independence*, a document that had not only brought the states together for a common political cause, but had also forced them to forge a degree of national identity.[106] Hamilton argued the Confederation was not designed to rectify debts contracted during the war for independence owed to foreign and domestic creditors, nor could it reinforce American trade laws nor strengthen free and fair trade with other nations. He asserted due to its slow process of state consensus government under the *Articles* was incapable of defending the fledgling nation against foreign aggression.[107]

The Anti-Federalists argued following the success of the Revolution the sovereignty of the British crown was transferred to the sovereign states, the exception being any and all powers ceded by them to invigorate a central regime. Oliver Ellsworth surmised the sovereignty of a central government was derived from the states and could not imagine a context in which the people envisioned themselves as citizens of both an individual state and a national collective.[108] The *Articles'* defenders reasoned they protected the relationship between a central authority and the sovereignty of the states. Richard Henry Lee, in his anonymously published *Letters of the Federal Farmer*, contended the Confederation was a structure which allowed the states to interact in friendship towards one another, and holding such a degree of respect that one would come to the mutual defense of all. The country had a definable structure of power that when utilized correctly was effective.[109] Moreover, in the opinion of James Winthrop, the idea of a dual sovereignty was ridiculous, for one would come into conflict with the other, and "[w]e shall find it impossible to please two masters."[110]

In James Madison's opinion, the *Articles'* foremost deficiency was in its design which strengthened the individual states, while unnecessarily weakening the central government, and concurrently relying upon the authority of the latter to unity the states into a cohesive whole.[111] The ineffectiveness of the central government during Shays' Rebellion had proven the necessity of a strong-centralized authority to coalesce the individual states against a common threat. The aim of the representatives to the earlier Annapolis Convention had been to amend the national charter. It was there the delegates agreed the *Articles* were unworkable in their present form and that powers should be ceded to invigorate a central governing authority. Unbeknownst to the majority of delegates their concerns over divided sovereignty initiated the foremost ideological debate in American political history: How much sovereignty should this central government possess at the expense of the state governments, or for that matter the American people?

The delegates who gathered at Philadelphia during the summer of 1787 represented a mix of ideologies. Because there were several divergent opinions and degrees of sentiment at the convention factions emerged.[112] According to historian M. E. Bradford, Roger Sherman of Connecticut was "almost an Anti-Federalist," who believed it was "in the interest of each and of the whole [Union] that they should be separate within their proper limits."[113] Oliver Ellsworth, also from Connecticut, shared similar views and insisted "[w]hat enriches a part enriches the whole, and the States are the best judges of their particular interest."[114] James Wilson of Pennsylvania claimed the union of the individual states represented the entirety of the nation, but that did not mean there was a political bond between them. George Mason of Virginia and John Dickinson of Delaware were Anti-Federalists who had concluded a centralized government was now necessary, as following Shays' Rebellion both had voiced their support for a political authority who could protect the Union. Centrist Pierce Butler of South Carolina supported "the powers of the General Government … [within limits] as not to destroy the Sovereignty of the Individual States."[115] Many of his centrist contemporaries such as Edmund Randolph of Virginia, William Richardson Davie and Hugh Williamson of North Carolina had also advocated a centralized authority of a limited scope subject to the final judgment of the states.[116]

The ardent Anti-Federalists were hostile to any plan which centralized power and were willing to do whatever they could to stop it.[117] Luther Martin of Maryland, the author of the proposal for the Electoral College, had not come to frame a new constitution, but to amend the *Articles of Confederation*. At the convention he railed against what he saw as an affinity for the larger states.[118] Robert Yates and John Lansing of New York believed state governments offered the best protection against the infringement of civil liberties. Throughout their brief stay at the convention, the two quarreled with their Federalist counterparts until they both left in disgust. Lansing insisted his state "would never have concurred in sending deputies to the Convention if she had supposed the deliberations were to turn on a consolidation of the States and a national government."[119] Gouverneur Morris of Pennsylvania and Alexander Hamilton of New York were the most ardent Federalists.

Because the political philosophers of the Enlightenment had neither delineated the parameters of popular sovereignty, nor defined the structure under which it could provide effective government, it was left to the American Framers to take on the task. As they debated republican tenets they discovered popular sovereignty too complex an idea to be encompassed by a single governing principle. The balance between local jurisdiction and central political authority was a unique proposition which had not been discussed in the democratic theories they had read. To reach an agreement they had to compromise, and instituted a government which operated on consensus and numerical majorities. In short, the Framers had also failed to define popular sovereignty in any specific manner as the philosophers before them.

The Preamble of the United States Constitution is the essential charge of American constitutional government. As in any legal contract, it is the mission statement which opens a flexible instrument of public policy, adaptable to changes within the society it regulates, both a living representation of the state which it governs, as well as its fundamental law.[120] Though the document established specific rights, the elastic clauses allow the government to adapt with time, as demonstrated by the Necessary-and-Proper Clause of Article I § 8 and the amending power of Article V.

At the onset this was the methodology involved in framing the Constitution and embodied by three specific goals agreed upon by both Federalists and Anti-Federalists. First, the Constitution was a governmental device intended to curb and control the social forces unleashed by the American Revolution. Second, it was constructed to protect and prolong the deferential society in which the lower classes were obligated to defer in governmental affairs to those of education, class and experience. Finally, it was designed to constrict, not to encourage, popular participation in government. The Constitution neither granted nor secured freedom: It sought to control the public while maintaining order. Furthermore, of the 'Bill of Rights', the first ten amendments to the Constitution, only the initial three actually declare 'rights' (and the Second with limitations). Amendments Four through Eight deal specifically with criminal procedure, while Amendments Nine and Ten were added solely to silence criticisms of the Anti-Federalists. Additionally, the Preamble set forth six essential charges as the basis of its contract with the American people. They are as follows:

> "[T]o form a more perfect Union"
> "Establish Justice"
> "Ensure Domestic Tranquility"
> "Provide for the Common Defense"
> "Promote the General Welfare"
> "Secure the Blessings of Liberty"

In the end there was still dissent. Luther Martin, Robert Yates, and John Lansing left the proceedings prior to the final vote on the grounds the Constitution marginalized the individual states. Others who remained such as Elbridge Gerry, George Mason, and Edmund Randolph refused their sanction on the same grounds. Gerry criticized popular participation in the legislature and the power of the judiciary. Mason objected to the exclusion of a Bill of Rights which guaranteed the dual sovereignty of the States. Randolph was furious when his proposals for restrictions on the federal judiciary, which he viewed as a tyrant waiting for an opportunity to arise, were not considered prior to the vote of the convention. Outside of the Constitutional Convention Richard Henry Lee, in a reply to George Mason's letter voicing his concerns, summarized what he saw as the dilemma of the new government: "If it should be established, either a tyranny will result from it, or it will be prevented by a Civil War."[121]

While serving as the Ambassador to the Court of St. James, John Adams read the document and voiced his apprehensions. The first was the executive had less authority than the legislature which made the balance of power unequal. Adams viewed the limitation on a president's autonomy with treaties as debilitating factors and would prove themselves to be unworkable.[122] But his foremost concern was sovereignty. Adams argued the balance of power between the three separate branches was unequal to the point of impotence and potentially anarchy.[123]

Thomas Jefferson also held concerns, though he thought there was not a citizen in the nation who approved of every measure. He was suspicious of a presidency without limitations on the terms of office, which he viewed as the equivalent to monarchy.[124]

Jefferson's greatest objection however was the exclusion of a declaration of rights which separated state authority from the federal governments under strict legal guidelines. In a letter to James Madison, Jefferson acceded to the document with the hope that it would later be amended.[125]

Political Scientist Bruce Ackerman argued the constitution was neither original nor ground breaking. In his book, *We the People: Foundations*, Ackerman stated the Framers had failed to recognize that in their own colonial governments they had "repudiated large chunks of their past and transformed their higher law to express deep changes in their political identities." Rather than searching for the means to address the controversies inherent within a new nation, they merely structured into law their defeat of a powerful enemy within a republican form of constitutional government.[126] He also alluded to "illegalities" in the ratification process, such as only a majority of states were needed to ratify the document, rather than every member state, hindering the Constitution from being an instrument of popular sovereignty.[127]

Historian Michael Kammen viewed the document as flawed for it failed to address the single most important question posed by the Anti-Federalists: How much authority would the states be required to grant to the federal government?[128] In his book *A Machine That Would Go of Itself: The Constitution in American Culture*, Kammen viewed this ambiguity as both its strength and its weakness. Because the Constitution itself was not clear in several key passages, representatives of many ideological persuasions have interpreted the clauses to mean a myriad of things. In the most critical of circumstances, the document was unsuccessful in explaining procedures vital to its operation, such as those of the Supreme Court. It was in these enigmatic passages, according to Kammen, what resulted was the greatest danger in American society itself: Most Americans have accepted a plethora of fallacies regarding the Constitution, as well as being oblivious to that fact.[129]

The Constitution is a charter which presented a standard by which the laws, the codification of American society's criterion of conduct, was to be constructed. As a prescription to remedy to a host of communal ills, law also embodies the aspirations of the civilization which created it. Its citizens accede to these mandates willingly for they believe they were constructed with the best interests of the entire public in mind. Under the best of circumstances justice is intrinsic, for neither bias nor malice interfered with the even-hand which determines proper punishment. Due to the rigorous attention to the letter of its written codes, coupled with a dedication to consistency with precedent, fundamental fairness was established and maintained as the norm, rather than the exception. Other nations recognize these patterns and express their respect for its achievements and this model provides a working example to the rest of the world.

Such is the public image of the American republic. In reality, this system has several defects. Laws are rarely wrought with the full beneficence of all citizens to the fore. Oftentimes the interpretation of fundamental law by the judiciary has caused controversy on any given issue rather than a convergence and/or willing acceptance. Furthermore, the previous two elements beg an important question: What if popular dissent against a law were so great it denied the legitimacy of the authority that created it?

This is the unpredictability of fundamental law made under the rule of democracy: Does a law remain legitimate if the populace does not recognize it as such? If a popular sovereignty of equals demands that legal mandates reflect the will of the majority, how does one justifiably enforce a rule opposed by that majority? And if the majority voices their discontent in a public forum, which group represents the genuine will of the people, the government established by the people, or the people themselves? What then constitutes a governing majority, and what role does it play within a democracy?

These questions originated with the 1787 constitutional convention and came to fore during the ratification debates which followed. The Constitution was of necessity a compromise between the communitarian values of the Federalists and the individualism of the Anti-Federalists. In their efforts to frame a document that would be ratified by the individual States, the framers failed to grasp an effective structure under which popular sovereignty could function. In an attempt to placate Anti-Federalists fears, Federalist James Wilson of Pennsylvania made the assertion that the Constitution had provided for a dual sovereignty in which central and state governments operated concurrent with one another within separate spheres of influence.[130]

As such the resulting charter of the new American nation was a hodgepodge of conflicting ideas with regards to sovereignty. And though the Constitution was ratified by a majority of the states, it also proved ineffective in defeating the strong advocacy of Anti-Federalists for the principles of confederation. James Madison recognized their dissent over the sovereignty issue and he agreed with them. It was his contention that among the most prominent controversies of the convention had been maintaining the balance between federal and state governments.[131] As a member of the House of Representatives Madison was instrumental in the passage of the Bill of Rights, which included a guarantee of state sovereignty embodied in the Tenth Amendment.

Thus within the framework of any philosophical discussion of political sovereignty, "We, the People" remains an abstract concept granted with a concrete application in terms of political administration. Though citizens did not have much in terms of a direct effect upon its democracy, their advocacy and active participation in the election process, as well as public debate, guaranteed their voice would be heard. It is in those outlets the United States is dependent upon the popular sovereignty of the people it governs, and without such participation the results are national dissention, disconnection, decay, and ultimately death.

Notes

1. Daniel C. Maguire and A. Nicholas Fargnoli, *On Moral Grounds: The Art/Science of Ethics* (New York: The Crossroad Publishing Company, 1991), 105.
2. *U. S. Constitution,* Article IV § 4.
3. Alexis de Tocqueville, *Democracy in America*, ed. Phillips Bradley (New York: Vintage Books, 1990), I: 243.
4. *Ibid.*
5. Ernest Gellner, *Nations and Nationalism* (Ithaca, NY: Cornell University Press, 1983), 6.
6. *Ibid.*, 43.
7. *Ibid.*, 39.
8. *Ibid.*, 55.
9. *Ibid.*, 126.
10. *Ibid.*, 15.
11. Sir James Gregory Frazier, *The Golden Bough*, 1995 reprint. (New York: Touchstone Books, 1922), 188.
12. Edith Hamilton, *Mythology* (Boston, MA: Little, Brown and Company, 1942), 207.

13. *Ibid.*, 200–4.
14. Geoffrey Ashe, *The Discovery of King Arthur* (London: Guild Books, Ltd., 1985), 16.
15. T. H. White, *The Once and Future King* (New York: G. P. Putnam's Sons, 1958), 195–7.
16. Geoffrey of Monmouth, *The History of the Kings of Britain*, ed. Lewis Thorpe (New York: Penguin Books, 1966), 222.
17. Frazier, 188.
18. Tacitus, *The Agricola and The Germania*, ed. Harold Mattingly (New York: Penguin Books, 1970), 43.
19. Suetonius, *The Twelve Caesars*, ed. Robert Graves (New York: Penguin Books, 1979), 111.
20. Michael Grant, *Constantine the Great: The Man and His Times* (New York: Charles Scribner's Sons, 1993), 151–2.
21. Livy, *Rome and Italy: Books VI–X of The History of Rome From Its Foundations*, ed. Betty Radice (New York: Penguin Books, 1982), 30.
22. Tacitus, *The Histories*, ed. Kenneth Wellesley (New York: Penguin Books, 1964), 15.
23. *Ibid.*, 272.
24. Norman F. Cantor, *The Civilization of the Middle Ages* (New York: HarperCollins Publishers, 1993), 55.
25. *Ibid.*
26. St. Augustine, *The City of God*, ed. Vernon J. Bourke (New York: Image Books, 1958), 326.
27. *Ibid.*, 392.
28. *Ibid.*, 444.
29. *Ibid.*, 88.
30. *Ibid.*, 118.
31. St. Thomas Aquinas, *The Pocket Aquinas*, ed. Vernon J. Bourke (New York: Simon & Schuster, 1960), 235.
32. *Ibid.*
33. *Ibid.*, 239.
34. *Ibid.*, 238.
35. Cantor, 12.
36. Richard Barber, *Henry Plantagenet 1133–1189: A Biography* (New York: Barnes and Noble, Inc., 1964), 1.
37. *Ibid.*, 16.
38. May McKisack and Hilda Johnston, quoted in Harold F. Hutchison, *Edward II: 1284–1327* (New York: David Bolt Associates, 1971), 145, 151.
39. *Ibid.*, 149–50.
40. Geoffrey Chaucer, *The Canterbury Tales*, ed. R. M. Lumiansky (New York: Washington Square Press, 1971), 34–5.
41. *Ibid.*, 21.

42. *Ibid.*, 34.
43. *Ibid.*, 88.
44. Jacques Maritan, *Man and the State* (Washington, DC: The Catholic University of America Press, 1951), 35.
45. Michael Grant, *The Founders of the Western World: A History of Greece and Rome* (New York: Charles Scribner's Sons, 1991), 178.
46. Lucretius, *The Nature of the Universe*, ed. Ronald Latham (Baltimore, MD: Penguin Books, 1951), 206.
47. *Ibid.*, 205.
48. *Ibid.*, 206.
49. Niccolo Machiavelli, *The Prince*, eds. Quinten Skinner and Russell Price (New York: Cambridge University Press, 1988), 63.
50. *Ibid.*, 59.
51. John Hale, *The Civilization of Europe in the Renaissance* (New York: Athenaeum Books, 1994), 368.
52. Thomas Hobbes, *Leviathan*, ed. Richard Tuck (New York: Cambridge University Press, 1996), 122.
53. *Ibid.*, 153, 231.
54. *Ibid.*, 139, 143.
55. *Ibid.*, 170.
56. *Ibid.*, 171.
57. *Ibid.*
58. *Ibid.*, 178.
59. *Ibid.*, 172, 175.
60. Jean Bodin, *Six Books of the Commonwealth*, ed. M. J. Tooley (Oxford, England: Basil Blackwell, 1955), 25.
61. *Ibid.*
62. *Ibid.*, 28.
63. *Ibid.*, 36.
64. John Locke, *Two Treatises on Government*, ed. Peter Laslett (New York: Cambridge University Press, 1960), 332.
65. *Ibid.*, 333.
66. *Ibid.*, 351.
67. *Ibid.*, 284.
68. *Ibid.*, 288.
69. *Ibid.*, 283.
70. David Hume, "Of the Original Contract," in *Social Contract*, ed. Ernest Barker (New York: Oxford University Press, 1960), 151.
71. *Ibid.*, 155.
72. *Ibid.*, 161.
73. *Ibid.*, 164.

74. Hubert Languet (as "Stephanius Junius Brutus"), *Vindiciae, contra tyrannos; Or, Concerning the Legitimate Power of a Prince over the People, and of the People over a Prince*, ed. George Garnett (New York: Cambridge University Press, 2003).
75. Juan de Mariana, S.J., *De Rege et Regis Institutione; Or, The King and the Education of a King* (London: Forgotten Books, 2017).
76. Francisco Suarez, S. J., *On Efficient Causality: Metaphysical Disputations 17, 18, and 19*, ed. Alfred J. Freddoso (New Haven, CT: Yale University Press, 1994), 330.
77. Sir Edward Coke, "Prohibitions Del Roy", in *The Struggle For Sovereignty: Seventeenth-Century English Political Tracts*, ed. Joyce Lee Malcolm (Indianapolis, IN: The Liberty Fund, 1999), I: 15–16.
78. William Goodwin, "Sermon Preached Before the Kings Majestie," in Malcolm, *Struggle for Sovereignty* 1: 31.
79. Ecclesiastes 8:2. *New International Version.*
80. Peter Heylyn, "A Briefe and Moderate Answer to the Seditious and Scandalous Challenges of Henry Burton, Late of Friday-Streete," in Malcolm, *Struggle For Sovereignty* 1: 82.
81. Algernon Sidney, *Discourses Concerning Government*, ed. Thomas G. West (Indianapolis, IN: The Liberty Fund, 1996), 222.
82. Thomas Lord Macaulay, *The History of England*, ed. Trevor Roper (New York: Penguin Books, 1979), 277–8.
83. *Ibid.*
84. David Hume, *The History of England from the Invasion of Julius Caesar to the Abdication of James the Second, 1688* (Boston, MA: Phillips, Sampson, and Company, 1850) VI: 287.
85. Bernard Bailyn, *The Ideological Origins of the American Revolution* (Cambridge, MA: The Belknap Press of Harvard University Press, 1967), 49–50.
86. Macaulay, 290.
87. Bailyn, 36–7.
88. John Trenchard and Thomas Gordon, "Of Plantations and Colonies," 8 December 1722, in *Cato's Letters, or Essays on Liberty, Civil and Religious, and Other Important Subjects*, ed. Ronald Hamowy (Indianapolis, IN: The Liberty Fund, 1995), II: 749.
89. https://en.wikiquote.org/wiki/John_Godfrey_Saxe. Accessed 4 June 2018.
90. Jack N. Rakove, *Original Meanings: Political and Ideas in the Making of the Constitution* (New York: Vintage Books, 1997), 15.
91. Jack P. Greene, *Negotiated Authorities: Essays In Colonial Political and Constitutional History* (Charlottesville: University Press of Virginia, 1994), 39.
92. *Ibid.*
93. Thomas Paine, *Common Sense*, ed. Issac Kramnick (New York: Penguin Books, 1986), 84.
94. *Ibid.*, 78.

95. John C. Miller, *Origins of the American Revolution* (Boston, MA: Little, Brown, and Company, 1943), 467.
96. Paine, 96.
97. Edmund Burke, *Reflections on the Revolution in France*, ed. J. G. A. Pocock (Indianapolis, IN: Hackett Publishing Company, 1987), 53–4.
98. Rev. John Witherspoon, quoted by Thomas Jefferson, in *Thomas Jefferson: Writings,* ed. Merrill D. Peterson (New York: The Library of America, 1984), 29.
99. Alexander Hamilton, "Essay #15", in *The Federalist,* The Gideon Edition, eds. George W. Carey and James McClellan (Indianapolis, IN: The Liberty Fund, 2001), 69.
100. James Bowdoin, "A Proclamation of Governor Bowdoin to the Commonwealth of Massachusetts," 2 Sep. 1786, in *The American Heritage History of the Presidency*, ed. Marcus Cunliffe (New York: American Heritage Publishing Co., Inc., 1968), 63.
101. Alexander Hamilton, "Essay #15", in *The Federalist*, 69.
102. Alexander Hamilton's views on sovereignty from "The Continentalist," essay #2, 19 Jul. 1781, in *The Papers of Alexander Hamilton*, ed. Harold C. Syrett (New York: Columbia University Press, 1975), 2: 688; and, "A Letter From Phocion To the Considerate Citizens of New York," Jan. 1784 in *Hamilton Papers*, 3: 489.
103. Alexander Hamilton, Letter to James Duane, 3 Sep. 1780, in *Hamilton Papers*, 2: 401.
104. Locke, 365.
105. Rakove, 163.
106. *Ibid.*
107. Alexander Hamilton's ideas summarized from essay #15, in *The Federalist*, 71–2.
108. Oliver Ellsworth, quoted in M. E. Bradford, *Founding Fathers: Brief Lives of the Framers of the United States Constitution*, 1994 Reprint. (Lawrence: University of Kansas Press, 1981), 35.
109. Richard Henry Lee's ideas summarized from *The Anti-Federalist: Writing by the Opponents of the Constitution*, ed. Herbert Storing (Chicago, IL: University of Chicago Press, 1981), 70–1. Herbert J. Storing, *What the Anti-Federalists Were For: The Political Thought of the Opponents of the Constitution* (Chicago, IL: University of Chicago Press, 1981), 10–1.
110. James Winthrop, quoted in Gordon S. Wood, *The Creation of the American Republic, 1776–1787* (Chapel Hill, NC: The University of North Carolina Press, 1969), 528.
111. James Madison, in "Essay #38", *The Federalist*, 192.
112. Rakove, 15.
113. Bradford, 21.
114. Oliver Ellsworth, quoted in *Ibid.*, 32.
115. Pierce Butler, quoted in *Ibid.*, 201.
116. Wood, 538.
117. Wood, 527.

118. Robert Yates, quoted in Ralph Ketcham, *James Madison: A Biography*, 1990 reprint (Charlottesville, VA: University Press of Virginia, 1971), 208–9.
119. John Lansing, quoted in Richard B. Morris, *Witness at the Creation: Hamilton, Madison, Jay, and the Constitution* (New York: Henry Holt and Company, Inc., 1985), 208.
120. Herman Belz, *A Living Constitution or Fundamental Law? American Constitutionalism in Historical Perspective* (Lanham, MD: Rowan & Littlefield Publishers, Inc., 1998), 1–2.
121. Richard Henry Lee, Letter to George Mason, 1 Oct. 1787, in *The Papers of George Mason*, ed. Robert A. Rutland (Chapel Hill, NC: University of North Carolina Press, 1970), 2: 997.
122. John Adams, Letter to Roger Sherman, 18 Jul. 1789, in *The Political Writings of John Adams*, ed. George A. Peek (New York: Liberal Arts Press, 1954), 168.
123. *Ibid.*
124. Thomas Jefferson, "Autobiography," in Peterson, *Thomas Jefferson: Writings*, ed. Merrill D. Peterson (New York: Literary Classics of the United States, Inc., 1984), 72.
125. Thomas Jefferson, Letter to James Madison, 20 Dec. 1787, in Peterson, *Thomas Jefferson: Writings*, 916.
126. Bruce Ackerman, *We the People: Foundations* (Cambridge, MA: The Belknap Press of Harvard University Press, 1991), 19.
127. *Ibid.*, 41.
128. Michael Kammen, *A Machine That Would Go of Itself: the Constitution in American Culture* (New York: St. Martin's Press, 1986), 5.
129. *Ibid.*, 13.
130. James Wilson, "Pennsylvania Statehouse Speech," 6 Oct. 1787, in *Friends of the Constitution: Writings of the "Other" Federalists*, eds. Colleen A. Sheehan and Gary L. MacDowell (Indianapolis, IN: The Liberty Fund, 1998), 102–3.
131. James Madison, "Essay #37"; in *The Federalist*, 182.

1

"In Order to Form a More Perfect Union"

The Social Contract and the Reclamation of American Independence

It was going to take a miracle. The urgency of events which had brought thirteen disparate colonies together to wage a successful war for independence had seriously eroded. Once the 1783 Treaty of Paris was signed, and the lands westward to the Mississippi River were in the hands of the victors, the individual states squabbled amongst themselves. As if to add tinder to the fire of disunion, a deep economic depression gripped the new nation which fostered local rebellions involving disgruntled citizens. It was also clear confederation was not strong enough to force the sovereign States to come back together for the common good. There seemed little holding the burgeoning country together.

Yet in this dire situation, a small group of men viewed it as an opportunity. They had seen American independence unravelling before their eyes and concluded only a strong central government would save their dream of self-determination. What they turned their attention towards was a new national charter: A social contract that would not only concentrate the country's political power, but also to put into place the necessary elements these men needed to realize the commercial juggernaut they envisioned for the budding nation.

The Constitution of the United States is a social contract and it is the culmination of a long evolution. Throughout recorded history there have been several written codes of law. With the fall of the Athenian aristocracy in the seventh century prior to the Common Era came the unique idea of a written charter to which all laws must be consistent. The oldest reference known to history of the social contract came from Aristotle when he argued in *The Politics* political sovereignty was derived from a relationship based upon mutual advantage and consent. People in the state of nature sought respite from their condition by granting their liberty to one of their own with the capacity for leadership for their mutual benefit.[1]

The first acknowledged written charter of government was constructed by the legislator Draco (c. 7th century BCE) as a table of laws enforced by the courts.[2] Draco's work has been a subject of debate, as they were termed within Aristotle's account of the *Constitution of the Athenians* as ordinances, rather than as a functioning governmental charter.[3] It was the constitution written by the chief magistrate and archon Solon (c. 638–c. 558 BCE) that stands as a structure of government, and of which there exists an account of its inception, construction and implementation.[4] Viewed by the people as one of its admired citizens, Solon was solicited to construct a foundation for the laws of Athens.[5] Its structure was as follows[6]:

I. Legislative Elaboration:
The procedures for choosing local representatives.
The duties of the magistrates and the Council of Five Hundred.
The duties of the Archons.
The qualifications and duties of Jurors.
The duties and procedures for the Arbitrators.

II. Executive Elaboration:
The duties of the Polemarch.
The duties of the Pytannes.
The duties of the Auditors.
The duties of the Receivers-General.
The duties of the Examiner-of-Accounts.
The duties of the City Commissioners.
The duties of the Commissioners of Repairs-of-Temples.
The duties of the Market Commissioners.
The duties of the Corn Commissioners.
The duties of the Commissioners of Weights-and-Measures.
The duties of the Commissioner of Public Worship.
The duties of the Commissioners of Public Contracts.
The duties of the Commissioners of Roads.

The duties of the Commissioner of Games.
The duties of the Superintendent of the Marts.
The duties of the Introducers of Cases.

III. Elaboration on Civil Duties:
The structure and qualifications for the voting franchise.
The structure and duties of the law courts.
The terms of mandatory military service.
The terms of public festivals.
The qualification and terms of banishment.

Emphasis was placed upon the regulation of those serving within executive office. When the legislative offices were compared with the executive positions there was a larger contingent of rules concerning conduct and specificity of duties for the latter than the former. This was an outgrowth of the successful struggle for independence by the citizens of Athens from the monarchy and the oligarchy which followed.[7]

The Federalists were inspired by Solon's efforts. James Madison respected Solon for his work in securing popular political participation in his governmental instrument.[8] He also praised solon for democratizing the Athenian government through his establishment of the Council of the Five Hundred, a legislative body elected by the people.[9] James Wilson proclaimed Solon should be admired due to the fact he chose not to claim despotic power for himself, and then placing his fellow citizens into bondage.[10]

The initial code of Roman law, the *Twelve Tables*, was instituted in 451 BCE.[11] Following their successful rebellion against the Etruscan King Tarquinius Superbus between 510 and 507 BCE a republican form of government was instituted.[12] Six decades later a group of commissioners under the direction of Consul Appius Claudius composed a charter of laws which were, according to the Roman historian Livy, "engraved on bronze and permanently exhibited in a place where all could read them."[13] Thus, the initial Roman constitution was, as the English legal philosopher Sir William Blackstone described it, a compendium of statues which had originated from sources ranging from the emperor, the senate or other public officials to the people themselves.[14] From the *Twelve Tables* the essential law of Roman Empire, the *Pax Romana*, grew into a complex charter of government which lasted until the advent of the Civil Wars. The *Constitution of the Romans*, as reconstructed by historians James Greenough and George Kittredge, was a more efficiently structured document than its Greek predecessor.[15]

- I. Citizenship and Orders of the State:
  1. Senatorial Order.
  2. Equestrian Order.
  3. Populus.
     - A. Roman citizenship.
     - B. Italian towns.
     - C. Provincials.
     - D. Freedmen.
- II. The Public Assemblies:
  1. Comitia Centuriata.
  2. Comita Tributa.
  3. Comita Curiata.
  4. Contio.
- III. The Senate:
- IV. The Executive:
  1. The Consols.
  2. The Prætors.
  3. The Quæstors.
  4. The Cursus Honorum.
  5. The Ædiles.
  6. The Lictors, the Insignia, and others.
  7. The Proconsuls and Proprætors.
  8. The Censors.
  9. The Tribuni Pleblis.
  10. The Auspices.
  11. The Augers.
  12. The Interrex.
  13. The Dictator.
- V. The Courts:

The most apparent influence of the Roman Constitution upon the American federal system was the division of governmental power into three separate branches: The legislature; the executive; and, the judiciary. Also, there was an abundance of specificity in the duties and authority of each of the delineated offices.

The impact of Rome's history and the *Pax Romana* upon the Framers cannot be understated. Writing under the pseudonym of 'A Citizen of Philadelphia', Federalist author Pelitiah Webster recounted how Rome had risen from its humble origins to become the greatest global power the world had ever known during its era of republicanism.[16] James Wilson argued the American constitution was superior to that of Rome for it had been the product of the people themselves through representatives they had chosen, and then submitted to the populace for ratification.[17] The Anti-Federalist author 'Brutus' contended republican governments were successful when they governed but a small area, but when they began their territorial conquests they evolved into a tyrannical power.[18] The Federalist author 'Atticus' agreed with that assessment, and contended Rome by that time had degraded itself to where anyone who assembled an effective army could claim the title of "Caesar".[19] 'The Federal Farmer' cautioned against adopting a system akin to Rome, for under its authority the rights of the people would be taken from them by the government as it so chose.[20]

There were three specific subjects of disagreement that warranted allusions to Roman history and its constitution: The legislature, the executive, and control of the military. In his defense of the structure of Article I and the legislative branch, Alexander Hamilton provided comparisons between the Roman senate and the American congress, and stated there was no difference between the two bodies.[21] But James Madison's historical comparisons were more succinct: The delegates to the Constitutional Convention had learned the lessons of Greek and Roman history and, as such, had improved upon those ancient models to achieve a balance between liberty and stability.[22] Noah Webster observed, penning under the pseudonym 'A Citizen of America', whereas membership in the Roman senate held the prerequisite of property ownership, in the American equivalent no such qualification was required.[23] Webster also contended the Constitution limited the power of Congress to where both the central authority and the rights of the people under a republican form of government were firmly guaranteed.[24]

Federalist James Madison, in his defense of Article II, drew the comparisons between Brutus following the destruction of the Tarquin monarchy to the duties of the president of the United States.[25] To make the argument for a strong chief executive, Alexander Hamilton correlated the fall of the Roman Republic and how due to weak leadership, it had been forced to accept first the rule of dictators, and then the creation of an imperial government which had threatened the existence of Rome itself.[26] Noah Webster claimed Rome's most potent source of political power was its military, and in comparing the structure and authority between the *Pax Romana* and the American constitution, the latter was specifically designed to control its defenses.[27]

'Cato' commented the constitution was weak in its the protections from military power. The author claimed the federal constitution lacked such specificity in its language that it would foster the ambitions of men who would be as brutal as Caligula, Nero and Domitian should they assume power.[28] Countering criticisms against its structure and limitations placed upon the military, Madison again evoked Roman history: "[T]he liberties of Rome proved the final victim of her military triumphs".[29]

In recounting the evolution of written constitutions, there are two other documents which deserve acknowledgement. The first is the *Corpus Juris Civilis*, better known as *The Institutes of Justinian.*[30] Rather than being a governing charter, it was a highly organized civil code of conduct. Sir William Blackstone contended it was important as a precursor to the English common law.[31] It was not the same with the second, *The Constitution of the Iroquois Nations*, a document produced between 1450 and 1500.[32] Within its text there are 16 sets of clauses under specific topics which declare the policies and instruments of governance. It structure is as follows:

I. The rights, duties and qualifications of the Confederation Council.
II. The rights, duties and qualifications of the Five Nation Lords.
III. The election of the Pine Tree Chiefs.
IV. The names, duties and rights of the War Chiefs.
V. Clans and consanguinity.
VI. Official symbolism.
VII. Laws of adoption.
VIII. Laws of immigration.
IX. The rights of foreign nations.
X. The rights and powers of war.
XI. Treason or secession of a Nation.
XII. The rights of the people of the Five Nations.
XIII. Religious ceremonies protected.
XIV. The installation song.
XV. Protection of the house.
XVI. Funeral addresses.

The pertinent lessons of history are its illustrations of how specific issues were addressed in the past, as well as a detailed account as how not to repeat its mistakes. This was a moral the American Framers applied from their readings in both Greek and Roman history. With the close attention to the instruments of government used in the past, they concluded such a structure was compulsory to both sovereign authority and the rights of the people. It was never the abstract concept of structure at question amongst them, but the substance of the clauses and the perimeters of authority granted that fostered debate.

In their frequent citations of ancient Greek and Roman history, the impact of that rich intellectual past upon the structure of the Constitution cannot be denied. What provided its specific tenets were the philosophical treatises published in the nearly two centuries prior to the Constitutional Convention of 1787.

Niccolo Machiavelli's *The Prince* was founded upon the premise the average human being was endowed with limited intelligence and, thus, easily led. The ruler's wellbeing rested upon his ability to be an effective shepherd of his flock. Power was the lone concern of every 'prince' and he must use a combination of intellect, intrigue and violence to attain it. Once taken power had to be prudently administered to maintain position. The control of political power was wrought through a balance between the admiration of the people combined with their fear of the ruler's wrath, and if a ruler must choose between them, the latter was preferable to the former.[33] As societies were fragile, a prince too timid or cautious unleashed wars that destroyed the polity, while the most ruthless held his realm together.[34] A firm hand was necessary coupled with an acute distrust of others who held the same ambition.

Several centuries before the advent of the theories of evolution and natural selection, Machiavelli had formulated a political doctrine of a "survival of the fittest". It was from this design of an iron-fisted regime that emerged the initial inklings of modern citizenship. Though citizens were afforded only the rights the Prince endowed upon them, nonetheless their fealty guaranteed a stability, and provided the laws enforced by the ruler. These edicts applied to everyone which made all citizens equal within it. There were benefits for both the sovereign and the citizens: The people recognized rights given them as enforceable law and, in turn, accepted their author as the sovereign.[35]

But which liberties were guaranteed to citizens under this Machiavellian model?

First, rather than discouraging popular participation in governance, the ruler invigorated it, for no other reason as to be seen as one among the ordinary citizens.[36] Policy and law were to have the input of those obliged to obey them. Once such a right was threatened the citizens withdrew their loyalty to that ruler. Secondly, it must guarantee fundamental fairness for citizens to eradicate any civil strife which would threaten social stability.[37] Civilizations cannot long function where there are disparities between the people whose labor maintains its viability; therefore, so long as social organizations were based upon elemental rules applied to all citizens, its basic functions continued to flourish. These rights were not borne out of benevolence, but to solidify power by keeping the people contented.[38] Civil liberty did not hold any guarantees for it was imperiled through internal political instability, disloyalty of the people, or the influence of the conquered.[39] Legal equality was the sole means by which the Prince maintained the affinity of the people.[40] Because citizens were fickle, the purveyance of rights were not always in the sovereign's best interests, for while citizens profited under the ruler they were loyal, but should they suffer deprivation they would withdraw their fealty.[41] Therefore, when the people no longer believed the prince to be just or effective, to maintain his power and social stability, he must force the people to believe.[42] Thus, the modern notions of nationalism as useful to social cohesion were first put forward by Machiavelli.

Thomas Hobbes expounded upon Machiavelli's theorem. He argued a ruler and his constituency entered into a social contract freely in which both were governed by an established code of law agreed upon by both parties.[43] Within this political construct the government was legally culpable for the welfare of its constituents.[44] In turn, constituents submitted themselves totally to the governing power of the state, delineated as the "sovereign". Once sovereignty was placed upon a leader his position was legitimized by either institution or by acquisition.[45] The ruler was then the embodiment of political and moral authority of the state and served to ensure the stability of the society against all forces threatening it, and once sovereignty had been placed with a monarch, power was absolute and civil disobedience was not tolerated.[46]

Hobbes' defined liberty as freedom impeded by the sovereignty of the state through its ruler.[47] A citizen practiced freedom to validate it, and doing so was consistent with the unlimited power of the sovereign, as it was he who had granted it in the first place.[48] The most stable form of liberty was dependent upon the silence of the law.[49] He cited the ancient republics as examples for his ideas.[50] Quoting a passage from Aristotle's *Politics*, he contended the Athenians were free because they had been educated to be free as the means of instilling within them the aspiration to protect the realm against all enemies, all while praising Athens and Rome as his models.[51] Yet Hobbes was not convinced their republican governments were effective, for they had divided power among the citizens.[52] This dissolution of authority created political factions that caused the destruction of both.[53] In his example of the Roman Republic, Hobbes presented the dysfunction of republicanism by denoting their civil wars which had destroyed the Republic and brought about imperial rule.[54] What had held the empire together was affording the people of their provinces the opportunity for citizenship under the rule of the emperor.[55]

Jean Bodin contended in the exercise of power a sovereign was the embodiment of the law and, as such, was bound to uphold not only his own edicts, but those of his predecessors.[56] This was especially true with national constitutions, for their clauses applied to all parties, and could not be violated at the whim of one against the other.[57] If all mankind were subject to the natural law of God, both ruler and subjects were bound by is derivative, which was the civil law.[58]

John Locke asserted the social contract was necessary for the stability of a society.[59] Due to the chaotic state of nature and the unity of society was precarious, a code of laws was a vital prerequisite to any contract.[60] As stated previously, man had bested the state of nature through a combination of labor and self-mastery, not through the coronation of a ruler.[61] The state of nature was not as a condition of evil and ignorance from which humans escaped to progress, but the stepping-stone from which all-human traits and rights originated. It was the conquest of the state of nature that was the beginning of civilization, for it bestowed upon a human being dominion over himself and his property: "The labor of his body and the work of his hands, we may say are properly his."[62] Locke pointed out the sole legitimate sovereignty was one the constituency consented to, and was best expressed in a popularly elected legislature designed to counterbalance the powers of the sovereign.[63] Because of the firm reliance of government upon a constituency's allegiance, a citizen could not waive his right to freedom, for such an action was morally wrong.

In his multi-volume work *The Rights of War and Peace* Hugo Grotius provided a rationale for the social contract which echoed Locke's contentions regarding property. The concept of war was the result of infringements upon the inalienable rights of citizens.[64] When rights and possessions, as either individuals or as a nation, were violated, it was a justification for war, as such an action violated the foremost term of the social contract.[65] According to Grotius the need for such an agreement arose from human social evolution.[66]

From this development came the awareness of property and ownership and its protection.[67] Anticipating the 'noble savage' argument of Jean-Jacques Rousseau, Grotius claimed if all things were owned equally there would be no essential need for either rulers or laws, for there would be no legitimate claims of sovereignty.[68]

Algernon Sidney advocated a commonwealth over a hereditary monarchy, and called upon the examples of the Athenian and Roman republics.[69] He again referenced these two republics in his restatement of Hobbes' paradigm, as well as portraying the Roman emperors in a dishonorable light by delineating the causes of the republic's fall.[70] Also, Sidney disparaged the Athenian historian Xenophon for his characterization of the two popular democracies as dreadful places where the indolent thrived and the industrious failed.[71] Sidney time and again referred to the Athenian republic in which the monarch and the representative body worked concurrently.[72] In the conduct and management of armed conflicts he proposed popular governments were more effective and specifically cited the Persian invasion of Athens found in Thucydides' *History of the Peloponnesian War* as a pertinent example.[73] Sidney put forward written constitutions were effective bulwarks against frivolous wars, as evidenced again by Pericles and the fall of the Athenian republic.[74] He also argued governments under a social contract were less prone to civil disturbances utilizing the example of the overthrow of the tyrants which led to Solon's constitution and the peace which reigned afterward.[75]

At the heart of Sidney's political theory was that efficient governments operated under a monarchy which possessed a democratic element, the two of which complemented each other, as evidenced by ancient Rome.[76] He also contended such governments also allowed for innovation, referencing the transition from the Republic to the rule of the Caesars.[77] The comparisons made between the rule of the Etruscan Tarquins and the Roman Caesars illustrated Sidney's assertion absolute monarchy was an invitation to tyranny.[78] He also recounted the dictatorial rule of Sulla and the cruelties of his reign.[79] The worst example repeatedly cited by Sidney was Caligula, a tyrant who committed such egregious acts he was rightly overthrown as an enemy of the Roman people.[80] Thus constitutions and codes of law were necessary not only to govern the people, but also to regulate the actions of monarchs, and Sidney cited the *Twelve Tables* following the end of Etruscan rule as his example.[81]

François Marie Arouet, known by his pen name Voltaire, put forward in his political treatises that society had been based upon protection of life to enhance the opportunity for prosperity, rather than a complicated stratum of conflicting interests, and political power was held by force. Once a ruler obtained sovereignty his constituents became as "[a]nimals accustomed to the yoke [who] present themselves for yoking of their own accord."[82] Thus, monarchical rule by divine right was against the laws of nature.[83] Voltaire agreed with Hobbes that liberty was dependent upon the law.[84] Yet, he also distrusted social sanctions as being arbitrary.[85] Mankind could not achieve a perfect state, for in a constitutional monarchy the greatest fear was confusion, and in a traditional monarchy it was the abuse of power and malfeasance.[86] Thus, the only viable solution to the problem of sovereignty and government was a "pure" democracy, the more simple being the more equitable.[87]

Charles Louis de Secondat, the Baron de la Brede et de Montesquieu, wrote *The Spirit of the Laws* as a comparative study of three modes of government—

despotism, monarchy, and republicanism—in which he utilized historical precedents to determine the form of government best for a world in political flux. Though Montesquieu argued in favor of a popular sovereignty of equals, he was not an advocate of social equality for it caused antagonism between those who demand and those who have earned.[88] The nature of democracy was conductive to conflict and, thus, violated the purpose of law.[89] Human societies were complex, so it followed government would have to be its mirror image to carry out its charge. Montesquieu agreed with Sidney on one crucial point: "[T]hat when the deputies represent a body of people…[representatives] should be accountable to those who have commissioned them."[90] Within a popular sovereignty there was no means to achieve jurisdictional balance, for every tributary who held power exercised it for his own advantage.[91] Therefore, the powers of government had to be separated, and that a competition between political subsidiaries equal in power and limited in their authority would achieve the desired political end.[92]

Montesquieu based his philosophical tenets upon his readings of ancient history and praised the Athenians and Romans for including their citizens in the legislative process.[93] Furthermore, only leaders elected by the people, as evinced with the commissioners of Athens and the counsels and praetors of the Roman Republic, held the trust of the citizens in congruence with the social contract.[94] In his analysis of the *Constitution of the Athenians* Montesquieu praised its strict controls over both the conduct of the military and its popular participation in voting.[95] Though Solon had acted in contrast to his own laws, he nonetheless proceeded in the spirit of equality when he cancelled all debt, including that incurred by their government.[96] Montesquieu referred to the Athenian archon either as an example, or as a counter to specific laws of various countries and principalities.

Throughout *The Spirit of the Laws*, the author either cited or alluded to Roman history and law as an example to follow in forming governments. With regards to the social contract, Montesquieu looked to the Roman model to provide an explanation of federalism: It was a settlement between several clusters of people to merge themselves into a single, larger political entity that also allowed others to combine with it.[97] He stated rights were the privilege of citizenship and originated from the state itself, a concept borne from the Roman laws governing the legal treatment of slaves.[98] Another governing paradigm the Romans observed was the doctrine of church and state separation.[99] Also exampled was that only the Roman senate could raise taxes in the realm, an example provided in the constitution's grant of such authority to congress.[100] In a precedent preceding the American constitution, prior to the ratification of the Seventeenth Amendment in 1917, the author recounted that Roman senators were not elected by the people, replacements were chosen by another body of representatives.[101] Providing a precedent for the constitutional requirement of a "state of the union" address from the president, Roman magistrates were required to publicly answer for their conduct.[102] Montesquieu also warned once the people identified with a strong executive it would be near impossible to return the people to supporting legislative government—as evidenced by the dictator Sulla's attempt to do so which, in turn, led to several civil wars in Rome.[103]

Montesquieu delivered many caveats for modern governments from the examples from within the broad swathe of Rome's history. Citing the ancient Roman historian Livy, he asserted when Servius Tullius dictated the consistency of the classes, he followed an aristocratic model which left the choice of public servants with the upper classes.[104] In turn, these aristocratic classes voted in secret which, according Cicero, was a root cause of the fall of the Roman Republic.[105] Though the Roman senate possessed the right to make laws, they were valid for a year unless the people voted their approval.[106] Also, he warned against the corrosive effect of poverty among the citizenry for it led to sedition, as it did in the Roman provinces.[107] Legal confiscation should only be practiced in cases of high treason—an issue which would not be addressed within the U.S. Constitution until the ratification of the Fifteenth Amendment in 1870.[108] Finally, among Montesquieu's most fervent admonitions was of empire itself, which was the outcome of citizens providing too much of their sovereignty to ambitious leaders.[109] As exampled by Rome, the military must answer to a civilian authority—a tenet mirrored in the notion of the president as commander-in-chief within the constitution.[110]

Jean-Jacques Rousseau asserted government had thwarted within the mind of civilized human beings their ardor for freedom and, furthermore, not only accept their bondage, but to actually hold an affinity for it.[111] If human nature was free, for government to be human it required full citizen participation and a civic commitment for the common good, manifested in what he termed 'the General Will'. Once a political system was established happiness was problematic, as government was an excuse to enslave man. By its representative nature, a republic abolished individual liberty by placing the sovereignty of a citizen in a body of surrogates, thus individual citizens had no direct recourse in the decisions of their government.

Rousseau refuted Locke's theory that the object of government was to secure the peace of society.[112] Social contentment was an outgrowth of the repose of the people under the sovereignty of their general will, and as such sovereignty rested upon the individual as a rational agent who was free.[113] Moreover, for a government to be a legitimate agent of the people, it must possess the true consent of the governed.[114] When mankind turned away from being hunters and gatherers, the process had led to the concept of ownership and property. Economic disparities created a caste system consisting of rich and poor and fostered war between the classes.[115] Though Rousseau argued a return to the state of nature was hopeless, a participatory democracy was not only preferable, but the best mankind in his social state could hope to achieve.[116] He drew upon examples from ancient Athens and Rome.[117] The author singled out Solon as having produced a civil government capable of exercising the general will.[118]

Rousseau utilized instances from Roman history to make his points. He spent an entire chapter in analysis of the Roman constitution, along with the evolution of its governmental practices.[119] Initially, the author stated Rome was to be commended for having established a government focused upon individual rights for all its citizens.[120] Such was the case with the establishment of the Republic after the fall of the Tarquins.[121] Later, with the Roman Empire under the rule of the emperors, the author cited Roman virtue—a love for the realm over the individual—as the essential element which provided for over five centuries of stable governance.[122]

Though these philosophers shared many of the same precepts of democracy, their differences point out the inherent problems of popular sovereignty. In their influential writings Hobbes had initiated the modern discourses on the rule of law and popular sovereignty. The critiques of Locke, Sidney, Montesquieu, Voltaire, and Rousseau provided the intellectual basis for the sovereignty debates among the Framers of the United States Constitution. This linkage created the philosophical foundation for the Federalist and Anti-Federalist framers in their public debates over the constitution, a document which embodied the philosophical foundations provided by the sapient works discussed.

The beginning of American constitutionalism—government under the aegis of a social contract—can be traced to John Adams' tract *Thoughts on Government,* published April 1776.[123] Within its scant pages Adams proposed a tripartite government with legislative, executive and judicial branches each with separate functions that provided a balance of power, as well as a declaration of rights.[124] Not only was the construction of his ideas consistent with the *Constitution of the Athenians*, but it also incorporated the paradigms put forward by the Enlightenment philosophers, especially John Locke. Adams began with a bold statement that the purpose of government was the contentment of the people.[125] Virtue, honor and the dignity of the human person were later added to this list in the author's discussion.[126] A republican form of government was considered best as it embodied a government of laws and not of mere human will.[127]

Adams maintained the legislature be bicameral, for a unicameral body would engage in crafting legislation of benefit to themselves, rather than of the entire polity.[128] It would also exclude itself from the laws it enacted for the citizens to adhere.[129] Referencing the historical example of the British Long Parliament, Adams concluded a single assembly would proclaim itself permanent, with life membership divorced entirely from the populace they were established to represent.[130] The assembly must not practice either executive power, or judicial authority, and proposed one branch of the legislature be directly elected to represent the people and the other elected to represent the government so a political equilibrium would be achieved.[131] The executive should have both command of the military and power to pardon.[132] For justice to be rendered in court decisions, all judges must be independent of the executive and the legislative branches, and be qualified by both their education and experience in the law.[133] One aspect of government which Adams stressed was popular participation: "Laws for the liberal education of youth especially of the lower class of people, are so extremely wise and useful that, to a humane and generous mind, no expense for this purpose would be extravagant."[134]

What made Adams' contribution unique was not only was its influence upon the design of the state constitutions of Virginia, North Carolina, New Jersey, and New York, but he himself used it as his model for the *Constitution of the Commonwealth of Massachusetts Bay* in 1780.[135] Its structure is as follows:

Preamble:
Part One: A Declaration of Rights:
Part Two: The Framework of the Government:

1. The Legislative Power—
    - A. the General Court;
    - B. the Senate;
    - C. the House of Representatives
2. The Executive Power—
    - A. the Governor;
    - B. Lieutenant-Governor;
    - C. the Council and the setting of elections;
    - D. Secretary, Treasurer; Commissary, and others
3. The Judicial Power—
4. Delegates to Congress—

5. The University at Cambridge, and Encouragement of Literature, etc.—
   A. the University;
   B. the Encouragement of Literature;
   C. Oaths and Subscriptions, etc.[136]

It was Adams' structure as put forward in *Thoughts on Government* James Madison of Virginia sought to implement at the Philadelphia Convention.

The first written constitution of the United States was the *Articles of Confederation and Perpetual Union* which, according to James Madison's account, was drafted by John Dickinson in July 1775 but not ratified until six years later.[137] Its structure was as follows:

Article I: The title of the country.
Article II: Statement of state sovereignty.
Article III: The mode of national government is a confederacy.
Article IV: The rights of citizens with both the country and the sovereign states.
Article V: Legislative elaboration.
Article VI: Limitations upon the sovereign states.
Article VII: Authority of the sovereign states in national military matters.
Article VIII: Financial elaboration.
Article IX: International Affairs.
Article X: Further legislative elaboration.
Article XI: Canada considered a member of the United States of America.
Article XII: Further financial elaboration.
Article XIII: Authority of the Articles over the sovereign states.[138]

The *Articles* proved themselves nearly worthless as a governing instrument. First, there was an economic recession that arose following independence which proved impossible to confront due to all thirteen States issuing their own currencies, abided by their own monetary policies, and were unwilling to assist one another.[139] Secondly, not only did the nation face an external threat from Great Britain due to its refusal to abandon its fortifications, but there were also interstate conflicts over western expansion.[140] Finally, there were popular rebellions in every one of the thirteen States in which governmental functionality had been either threatened or shut down completely. Two examples were the Hatfield Uprising of 1786 and Shays' Rebellion of 1787. In both cases, the representatives in Congress were required to authorize an armed force—which had to be raised from scratch and trained before deployment—before a unified action could be taken against the rebels.[141] The rebellions broke up under their own volition before the Confederation force could be employed.[142]

In between these uprisings twelve delegates from five states met at Annapolis, Maryland to discuss necessary changes to the *Articles*.[143] In his account of the proceedings James Madison stated after surveying the document the delegates agreed they were unworkable and needed revision, but the sovereign states would be adversarial in the effort to make any changes.[144] It was decided to call a full convention to consider both amending and restructuring the *Articles* the following year.[145] Though the meeting was eventually called for the 14th of May 1787, the first of the delegates did not arrive until nine days later.[146]

It was Edmund Randolph of Virginia who put forward a list of grievances against the *Articles*, which were:

1. Confederation government provided no effective bulwark against foreign invasion—
2. Confederation government could neither intercede between the sovereign states, nor quell a popular rebellion—
3. A new structure of government would provide an expanse of benefits which were restricted under the *Articles of Confederation*—
4. Confederation government could not cease and desist infringements upon the authority of the central government.[147]

Randolph described continuing under its authority as ludicrous and that the republic was in real danger of imploding.[148] James Wilson of Pennsylvania determined the deficiency of the *Articles* was the central authority had too little power, and as such was incapable of acting congruent with its constitutional charges[149] In Wilson's assessment to address and rectify the dysfunction of the confederacy was the essential reason the delegates had been sent to the convention in the first place.[150]

At the time the federal constitution was framed there was a national crisis at hand: James Madison argued the separate States were tottering on the brink of disunion due to internal dissention along with the threat of foreign invasion.[151] It was his conviction a new written instrument of government would strengthen the Union, as well as foster more cordial relationships among the sovereign states.[152] Alexander Hamilton was blunt in his statements. Due to its foundation upon State Rights, the *Articles of Confederation* were not strong enough to hold the country together.[153] It lacked the authority to force the individual States to abide by the nation's essential edicts, as well the authority to influence its members into compliance.[154] As such, the *Articles* had portrayed the United States as a country that could not govern itself, much to the amusement of the rest of the world, due to its virile attachment to the authority of state governments.[155] He also contended the resolve of the federal constitution was to provide necessary central authority to hold the country together.[156] Its purpose was to protect the nation as a whole as well as its individual states, preserve the peace between them, and to oversee free trade internally between the States and with other countries.[157]

The Anti-Federalists were leery of the consolidation of state-based political power into a central government. 'Brutus' posed their foremost question: Whether under this new federal constitution the states would be amalgamated into one large nation, governed by laws passed by a single legislative body, administered by a single executive, and adjudicated by one set of judges.[158] Later, he put forward the tenets of social contract theory as the basis of free government: That the people themselves must agree to any government whose authority under which they must live.[159] The author then placed the United States into a historical comparison with other known republics, and fretted the U.S. would become the largest republican government in recorded history, specifically noting those of Athens and Rome.[160] It would inevitably follow the same path of those ancient polities in pursuit of territorial conquest, as well as abandoning republican principles to become akin to a tyrannical imperial state.[161] This change would be wrought in a subtle manner, as it had in both ancient Athens and Rome, in which the rule of law over the many would become the rule of one whose will was absolute.[162]

'Brutus' specifically cited Article I § 8's Necessary and Proper Clause which gave the Congress the authority to pass laws as it saw fit.[163] He then coupled the previous citation with Article VI's Supreme Law Clause, and concluded as the broad power to execute the functions of government were ratified, under this federal constitution state governments were unnecessary.[164] According to 'Brutus', the constitution was not a document which limited the power of government, but centralized and consolidated political power to the detriment of the individual states.[165]

'Brutus' described the power of the Supreme Court, as put forward in Article III, as limitless, for it possessed the authority to adjudicate all cases concerning the construction of the Constitution without any higher court for appeal.[166] Once its power was proclaimed, the Court held an authority above both the legislative and executive branches, as well as those above the individual sovereign states.[167] It would influence those appointed to the bench to act unilaterally, for there was no oversight practiced upon them from the other two branches.[168] He also argued the Supreme Court presupposed justice was unobtainable under the authority of the state courts, and the latter would lose many of the rights already afforded them.[169] As such, this notion ran counter to the duties and authority for which it was originally intended to exercise.[170] But the author agreed with the Federalists regarding the independence of the judiciary, so that "they may maintain firmness and steadiness in their decisions."[171]

'The Federal Farmer' argued equitable representation under a unified government was impossible due to the size of the population.[172] The author contended there was no way all of the divisions could be represented in one large body, though in comparison, it was possible in the state governments due to their locality and specificity.[173] The constitution focused the bulk of its authority in a central location far removed from the citizens of the states who would, at that point, have little recourse in correcting errors in legislation.[174] The author bemoaned the federal government's ability to act unilaterally upon citizens, rather than by a political authority that was in close proximity to them.[175] In concurrence 'An Old Whig' asserted whereas the *Articles* had stated all powers not provided for the central government were reserved for the states, the federal constitution was void of such a clause.[176] The author also argued for the inclusion of a bill of rights, as well as for more stringent control of the executive in the capacity of commander-in-chief.[177]

'Cato' argued the constitution placed the federal government's authority above the individual states, which was a mistake, as the citizens of the states were too varied in their culture and interests to thrive and flourish under a general government.[178] 'Centinel' warned it was folly to trust a constitutional system of checks-and-balances to the protection of their rights and liberties.[179] The author was also in agreement with 'Brutus' as to the potential for the abuse of power of the Supreme Court.[180] He warned the consolidation of the states into a single federal union would inevitably result in despotism.[181]

Of all of the Anti-Federalist essayists 'John DeWitt' was the arguably the most articulate. 'DeWitt' defended the *Articles* as a government constructed and chosen by the people.[182] The new federal constitution was neither a revision of the *Articles*, nor a stop-gap measure—it was a fully formed federal system of government that if ratified would be in perpetuity.[183] The document was difficult to change, an amendment needing a large majority in both houses of congress and the state legislatures, which meant should problems arise they would remain unaltered.[184] Also, there was no Bill of Rights expressed within it.[185] 'DeWitt' asserted without such a statement of rights, the government possessed a monopoly of power over its citizens.[186]

This debate focused upon a difficult question. How could a centralized authority deliver greater efficacy than one divided between thirteen sovereign states without reducing their relevancy? In a careful examination of the structure of this governmental instrument, the Constitution itself provided few answers. Furthermore, only time could reveal the truth.

The Constitution of the United States was a negotiated government instrument wrought through debate and compromise over a period of three-and-a-half months. The structure of the federal constitution is as follows:

Article I—Congressional Elaboration:
- §1 Definition of Congress as bicameral—
- §2 Qualifications for the House of Representatives—
- §3 Qualifications for the Senate—
- §4 Specifications for congressional elections—
- §5 Powers and Duties of both Houses of Congress—
- §6 Rights and Restrictions on Congress members—
- §7 Legislative powers of both Houses of Congress—
- §8 Powers of Congress—
- §9 Powers Denied to Congress.

Article II—Presidential Elaboration:
- §1 Nature of Presidential Power—
- §2 Powers and Duties of the President—
- §3 Execution of Laws and the State of the Union Address—
- §4 Presidential Impeachment.

Article III—Judicial Elaboration:
- §1 Powers of the Judiciary—
- §2 Jurisdiction of the Supreme Court—
- §3 Definition of and Trials for Treason.

Article IV—Interstate Relations:
- §1 Full Faith and Credit—
- §2 Privileges, Immunities, Extradition, Non-discrimination—
- §3 Admission Procedures for Statehood—
- §4 Republican Form of Government.

Article V—Amending Power: Procedures for Amendment.

Article VI—Supremacy Power: Supremacy of the Federal Government.

Article VII—Ratification.

Writing fifteen years following the ratification debates, law professor St. George Tucker penned two exquisite disquisitions: one on the national charter titled *View of the Constitution of the United States* and *On the Several Forms of Government*, an examination on political systems and ideologies. Together they represent a congruence of the Federalists' contention of the necessity of a central government, while given credence to the Anti-Federalist argument as to the role of the individual states. In his former treatise, Tucker defined the Constitution as a compact in which sovereign states had united within a confederacy without losing their individual political identity.[187] Thus, the document created a power-sharing political venture operating within two separate spheres of influence—a doctrine adopted by the U.S. Supreme Court in its decision in *Charles River Bridge v. Warren Bridge* (1837).[188] Furthermore, the Tenth Amendment guaranteed this relationship: "the powers not delegated to the United States by the constitution, nor prohibited by it to the states, are reserved to the states respectively, or to the people."[189] The document assured the country and its individual states a republican government.[190] Because the constitution had been framed by representatives of the people, as well as ratified in conventions by members of their individual states, it was a contract in which all the people were a party to.[191] Rather than being a staid instrument of government, the constitution had procedures to amend it: A safeguard which allowed for any changes to be wrought through the will of the American citizens themselves.[192]

According to Tucker, the federal government was founded upon "the free consent and suffrages of the people of the several states, separately, and independently, expressed."[193] Citing the *Constitution of the Athenians*, the author reasoned every charter of government must prevent the tyranny of a single ruler while preventing the citizens from disregarding its tenets.[194] Tucker also issued a warning should the democratic man renege upon his charge to uphold the principles of democracy, he ultimately becomes the tyrant he so feared.[195] The purpose of the American social contract was to do for the people through representatives chosen by themselves to perform both the administrative duties of government, as well as to preserve the amity between the individual states.[196] It was in this manner both the Federalists and the Anti-Federalists had both received what they had sought.

In hindsight it was a fairly simple task to discern which side held the most correct position, but at that time no one could have known what the consequences of their actions would be. That something needed to be done to halt the political disintegration of the country was apparent to a specific group later termed the 'Federalists'. Yet there were a further clutch called the 'Anti-Federalists' who perceived nothing to be wrong with it. During the Annapolis convention delegates from five states carefully examined the *Articles of Confederation and Perpetual Union* and found them lacking, and they set their sights on a further gathering the following year in Philadelphia to design a new governing charter for the United States.

In the construction of a governmental organization, they drew upon historical models, philosophical concepts, and legal precedent. When discussing the purpose of such a document, the delegates were faced with five perplexing abstract questions: 1) what was the nature of justice and how could it be proficiently rendered; 2) how could political power be balanced between the need of one final political authority and the existence of several individual sovereign States; 3) how could a central government control a military created to defend the burgeoning country without that organization evolving into an all-consuming instrument of empire building; 4) what was in the best interests of the people and how could government be a tool in obtaining it; and, 5) how did a political authority define liberty, construct it within a governmental framework, and maintain it in perpetuity?

The Framers were given an undertaking which involved careful consideration on several divergent dimensions and incorporating them into a flexible instrument of government. Thus, the construction and ratification of this social contract was the beginning of a journey, not its conclusion, and one which we, their descendants, are still rightfully engaged upon.

Notes

1. Aristotle, *The Politics*, ed. William Ellis (Buffalo, NY: Prometheus Books, 1986), 2.
2. Aristotle, *The Constitution of the Athenians*, trans. Sir Frederick G. Kenyon; at The Internet Classics Archive; Section I, Part 3. http://classics.mit.edu/Aristotle/athenian_const.mb.txt. Accessed 30 August 2016.
3. *Ibid.*, Section I, Part 4.
4. Plutarch, *The Complete Collection of Plutarch's Parallel Lives*, trans. John Dryden (CreateSpace Independent Publishing Platform from Outskirts Press, 2014), 32–4.
5. *The Constitution of the Athenians*, Section I, Part 5.
6. *Ibid.*, Sections II, Parts 42 to 44 and Section III, Parts 45 to 69.
7. *Ibid.*, Section I, Parts 2 and 3.
8. James Madison, "Essay #38"; in *The Federalist,* The Gideon Edition, eds. George W. Carey and James McClellan (Indianapolis, IN: The Liberty Fund, 2001), 186–7.
9. James Madison, "Essay #63"; in, *Ibid.*, 329.
10. James Wilson, "Oration on the Fourth of July 1788", in *Friends of the Constitution: Writings of the 'Other' Federalists 17878–1788*, eds. Colleen A. Sheehan and Gary L. McDowell (Indianapolis, IN: The Liberty Fund, 2001), 503.
11. Michael Grant, *History of Rome* (New York: Charles Scibner's Sons, 1978), 75.
12. Livy, *The Early History of Rome*, trans., Aubrey De Sélincourt (New York: Penguin Books, 1960), 105. Grant, 67.
13. Livy, 247–8.

14. William Blackstone, *Commentaries on the Laws of England*, ed. William Draper Lewis, reprint of 1922 edition (Clark, NJ: The Lawbook Exchange, 2004), I: 69. Italics are that of the author.
15. "Introduction: VI. The Roman Constitution"; from *Select Orations and Letters of Cicero*. eds. J. B. Greenough and G. L. Kittredge. (Boston, MA: Ginn and Company, 1902). At http://www.uah.edu/student_life/organizations/SAL/texts/misc/romancon.html. Accessed 22 March 2016.
16. "A Citizen of Philadelphia" (Pelitiah Webster), "The Weakness of Brutus Exposed" (1787); in *Friends of the Constitution*, 194.
17. James Wilson, "Oration on the Fourth of July 1788", in *Friends of the Constitution*, 503.
18. "Brutus", "Essay #1", 18 October 1787, *The Anti-Federalists: Selected Writings and Speeches*, ed. Bruce Frohnen (Washington, DC: Regnery Publishing, Inc., 1999), 380.
19. "Atticus", "Essay #1", 8 August 1787; in *Friends of the Constitution*, 330.
20. "The Federal Farmer", "Letter #8", 8 January 1788; in *The Anti-Federalists*, 208.
21. Alexander Hamilton, "Essay #34"; in *The Federalist*, 162–3.
22. James Madison, "Essay #63"; in *The Federalist*, 328.
23. "A Citizen of America" (Noah Webster), "Leading Principles of the Constitution", 17 Oct. 1787; in *Friends of the Constitution*, 385.
24. *Ibid.*, 405.
25. James Madison, "Essay #38"; in *The Federalist*, 186.
26. Alexander Hamilton, "Essay #70"; in *The Federalist*, 362.
27. "A Citizen of America" (Noah Webster), "Leading Principles of the Constitution", 17 Oct. 1787; in *Friends of the Constitution*, 397, 398.
28. "Cato", "Letter #5", 22 November 1787, in *The Anti-Federalists*, 21.
29. James Madison, "Essay #41"; in *The Federalist*, 209.
30. *Corpus Juris Civilis* (The Institutes of Justinian), ed. J. B. Moyle. At http://www.gutenberg.org/files/5983/5983-h/5983-h.htm. Accessed 29 March 2016.
31. Blackstone, I: 63.
32. *The Constitution of the Iroquois Nations*. At http://www.indigenouspeople.net/iroqcon.htm. Accessed 30 March 2016.
33. Niccolo Machiavelli, *The Prince*, eds. Quentin Skinner and Russell Price (New York: Cambridge University Press, 1988), 59.
34. *Ibid.*, 34–7.
35. *Ibid.*, 18–9.
36. *Ibid.*, 35–6.
37. *Ibid.*, 30, 79.
38. *Ibid.*, 15, 66.
39. *Ibid.*, 17–18.
40. *Ibid.*, 26, 35.

41. *Ibid.*, 59.
42. *Ibid.*, 21.
43. Thomas Hobbes, *Leviathan*, ed. Richard Tuck (New York: Cambridge University Press, 1996), 122.
44. *Ibid.*, 153, 231.
45. *Ibid.*, 139, 143, 150–2.
46. *Ibid.*, 121, 139, 227.
47. *Ibid.*, 171.
48. *Ibid.*, 172, 173.
49. *Ibid.*, 178.
50. *Ibid.*, 149.
51. *Ibid.*, 150, 255. Aristotle, 362.
52. *Ibid.*, 222–3.
53. *Ibid.*, 225.
54. *Ibid.*, 67–8.
55. *Ibid.*, 137–8.
56. Jean Bodin, *Six Books of the Commonwealth*, ed. M. J. Tooley (Oxford, England: Basil Blackwell, 1955), 28.
57. *Ibid.*, 30.
58. *Ibid.*, 36.
59. John Locke, *Two Treatises on Government*, ed. Peter Laslett (New York: Cambridge University Press, 1960), 333.
60. *Ibid.*, 351.
61. *Ibid.*, 284.
62. *Ibid.*, 288.
63. *Ibid.*, 283.
64. Hugo Grotius, *The Rights of War and Peace*, ed. Richard Tuck (Indianapolis, IN: The Liberty Fund, 2005), II: 420. Italics are that of the author.
65. *Ibid.*, II: 420–4.
66. *Ibid.*, II: 426.
67. *Ibid.*
68. *Ibid.*, II: 435–6.
69. Algernon Sidney, *Discourses Concerning Government*, ed. Thomas G. West (Indianapolis, IN: The Liberty Fund, 1996), 30.
70. *Ibid.*, 101.
71. *Ibid.*, 175. Xenophon quoted from the *Constitution of the Lacedaemonians* 1.2–10.
72. *Ibid.*, 166.
73. *Ibid.*, 201.
74. *Ibid.*, 203.
75. *Ibid.*, 221.
76. *Ibid.*, 167.

77. *Ibid.*, 170–1.
78. *Ibid.*, 174.
79. *Ibid.*, 262–3.
80. *Ibid.*, 226–7.
81. *Ibid.*, 391.
82. Voltaire, "Thoughts on Public Administration," in *Political Writing*, ed. David Williams (New York: Cambridge University Press, 1994), 213.
83. Voltaire, "Politique," in *Ibid.*, 84.
84. Voltaire, "Thoughts on Public Administration," in *Ibid.*, 216.
85. Voltaire, "Laws," in *Ibid.*, 19.
86. Voltaire, "Thoughts on Public Administration," in *Ibid.*, 217.
87. Voltaire, "Laws," in *Ibid.*, 18.
88. Montesquieu, *The Spirit of the Laws*, eds. Anne Cohler, Basia Miller, and Harold Stone (New York: Cambridge University Press, 1989), 46.
89. *Ibid.*, 114.
90. *Ibid.*, 159–60.
91. *Ibid.*, 169.
92. *Ibid.*, 510.
93. *Ibid.*, 12, 15.
94. *Ibid.*, 11–12.
95. *Ibid.*
96. *Ibid.*, 45, 205.
97. *Ibid.*, 131.
98. *Ibid.*, 247.
99. *Ibid.*, 501–2.
100. *Ibid.*, 164. *U.S. Constitution*, Article I § 8.
101. Montesquieu, 15. *U.S. Constitution*, Seventeenth Amendment.
102. Montesquieu, 54.
103. *Ibid.*, 22.
104. *Ibid.*, 12–3. Livy, 81–2.
105. *Ibid.*, 14. Cicero, *On the Commonwealth and On the Laws*, ed. James E. G. Zetzel (New York: Cambridge University Press, 1999), 112–4.
106. Montesquieu, 15.
107. Montesquieu, 64.
108. *Ibid.*, 65. *U. S. Constitution*, Fifteenth Amendment.
109. Montesquieu, 143.
110. *Ibid.*, 165. U.S. Constitution, Article II § 2.
111. Jean-Jacques Rousseau, "A Discourse on the Moral Effects of the Arts and Sciences", (1750); in Jean-Jacques Rousseau, *The Social Contract and Other Later Political Writings*, ed. C. D. H. Cole (Rutland, VT: Charles E. Tuttle Co., Inc., 1973), 5.
112. Locke, 359.

113. Jean-Jacques Rousseau, "Discourse on Political Economy", (1755); in, *The Social Contract and Other Later Political Writings*, ed. Victor Gourevitch (New York: Cambridge University Press, 1996), 6–7.
114. Jean-Jacques Rousseau, "Of the Social Contract", (1762); in, *Ibid.*, 57.
115. *Ibid.*, 162–4.
116. *Ibid.*, 167.
117. Rousseau, "Discourse on Political Economy"; in, *Ibid.*, 8.
118. Rousseau, "Of the Social Contract"; in, *Ibid.*, 60.
119. Rousseau, "Of the Social Contract"; in, *Ibid.*, 127–42.
120. Rousseau, "Discourse on Political Economy"; in, *Ibid.*, 18.
121. Rousseau, "Of the Social Contract"; in, *Ibid.*, 72.
122. Rousseau, "Discourse on Political Economy"; in, *Ibid.*, 22.
123. John Adams, "Thoughts on Government", (1776); in *The Revolutionary Writings of John Adams*, ed. C. Bradley Thompson (Indianapolis, IN: The Liberty Fund, 1987), 287–93.
124. *Ibid.*, 289.
125. *Ibid.*, 287.
126. *Ibid.*, 287–8.
127. *Ibid.*, 288.
128. *Ibid.*
129. *Ibid.*
130. *Ibid.*
131. *Ibid.*, 288, 290.
132. *Ibid.*, 291.
133. *Ibid.*, 291–2.
134. *Ibid.*, 292.
135. Page Smith, *John Adams* (Garden City, NY: Doubleday & Company, Inc., 1962), I: 439–44. *Revolutionary Writings*, 286.
136. *The Founders' Constitution*, eds. Philip B. Kurland and Ralph Lerner (Indianapolis, IN: The Liberty Fund, 1987), I: 11–23.
137. James Madison, *Notes of Debates in the Federal Constitution of 1787* (Athens, OH: Ohio University Press, 1966, 1985), 5.
138. *The Founders' Constitution*, I: 23–26.
139. Forrest McDonald, *E Pluribus Unum: The Formation of the American Republic 1776–1790*, 1979 reprint (Indianapolis, IN: The Liberty Fund, 1965), 46–7.
140. *Ibid.*, 41–2.
141. McDonald, 249–56. Gordon S. Wood, *Creation of the American Republic 1776–1787* (Chapel Hill, NC: University of North Carolina Press, 1969), 412–3. *Articles of Confederation*, Article IX, Clause 5.
142. McDonald, 249–56.
143. McDonald, 239–40. Wood, 327.

144. Madison, 10.
145. *Ibid.*, 13.
146. *Ibid.*, 23.
147. *Ibid.*, 29–30.
148. *Ibid.*, 127.
149. *Ibid.*, 296.
150. *Ibid.*
151. James Madison, "Essay No. 20"; in, *The Federalist*, 98.
152. *Ibid.*
153. Alexander Hamilton, "Essay No. 21"; in, *The Federalist*, 99.
154. *Ibid.*
155. *Ibid.*, 100, 1011.
156. Alexander Hamilton, "Essay No. 22"; in *The Federalist*, 112.
157. *Ibid.*, 113.
158. 'Brutus', "Essay #1", 18 October 1787; in *The Anti-Federalist: Writings by the Opponents of the Constitution*, ed. Herbert Storing (Chicago, IL: University of Chicago Press, 1981), 109.
159. *Ibid.*, 114.
160. *Ibid.*, 113.
161. *Ibid.*
162. *Ibid.*, 114.
163. *Ibid.*, 110. *U.S. Constitution*, Article I § 8.
164. *Ibid.*, *U.S. Constitution*, Article VI.
165. *Ibid.*, 112–13.
166. *Ibid.*, 164, 165.
167. *Ibid.*
168. *Ibid.*, 166.
169. 'Brutus', "Essay #12", 14 February 1788; in *The Anti-Federalist*, 171, 172.
170. 'Brutus', "Essay #13", 21 February 1788; in *The Anti-Federalist*, 173.
171. 'Brutus', "Essay #16", 10 April 1788; in *The Anti-Federalist*, 187.
172. 'The Federal Farmer', "Letter #2", 9 October 1787; in *The Anti-Federalists*, 151.
173. *Ibid.*, 152–3.
174. *Ibid.*, 154–5.
175. 'The Federal Farmer', "Letter #17", 23 January 1788; in *The Anti-Federalists*, 290–2.
176. 'An Old Whig', "Essay #2", 17 October 1787; in *The Anti-Federalists*, 322.
177. 'An Old Whig', Essay #5, 1 November 1787; in *The Anti-Federalists*, 341.
178. 'Cato', "Letter #3", 25 October 1787; in *The Anti-Federalists*, 9–10.
179. 'Centinel', "Letter #1", 5 October 1787; in *The Anti-Federalists*, 37–8.
180. *Ibid.*, 39–40.
181. 'Centinel', "Letter #5", 4 December 1787; in *The Anti-Federalists*, 82–3.
182. 'John DeWitt', "Essay #1", 22 October 1787; in *The Anti-Federalists*, 491.

183. 'John DeWitt', "Essay #2", 29 October 1787; in in *The Anti-Federalists*, 495.
184. *Ibid.*, 496.
185. *Ibid.*
186. *Ibid.*, 497.
187. St. George Tucker, "View of the Constitution of the United States" (1803); in, *View of the Constitution of the United States, with Selected Writings*, ed. Clyde N. Wilson (Indianapolis, IN: The Liberty Fund, 1999), 92.
188. *Ibid. Charles River Bridge v. Warren Bridge*, 36 U.S. 420 (1837); at https://supreme.justia.com/cases/federal/us/36/420/case.html. Accessed 12 May 2016.
189. *U.S. Constitution*, Tenth Amendment. Tucker quoted the entirety of the Tenth Amendment of the U.S. Constitution; in "Views of the Constitution of the United States", 93–4.
190. Tucker quoting the Government Clause of the U.S. Constitution; in "Views of the Constitution of the United States", 94. *U.S. Constitution*, Article I § 4.
191. *Ibid.*, 120.
192. *Ibid.*, 121.
193. St. George Tucker, "Of the Several Forms of Government" (1803); in, *View of the Constitution of the United States, with Selected Writings*, 34.
194. *Ibid.*, 42.
195. *Ibid.*, 42.
196. *Ibid.*, 124.

2

"Establish Justice"

Impartiality and Equity under a Federal Constitution

Among the ironies of human beings is that they are the sole species to grasp the abstract concept of justice, yet they are incapable of achieving it. To obtain what is just one must be aware of what it is not. It is by experiencing injustice people to discover for themselves that which is just. It begs the question: If something is unjust, how can it be rectified as to not cause further injustice?

Justice is a concept defined by each individual's understanding of it. What is just to one will not necessarily be so for another. What makes it more murky are the words associated with what is "just"—fairness, equity, honesty, righteousness, morality—are also subject to personal interpretation. This infers justice must be consciously and continuously sought. It also presupposes several revealing questions: Is justice a self-evident but unyielding trait, or is it dependent upon circumstance? If justice is defined solely by one's belief or bias, how can anything be truly 'just'? Is it out of the ordinary for two people searching for a just solution to come to different logic-based conclusions? How does a society conclude what is just for all if the concept is as individual as each citizen residing within it?

Then there are others who argue that only within a social construct in which each individual comports themselves autonomously in an equitable manner can a just society be achieved. But is it not out of the realm of possibility to conclude the pursuit of justice, a noble cause of itself, can be rationally perverted into a vain pursuance of power? This is because what is right for the few or the one is not always applicable to the many. The general course and specific events of our existence shape our perceptions of right-and-wrong, and these acuities continuously change over the course of our lifetimes. Thus, it is not illogical to conclude morality is neither staid nor unyielding.

This is at the heart of why human beings disagree on what is just. Each one of us grasp for order and meaning in our lives, and we champion such tenets which allow us a reasonable amount of stability. Yet a society which cannot concur upon the most generalized ethical principles will inevitably destroy itself over rectifiable situations. If people cannot agree on what is just, and if we choose to cease-and-desist from our search for justice, society would have reached what philosopher Friedrich Nietzsche explained as tyranny, with extinction as its unavoidable destination.[1]

Laws have been made since the dawn of civilization, the oldest extant example being the Neo-Sumerian Code of Ur-Nammu of ancient Mesopotamia written c. 2000 BCE.[2] It was in that region during the 17th century BCE the first known codes of justice, written protocols of jurisprudence, flourished. The first known written statements of civil rights and liberties were embedded in the Code of Hammurabi, another ancient Mesopotamian ruler, written in the mid-seventeenth century BCE.[3] Several Greek city-states also possessed written constitutions from which codes of law were constructed, as evidenced in *The Histories* by Herodotus.[4]

It is not difficult to appreciate the impact of the *Constitution of the Athenians* upon its American counterpart.[5] Several of the clauses were important predecessors to the Framers' concepts of social rights and justice under a structured government. For example, one tenet of relevance to our time and included within the text itself was the account of how the majority of the Athenian people had been enslaved by debt to the wealthy class, rose up against them, and with the composition of Solon's constitution, stripped them of their influence.[6] Both the philosopher Aristotle and the historian Herodotus recounted the circumstances under which Solon had drawn up a constitution and mandated all Athenian citizens and governing officials swear an oath to act in accordance.[7] Under this code citizens were provided with four inalienable rights:

1. The prohibition of slavery through money lending—
2. The right of a citizen to legal redress of wrongs committed by others against them—
3. The right of a citizen to an appeal of a judgement of the court—
4. The right of a citizen to vote in an election.[8]

Among the democratic innovations instituted by Solon was the establishment of the Council of the Five Hundred: A parliamentary forerunner to what contemporary Americans recognize as 'Congress'.[9]

Such reforms were in contrast to the governments of neighboring kingdoms such as Persia, with whom Greece later fought a grueling war for their survival. As Herodotus recounted, most nations were under the absolute rule of a king who governed by whim, rather than by written law.[10] Under absolute monarchy the sovereign issued death sentences at will regardless of evidence of innocence, forced women to service his sexual desires, and could not be held accountable for his actions.[11] The Persians had rejected democracy as they were convinced differences of political opinion led to civil war.[12]

The code of laws written by Solon were fashioned with legal reforms that included the right of the accused to examine all evidence and witnesses against them.[13] The voting franchise was given to all, provided they were 18 years-old and were born citizens of the realm.[14] In a measure to encourage popular political participation each government member, the exception being members of the War Council and their generals, were limited to a single term of service in any one office, and received a meager salary payment only upon attendance at a legislative session.[15] The satellite cities and towns were granted the right of self-government and remained citizens of Athens.[16] All matters concerning the prosecution of crimes and the required punishments following a guilty verdict were within the purview of the authorized courts of law.[17] Public servants were not immune from court cases brought against them by citizens if they were perceived as having acted unlawfully.[18] Among the duties of the Council was the administration of state funds provided for those affected either by poverty, or incapacitated by illness—the harbinger of modern social responsibility programs.[19]

While the Greek Islands were involved in the long and destructive Peloponnesian War, the city-state of Rome was engaged in designing its own code of civil law. The final product was the *Leges Duodecim Tabularum* (*The Law of the Twelve Tables*).[20] Though no copies are known to be extant, from the fragments scholars have pieced together it was a work based upon Solon's *Constitution of the Athenians*. The Roman statesman Cicero indicated the tables were centered upon "war and peace, the position of our allies, the levying of taxes, and the legal rights assigned to rank and age."[21] Of the last item, citizens were imbued with explicit rights of criminal procedures which were exempt from the rescission of government.[22] The historian Livy specified the *Tables* were forged in bronze and located where all citizens had access to them.[23] Over time they became outdated and, according to historian Edward Gibbon, affluent Romans found amusement in breaking the law and paying whatever fine was levied against them.[24]

The *Ius Civile Romanarum*—the Roman civil law—was the outgrowth of the *Twelve Tables* and the founding of the Roman Republic. Under its edicts either commanders of the legions or the judges of the civil courts were given the title of "praetor", and though they were not bound by the edicts of a predecessor, they were aware of past decisions and sought to decide cases in a consistent matter.[25] With this development came the idea of legal precedent.[26] By the onset of the Classical Era the codes evolved into an intricate system of civil law, accompanied by Sulla's expansion of the legal courts.[27] Among its more significant innovations was the development of rights concerning possession and ownership.[28]

With the advent of Imperial Rome came vital reforms in the *Ius Civile*. First were expansions of the legal system which guaranteed even the poorest of Romans could participate, as well as safeguards for the treatment of slaves.[29] Julius Paulus' seminal work *Sententiae* (*Opinions*) was a personal analysis of civil law which sought to transform traditional Roman values of family and property towards a more democratic and philanthropic direction.[30] His argument was with the relief of poverty came a respite in the discontent against the Roman government.[31] Domitus Ulpianus (Upian) contended all persons were born in a state of freedom, therefore slavery was an unnatural state—an argument made not on the basis of morality, but to calm the growing restlessness towards Rome.[32] The single most vital development of this time was that jurists, lawyers and legal philosophers wrote long explanatory theses upon the *Ius Civile* which have been preserved and translated, and out of this was born the concept of judicial opinions explaining specific interpretations of the law.[33]

Historian Frederick William Maitland in his work *The Constitutional History of England* explained how the country's canon law, instituted during the reign of King Stephen, was directly influenced by a renewed study of Roman law.[34] The beginning of British constitutionalism arose with the forced acceptance by King John of the *Magna Carta* in 1215. With the recognition of the Great Charter, asserted by historian Thomas Lord Macaulay, the Constitution to which all others afterward has been modeled, became recognized as a noble instrument of citizenship rights.[35] Though in the assessment of historian David Hume the document was most favorable to the barons, it did feature important clauses containing ideas which found their way into both the U.S. Constitution and its initial ten amendments.[36] Clause 39 asserted the right of both a trial by a jury of one's peers and a just sentence to be rendered.[37] These clauses were the direct result of the king standing publically accused of selling verdicts and pardons to the highest bidder.[38] In the assessment of legal historians Frederick Pollard and Frederic Maitland, "[King] John, in these last years, had been breaking the law; therefore, the law must be defined and set in writing."[39]

Though the *Magna Carta* limited the rights of the king, it also provided leeway for him to conduct the nation's business as he saw fit.[40] Historian David Hume praised the document as a milestone in the development of constitutionalism, as it forged legal justice and the rights of property all citizens enjoy.[41] Refuting such praise historians Pollard and Maitland argued "some of these celebrated clauses are premature, while others are vague and can be eluded."[42]

The next crucial development in the concept of justice was *The Petition of Right* (1628): A measure introduced in parliament prior to King Charles I dismissing it in 1629.[43] Among the members' complaints was the monarch had given his ascent to government officials forcing private citizens to loan money to the government on threat of imprisonment, of which Parliament accused the King of acting beyond his authority.[44] After the measure had received the approval of the House of Commons, King Charles I was read the petition and agreed to its provisions.[45] Its passage meant he could not impress into service any private supplies for his military, abolished military tenure, and stated the King lacked the authority to raise taxes without the consent of Parliament.[46] More substantially, *The Petition of Right* led to the institution of the *Habeas Corpus Act of 1679*, which not only demanded an impartial judicial review to determine the validity of charges against the accused, it required a protection against illegal imprisonment, and assured the independence of the British judiciary.[47]

The English Bill of Rights of 1689 declared that though the monarchy remained as the titular head of government, it also was obligated to abide by and enforce the essential law of the realm.[48] Due to its position as head of the Church of England, it also barred either king or queen from extolling or adopting other religious faiths under threat of forced abdication.[49] The document directed Parliament be held on a frequent basis as to assure the right of citizens to redress their grievances to their government, as well as amending the laws.[50] As to the legislative power, other than administrating the laws, the monarchy's authority to dispense with the law was made illegal, as was its ability to raise money through taxation without parliamentary consent.[51] Finally, it reaffirmed the independence of the English judiciary, along with the abolition of excessive bail.[52]

Niccolo Machiavelli had little positive to convey regarding sovereigns and the pursuit of justice. Leaders who conducted themselves in a just manner were nearly always deposed, or killed, or both.[53] Even the most righteous of rulers, to strengthen and maintain their political power, engaged in immoral deeds.[54] A sovereign was bound to conduct his affairs with proven allies in a respectful and judicious manner, as doing so guaranteed their loyalty even in defeat.[55] It was more beneficial to be seen by the public as a strong leader than a just one, for justice did not guarantee a nation's survival and strength did.[56]

Jean Bodin began his discussion on justice with the premise that it provided the motivation for a ruler to govern, for to do so was to gain the reverence and obedience of his subjects.[57] Thus, the internal preservation of a commonwealth was dependent upon the manner and the degree of justice the sovereign dispensed to the citizens.[58] As all subjects were suspicious of those who held power, so to maintain their loyalty, a ruler must act in a just fashion. A sovereign should also be mindful his officers and delegates exercised only legitimate powers, as any fissure in this responsibility would be accredited to the ruler.[59] Any breach was viewed by the citizenry to be unjust, and it either undermined the authority of the ruler, or caused the destruction of the realm.[60]

Thomas Hobbes cast a cynical eye upon justice and his discussion was centered upon human beings in the state of nature. He described this early period as a constant state of war which held no place for such lofty notions as ethics and justice.[61] The concept of justice was dependent upon every one taking care of themselves.[62] Without the existence of a government which recognized the rights of citizens to own property, justice defined as the right of ownership was a moot point.[63] Distributive justice was dependent upon a political entity which enforced laws that imposed it.[64] Hobbes scoffed at the notion of justice ascribed to people: "Justice is but a word, without substance".[65]

Algernon Sidney reasoned no right was the product of conquest, and if they were involved in conflict, it was meant to preserve the right, not to establish it.[66] Neither political rights, nor justice were products of fear wrought by a sovereign.[67] If the law was administered by less-than-honorable magistrates they had no effect, for though they were put into place to establish justice, and their corruption rendered it moot.[68] Thus, if justice was reliant upon the equal distribution of rights and laws a magistrate could neither assign, nor an executioner carry out a sentence of death for all concerned were citizens of equal standing within the community.[69]

A law not founded upon what was just was unenforceable, and the citizen not only had the right, but the duty not to obey it.[70] Because civilizations were founded upon the equal dispensation of the law, citizens were not obligated to suffer the unfair edicts or punishments rendered by their sovereign.[71] No one who lived within the boundaries of the community was above the law.[72] Sovereigns possessed neither the authority to grant nor to rescind rights, for they were not sanctioned by the citizens to do so.[73] It was the responsibility of the citizens themselves to reward sovereigns who sought to benefit the people, as well as punish those who acted against their wishes.[74]

Hugo Grotius argued natural and civil law were products of the same source and, as such, both nations and their citizens were required to act consistent with them.[75] Under these same conditions the citizen was the most responsible for the content of the laws as instruments of justice.[76] Attributing his understanding of its concept to Aristotle, Grotius provided a legalistic illustration in his delineation of justice: If someone else had taken possession of property that was rightfully yours, the social contract provided the justification to retrieve that which you rightfully owned.[77] Civic morals and conduct, acts which could be attributed to justice, were imperfect, yet they defined the just and prudent administration of government.[78] The social contract had been based upon attributive justice—that which belonged to the entire community—thus, injustice was defined as that which was repugnant to a reasonable citizenry.[79]

Grotius articulated the twin concepts of rights and justice were not interchangeable. In his clarification whereas the former applied specifically to each individual person, the latter pertained to the entirety of a society or civilization.[80] The goal of punishment was equity between the crime committed and the amount of retribution due it, as well as that the perpetrator be found by impartial means to have deserved the punishment inflicted.[81] Any judge who passed sentence must legitimately possess the right to do so.[82] In rendering verdicts they should take great care to evade generating an injustice.[83] Though it is not documented whether Cesare Beccaria had read *The Rights of War and Peace*, his work *On Crimes and Punishments* is an extensive exegesis upon the principles put forward by Grotius.

In his eight-volume opus, *Of the Law of Nature and Nations*, Baron Samuel Von Pufendorf combined Hobbesian social contractarianism and Aristotelian natural law philosophy to define justice as a social utility. Justice was the product of human reflection upon the natural world, therefore it was both inherent and apparent in its disposition. The most profound force within the universe was human kind's ability to rationalize and to continue to prosper intellectually even when his conclusions were imperfect.[84] People were judged upon the comportment of morals and manners which were entirely of their own creation.[85] Moral precepts were not substantially found within nature, but were perceived by people upon the reflection of the natural state of non-animate substance.[86] Whereas human beings evolved in their moral judgments, nations were constrained in moral behavior by their customs and constitutions.[87] This was the basis for civil law, the vital aim being a serene society.[88] A citizen who violated the civil law was subject to just punishment, but the sovereign who sullied it risked the rejection of his subjects and their withdrawal from the social contract.[89]

The discussion of justice took on a partisan veneer with John Trenchard and Thomas Gordon under the pseudonym 'Cato'. In their initial statement on justice, they mocked the idea of empathy.[90] They railed against using public funds towards the reformation of convicted criminals and were equally angered by any laws or allocations which aided the wealthy class.[91] Economic policies which did not benefit all the people were unjust. They argued the existence of law was the foundation of justice, and neither innovations, nor revenge in the punishment of convicted criminals was acceptable.[92] The principal task of a government was to protect citizens from harm, punish those who sought to subjugate them, and therein justice resided.[93] Trenchard and Gordon referred to Sidney's model of good and bad magistrates as an example of just and unjust political administration.[94] Both illustrations relied upon personal virtue to measure the level of justice.

Baron de Montesquieu maintained the prime element of republican governments was virtue.[95] He was unwilling, however, to concretely connect the words "justice" and "virtue" into a single concept. Instead, he chose to define injustice as a lack of virtue.[96] Government was the product of social customs, and those congruent with the traditions of their constituency lasted the longest.[97] Though democracies were obligated to provide for the people political liberty—Montesquieu's definition of justice—they often entailed denying the people what they had asked for.[98]

Jean-Jacques Rousseau contended the body politic was "a moral being that has a will, a general will, common to the whole, which always tends towards the preservation and the well-being of the whole, and of each part".[99] The concept of justice and the law of nature were entwined.[100] Thus, the sole guarantor of freedom and justice was the law equally enforced and applied.[101] He maintained that the terms of the social contract mandated each member of the society enjoy a quality of life consistent with the greatest good for the greatest number, a definition of the general welfare, which is also a mandate presented within the Preamble of the Constitution.[102]

The philosophical underpinnings of the American criminal justice system are found within the work of the Italian philosopher Cesare Beccaria. His book *On Crimes and Punishments* was a dissertation on the then-current standards of rendering justice under the law. Beccaria examined the legal practices of his time and concluded in its administration, as well as trial and sentencing, bias ran rampant in favor of wealthy citizens. The author's goal was to put forward a series of reforms consistent with the public good, as well as fair to those convicted, and just to the degree of the crime.[103]

Becarria criticized the civil law as being the result of passion and personal prejudices, rather than the outcome of men in the pursuit of justice.[104] Punishment was a remnant of ancient and unenlightened codes of law based upon the need of human beings to treat those who trespassed against them with revenge rather than with mercy.[105] He criticized this approach for punishment as tyranny as the product of those who rendered punishment in excess to the degree of the offense.[106] Any penalty prescribed should be within the fundamental law and the boundaries of the social contract itself, for anything that violated either of those tenets was tyranny.[107] He contended not only were laws written in an obscure manner, but also human tradition often forced itself into their interpretation and, thus, obscured the just punishment from the presiding judge.[108] Such elements kept punishment from detering others from engaging in the same offense.[109]

Among other complications was discerning the proper degree of offense rather than one perceived with fear.[110] Any case brought against a citizen must be done in a timely manner within the limits placed upon it by law.[111] No evidence produced under torture was reliable, as one admitted to all offences under the duress of extreme pain.[112] After the prosecution has presented the evidence of crime, those accused must be allowed the opportunity to examine all evidence and witnesses against them.[113] For this purpose one accused should be held accountable for a crime through a verdict rendered by a jury consisting of one's peers, as they would comprehend both the context and circumstances under which the crime, if any, was committed.[114] Following the jury's verdict, if the legislation had been written in a clear and precise manner, it would be an effortless task for the judge to render a just decision as to punishment.[115]

On Crimes and Punishments was widely read. A version translated into French contained an introduction penned by the French thinker Voltaire and was read by both John Adams and Thomas Jefferson. In his *Commentary on the book 'On Crimes and Punishments'*, published anonymously in 1766, Voltaire not only wrote of his agreement with Beccaria's assessment of the brutality associated with then-contemporary criminal retribution, but within its closing paragraph he offered several reforms, many of which are familiar to us in our time: The right of the accused to the services of an attorney; the trial of the accused be held in the jurisdiction closest to where to the crime took place; a trial by a jury of one's peers; a separation between church and state, and no arrests without warrants authorizing them.[116]

In his work *An Inquiry into the Wealth of Nations* economist Adam Smith stated the charge of any sovereign power was to protect subjects from injustice and oppression.[117] Smith recounted the dual history of law and justice along with the pursuit of revenue, and found in most eras the former was subservient to the latter.[118] Even in more contemporary times, when justice was said to be administered *gratis*, so long as there were court costs and attorney's fees it would never be the case.[119] He argued for "justice to be fairly rendered and separated from the gathering of revenue, and that justice rendered without considerations of this manner would be of benefit to all of society."[120]

The English legal tradition dates back to the kingdoms of Kent, Wessex and Mercia in the 7th century. King Offa (757–96) of Mercia issued laws in his name though none are now extant.[121] Within the annals of English statues are laws written by King Alfred (871–99) which provide the basis of its unwritten constitution.[122] King Canute I (1016–35) was the English first monarch to formally publish a code of law, an outcome of his visit to Rome in 1027.[123] Following the Norman victory at the Battle of Hastings on 14 October 1066, much of the prior legal traditions were incorporated into the codes of law enacted by King William I (1066–87).[124] Ancient Roman law was later merged into the Norman civil codes by King Henry I (1100–35) who was intrigued by its demand of obedience from its citizens.[125]

As recounted in Frederick Maitland's *The Constitutional History of England*, a four-step progression took place in the management of justice. The British legal institution found its origins in "the very ancient courts of the shire", which the historian characterized as "communal courts" whose membership consisted of "the free-men of the district".[126] These bodies had jurisdiction over all criminal and civil matters.[127] The authority of these bodies was immense for prior to the ascension of King William I, a reigning monarch refused to hear any case of a citizen which had not been presented beforehand to these courts.[128] The Feudal courts were the next step in this process in which service was based upon one's status as a lord or baron of a manor or estate.[129] These bodies held jurisdiction over civil matters, as the lord or baron reserved authority over criminal matters involving his vassals.[130] Thirdly, there were courts specifically authorized by the reigning monarch and served three essential functions: 1) a court of last resort in a similar manner to the U.S. Supreme Court[131]; 2) a court for the tenant-in-chief ruling on feudal principle[132]; and, 3) a court which examined legal matters brought forward by the monarch.[133] Many offenses under the jurisdiction of the King's Court were placed under the legal umbrella of 'the King's peace' from as far back as Canute I.[134] By the reign of King Edward I (1272–1307), the King's Court had evolved into the superlative forum of litigation within the country.[135] Completing this process were the visitational courts held under the authority of the monarch's justices who traveled throughout the realm, during the reign of the King Henry II (1154–89).[136] It was also this monarch who began the practice of judgements rendered by a jury of one's peers as a legal device for rendering justice under the law.[137]

A further innovation that occurred during the reign of Henry II was the indictment and appeal.[138] By the close of King Edward I's reign trial-by-jury was standard practice in the trial of criminal cases.[139] Also, at that time the King's Court was separated into three separate courts with their own jurisdictions: 1) the King's bench, a court of appeals held by the monarch accompanied by his justices which held the authority to overturn the verdicts of inferior courts; 2) the Court of Common Pleas, a court of general jurisdiction in all civil cases between two or more parties; and, 3) the Court of Exchequer, an appellate court of civil actions as well as serving administrative functions.[140] During the reign of King Henry VII (1485–1509) important reforms in the administration of justice took place, the most weighty being the ascendency of the King's Court as being the foremost judicial entity of the realm, along with the demise of the communal and feudal courts.[141] Also the grand jury was instituted as a decision-making body in criminal cases replacing the past function of the petty and trying juries; and, the initiation of the House of Lords as a judiciary body provided with the authority to render judgments on the criminal activities of its peers.[142]

With the passage of the *Act of Settlement of 1701,* the independence of judges was secured by law.[143] Prior to this precedent, a judge who issued a decision which conflicted with the will of the monarch faced consequences ranging from a significant reduction in salary to immediate dismissal.[144] Through the guarantee of a judge's independence came the imperative all judgments were to be rendered solely upon the text of the law.[145] Along with these key developments came the institution of *habeas corpus*, a legal procedure against unlawful and arbitrary incarceration, and the abolition of excessive bail for all prisoners except those accused of treason against the realm.[146] Also, impeachments of government officials for 'high crimes and misdemeanors' occurred during the reign of Edward III (1327–77), but were rampant in the time of James II (1685–88) and afterwards. The King's Court, in its decision in *R v Richardson* (1758), allowed for the impeachment of government officials who had committed acts of malfeasance in their official capacity.[147] Finally, laws regarding treason and attainder were left in place, though modified to allow for the accused a legal defense on their behalf.[148]

As for justice, Sir William Blackstone centered his definition upon the freedom and contentment of society.[149] All his analyses were placed within a strict legal context, though he never forthrightly defined what justice was. Blackstone stated interpretations of the law must be flexible to achieve justice.[150] Injustice occurred when a case was either unduly delayed, or when a lower court overstepped its authority.[151] The legal system as administered by the courts was not allowed to practice "against public *justice*, against the public *peace*, against the public *trade*, against the public *health*", for to do so was to compel crimes against the community itself.[152] Once a judgment was rendered it was to be carried out to its letter: Any course either less or more severe was unjust.[153]

Many of the concepts of legal rights analyzed by Blackstone found a home within the first ten amendments to the U.S. Constitution. The Fifth Amendment states "No person shall be held to answer for a capital, or otherwise infamous crime, unless on a presentment or indictment of a Grand Jury".[154] A grand jury was but one of several legitimate processes for a criminal case to be prosecuted, an English legal tradition which began under King Ethelred of Wessex in the mid-ninth century.[155] Their sole charge was to be instructed in the specific articles of inquiry and to hear evidence put forward by the prosecutor to decide upon the charge's legitimacy.[156] That same constitutional amendment stated no one shall "be deprived of life, liberty or property without due process of law".[157] Another protection granted in the Constitution's Fifth Amendment against self-incrimination was also found in Blackstone's treatise.[158]

Further examples of Blackstone's influence are found in the Sixth Amendment's assertion of every person accused of a crime possessed the right to the examination of all witnesses and evidence used against him.[159] He asserted such a right had existed within the purview of English law since the era of Queen Elizabeth I (1558–1603).[160] The tradition of trial by a jury of one's peers originated from the creation of the first primitive Saxon governments, and achieving its fundamental structure during the time of King Egbert of Wessex in the early-to-mid-9th century.[161] It was reaffirmed in 1215 by Clause 39 of the *Magna Carta*.[162] It was a constitutional right and possessed a legal duality, a citizen may find themselves under its authority, as well as serve as a juror in another's trial.[163]

The Eighth Amendment to the Constitution forbade all forms of "cruel and unusual punishment", but according to Blackstone this notion had always been a part of the English law.[164] Capital punishment was only valid for crimes against the state which presented a real danger to the realm and its inhabitants.[165] The society was responsible for preventing grievous bodily harm or murder without justification of the law.[166] Statutes governing punishments should never be allowed to lose their foundation in humanity itself, and those who must decide cannot waver in the perimeters of their warrant.[167] Blackstone ended his discussion with the axiom any severe punishment will not have the desired effect of prevention if inflicted broadly.[168] As has been proven by an examination of his *Commentaries*, several of the legal concepts argued by Cesare Beccaria were not unknown within English law.

The question before the delegation of the constitutional convention was how to incorporate the many interpretations of justice into a workable governmental context. Upon a close examination of Article III, the section of the Constitution which details the consistency and authority of the judicial branch, what is noticeable is its scant specificity. It goads speculation as to the reason for such ambiguity: 1) Whether the delegates were suitably concerned; or, 2) Whether they were content to allow the judiciary a high degree of legal latitude. The truth is the language was the most the majority of the delegates could agree upon. Though James Madison's notes on the convention proceedings accurately detail the order and content of the clauses, there is only limited information regarding debates on the judicial branch.

On 13 June 1787, a proposal for the establishment of the national judiciary was introduced.[169] The Supreme Court was to preside over cases concerning tax collection and impeachments.[170] Elbridge Gerry of Massachusetts contended disqualifying people from serving as a member of the national judiciary due to debt was a detriment to justice.[171] On 6 August 1787 the report of the Committee of Detail chaired by John Rutledge of South Carolina was read which included a draft of Article III detailing the powers and qualifications of the judicial branch, and was formally accepted.[172] A clause was later added stating no one serving in the federal government could simultaneously hold offices in more than one branch at any one time.[173] As the structure became more refined James Madison of Virginia sought to limit the Supreme Court's jurisdiction to cases involving controversies of constitutionality, which was accepted and the language further improved and modified.[174]

Of greater concern to the delegates was the Constitution's lack of protections against abuse by its serving officers, though there was an inordinate amount of time devoted to misconduct in public office, and impeachment for crimes committed while in public service. Gunning Bedford of Delaware argued the probability of impeachment was an ineffective deterrent for underqualified candidates seeking the presidency, as it covered malfeasance while holding office, but not in seeking election.[175] George Mason of Virginia voiced his concern that if his colleague's proposal was adopted, the new government would prohibit the removal of an unfit government officer.[176] On the 13th of June 1787 the first resolution on the subject was put forward and agreed upon by the Committee of the Whole, which stated elected officials were subject to impeachment and conviction of crime during service to the government.[177] Five days later it was proposed a special court preside over by the Chief Justice be the venue for impeachment of federal officers expanded upon by Gouverneur Morris of Pennsylvania and Luther Martin of Maryland.[178] Only Charles Coatesworth Pinckney of South Carolina argued that the president not be liable to impeachment during his term of office as it could lead to governmental gridlock, to which George Mason countered: "Shall any man be above Justice?"[179] Throughout the rest of the proceedings Pinckney and Mason debated their stances until the language and procedure was settled as it appears in Article I § 3.[180] More time and effort were devoted to debating the procedures for impeachment than any other issue of justice debated during the Constitutional Convention—more so than of treason.

The first mention of treason was made in a report by the Committee of the Whole defining the authority of the executive. It stated the president possessed the power of granting an executive pardon for all offenses with the exception of treason, which would require the approval of the senate.[181] A definition of what constituted treason was not offered until 6 August 1787 in a report issued by the Committee of Detail chaired by John Rutledge, which was demarcated as in levying war against either the United States, or the individual states themselves.[182] Citing the *Treason Act of 1351*—which included inciting and waging war against the realm and threatening the lives of the monarch, the royal family, and the officers of the government—James Madison contended such authority be left to the State Legislatures, to which George Mason agreed.[183] Gouverneur Morris argued the authority to prosecute treasonous activities must be left to the federal government, for to allow such a division of authority could create disparate laws between the federal government and the individual states, to which Rufus King of Massachusetts agreed.[184] As a compromise Edmund Randolph of Virginia offered the clause that read providing enemies with aid and comfort.[185] Later in the debate King asserted treason must be uniformed in that committing such an act against an individual state was to ensure the same against the United States.[186] The language as it appears in Articles I § 6, III § 3, IV § 2 was finalized on 12 September 1787 with the approval by the entire assembly of the report of the Committee of Style.[187]

Two legal issues concerning justice the delegates debated were ex-post-facto laws and bills of attainder. Ex-post-facto laws are statutes which include acts made illegal by legislation which applied to actions perpetrated prior to its adoption. Elbridge Gerry argued in favor due to the larger the number of federal and state legislators the more likely they were to be passed, to which John Rutledge agreed.[188] Hugh Williamson of North Carolina also spoke in support stating though there was such a clause in his state's constitution and it was regularly violated.[189] John Dickinson of Delaware, citing Blackstone's *Commentaries*, put forth a proposal that such restrictions be applied to criminal cases only, not civil statutes.[190] On 14 September 1787 George Mason recommended the deletion of the clause all together as it lacked specificity, which the delegates voted down.[191] A bill of attainder is a statute which declared any group guilty of a crime, in most cases without a trial, that allowed for property forfeiture and confiscation. The majority of delegates had no problem with abolishing such laws, perhaps because many were practicing lawyers who had argued in court against such cases. George Mason claimed due to the prohibition of bills of attainder clauses governing impeachment must be strengthened.[192] The language for both clauses were passed on 14 September 1787 by the assembly without any objections and are found in Article I § 9 of the Constitution.[193]

Habeas corpus is the legal requirement anyone under arrest be brought in person before the judge who is adjudicating their case; thus, providing all judgments made on their behalf be made in the accused's presence. The language of this clause was placed into the official record on 20 August 1787 with no objections.[194] Eight days later when it was brought up for revision, John Rutledge argued for not only its inclusion, but for it being inviolate, to which Gouverneur Morris agreed.[195] James Wilson of Pennsylvania added he did not foresee any context by which a suspension of such a right would be accepted under any state law, let alone federal statutes.[196] This clause was accepted on 12 September 1787 and was also included within Article 1 § 9 of the Constitution.[197]

The Federalists were convinced justice was achieved by stringent laws which strictly controlled the public, along with a governmental structure contusive to enforcing such regulations. Of the reasons to 'establish justice', they were pessimistic this could be achieved under the best of circumstances. James Madison maintained the federal government as constructed was the best guarantee of justice within the Union.[198] Yet in his assessment, because people if given the power to make such decisions they would consistently decide in their own favor, true justice was unobtainable.[199] Alexander Hamilton pessimistically concluded the individual states did not possess the ability to curtail the ambitions of aspiring men.[200] He argued there were, indeed, areas where the administration of local tasks were best left to the state governments, in which case the federal government would not usurp such authority.[201] Under the federal system it was a much easier task for the states to impinge upon federal authority than it was the other way around.[202] It was the reason for the construction of a republican form of government rather than a true democracy to continue in the cause of justice.[203]

The Federalist author "The State Soldier" reiterated Hamilton's points and further explained how jealousy between the individual states had thwarted public justice in the country.[204] Tench Coxe, writing under the penname 'An American Citizen', lauded the strong judiciary, adding when combined with the state courts and inferior federal courts, justice would prevail because they were stringently controlled by the federal government.[205]

The Anti-Federalists were united in their support for a declaratory statement of rights within the body of the Constitution. In their view if such liberties were included within the original document they would provide an effective bulwark against abuses of power and federal government encroachments. 'The Federal Farmer' examined the federal judiciary as proposed, and concluded it was not a system to meet the needs it was designed for.[206] Furthermore, traveling the distances necessary to be heard in a court of law for some residents involved tremendous expense and imposition of time and, thus, proved itself impractical.[207] Without a written declaration of rights there was also a problem in discerning which specific rights the people possessed.[208] Under such conditions the state governments would be unnecessary and, as a result, the people would exist under the federal government solely.[209] 'Brutus' restated the criticisms of the federal judiciary put forward by 'The Federal Farmer'.[210] Whereas public order and criminal justice matters were best left to the States, the federal government should concern itself solely with the military defense of the nation.[211]

'Centinel' was focused upon economic justice and class.[212] The Constitution was the product of the wealthiest of the country who sought to institute a feudalistic system upon the American people.[213] Citing John Adams' *Thoughts on Government* as the antecedent to the Constitution, the author claimed the document's most disturbing flaw was that it coddled private interest to the detriment of the public good.[214] Both the president and the justices of the federal judiciary were not subject to election by the people.[215] Thus the federal government created by the Constitution was bereft of any legal mechanisms to hold public servants accountable for their actions by the people.[216]

'An Old Whig' objected to the multi-tiered process of amending the document as found in Article V, and claimed it was unjust to deny citizens the right to either criticize or make changes to their government.[217] Once amendments were proposed, the author maintained, they would never cease, and when the process of amendment had begun the representatives of the other states would never agree to them: Henceforth, a deadlock would occur.[218] When the amendments were finally rejected the debates would prove so raucous the country could find itself worse off than it was prior. The writer's suggestion was to offer them all at once, or not at all.[219]

The debates over the ratification of the Constitution were not specifically centered upon achieving justice: They concerned the consolidation of power by a strong central government that would put an effective end to the interstate squabbling which threatened to cut the nation asunder. Supporters of the *Articles of Confederation* were leery of the claims such a government allowed for both the concentration of political power while ensuring the sovereignty of the individual states. They wanted safeguards within the document itself.

Among the best displays of this debate was centered upon the No-Religious-Tests Clause of Article VI which assured no citizen was obligated to pronounce their adherence to a specific religious faith to hold office within the government.[220] James Madison recognized even in his time no single issue had fostered more anger within the populace, or had been the primary cause of political division, than the subject of religion.[221] People who claimed to strictly adhere to a defined theology were no more immune from political corruption than any other.[222] The governance of the nation should be placed with those who were concerned with the wellbeing of the country, rather than those who were primarily driven by their faith.[223] He was circumspect of those who placed their religion above governance, for they would pervert their specific theology into a political party, much to the detriment of the country.[224] Making his point Madison alluded to Europe's Thirty Years War—a succession of military conflicts between Protestants and Catholics which plagued Central Europe between 1618 and 1648—as an example of what would occur in the United States of America if religion were allowed any traction within government.[225] Alexander Hamilton added a stern declaratory statement, utilizing the differences between spiritual and civil religions: Under the Constitution the government of the country had its jurisdiction, and the separate religions had theirs, and they should never be allowed to merge.[226] 'The Federal Farmer' queried why the freedom to practice the religion of one's choice had not been established in the first place.[227]

The Anti-Federalists advocated a bill of rights be added to the Constitution as a specific section, as John Adams had delineated in his tract *Thoughts on Government*.[228] They ultimately triumphed for the *Bill of Rights*, embodied by the initial ten amendments, was proposed and passed during the initial session of the Congress and added to the Constitution on 15 December 1791. Within the body of these amendments three clearly defined sections emerge: The first three amendments were rights guaranteed to the people which are exempt from government rescission, as championed by the Anti-Federalists, with the exception of times of war in which the country itself was threatened:

1. Freedom of Speech, assembly, religion, and petition of government.
2. The right of the state and/or national militias to bear arms.
3. Quartering of soldiers on private property prohibited without the consent of the owner.

Consistent with the thoughts of philosopher Cesare Beccaria and legal historian Sir William Blackstone, amendments four through eight were guarantees of specific procedures due the public in what is in contemporary times termed "criminal justice":

4. Illegal searches and seizures prohibited.
5. Establishment of grand juries; prohibitions of self-incrimination and double jeopardy; due process of law; and, eminent domain.
6. Criminal court procedures.
7. Trial by jury in common law cases.
8. Bail and the prohibition of cruel and unusual punishment.

The final two amendments provide restrictions to federal government authority in its relationship with both the individual states and the residents of those states:

9. Rights retained by the people under the Constitution.
10. Reserved rights of the individual states.

Though these amendments have been touted as iron-clad protections, this is not entirely the case, especially concerning amendments nine and ten. Article I § 8 guarantees to Congress the authority to pass laws deemed "necessary and proper" without any guidelines as to how those terms are specifically defined.[229] Coupled with this authority is Article VI which states all laws passed under the authority of the U.S. Constitution are the "supreme law of the land": A statement of federal sovereignty over the individual states.[230] When taken together and coupled with the president's authority to sign bills into law,[231] it makes plain Congress can pass any law it sees fit and, so long as the chief executive approves it, and its legality is affirmed by the Supreme Court, it is indeed the "supreme law of the land".

This begs an important constitutional question: With such powers authorized within the purview of Congress and the president, what powers are actually delegated to the individual states? Only those the federal government has seen fit to allow them. This is a demonstration of the Hobbesian principle of negative freedom: The liberty of state action lies within the silence of federal law. In his per curiam opinion in *Calder v. Bull* (1798), Associate Justice Samuel Chase reaffirmed this paradigm:

> An act of the Legislature (for I cannot call it a *law*) contrary to the *great first principles* of the *social compact*, cannot be considered a *rightful exercise of legislative* authority. The obligation of a law in governments established on *express compact, and on republican principles*, must be determined by the *nature* of the *power*, on which it is founded.[232]

Ill-defined powers are transitory by their nature.

In spite of their limitations the first ten amendments have remained a popular bulwark against encroachments upon the rights of citizens by both federal and state governments. Though we as citizens may not always remember what they specifically entail, these rights are justly non-retractable—especially when we speak up for them when they are criticized or attacked. Seven years following the ratification of the first ten amendments, the Supreme Court ruled consistent with the Federalists' contention of intrinsic rights. The Court in *Calder v. Bull* (1798), speaking through Associate Justice Samuel Chase, mandated a policy of "substantive due process": A reading of the Fifth Amendment's Due Process Clause which guaranteed rights not expressly found in the Constitution. The Court speaking through Justice Chase affirmed: "There are certain *vital* principles in our *free Republican governments*, which will determine and over-rule an *apparent and flagrant* abuse of *legislative* power; as to authorize *manifest injustice by positive law*; or to take away that security for *personal liberty*, or *private property*, for the protection whereof the government was established."[233]

In his 1924 book *The Growth of the Law* future Associate Justice Benjamin Cardozo wrote: "Justice is not to be taken by storm. She is to be wooed by slow advances."[234] The Framers of the Constitution viewed justice in the same light as Cardozo. They understood what constituted justice in their time would ebb, flow and progress over time. While the Federalists argued all the necessary protections for individual rights were included within the document itself, the Anti-Federalists demanded a declaration of rights be included within the Constitution, or they would work to defeat its ratification. In the end both sides triumphed.

In their effort to construct a governing charter that would stand as fundamental law, they also allowed for amendments as to promote a living body of governing principles to reflect the timbre of the current times. American history has proven them correct. Over the years there have been substantial changes wrought by new perspectives on issues ranging from ending human chattel slavery to equality of cultural and gender minorities. In each case the Constitution has proven both flexible in its language, yet firm in its protections. As justice has evolved so has the depth and breadth of our constitutional understanding.

It is a glorious sight to behold when new light shines through old windows. With each constitutional innovation not only do we see the brilliance of the Framers, but we also experience for ourselves the magnitude of their creation, not just a document of their time, but for all time. With each advance the American nation moves ever closer towards "a more perfect union", not just of states, counties and towns, but as a nation. Time and again Americans wonder how their country will fare in dire times, and yet in the pages of our history we see all along it was our constitution, the product of intellect, which has sustained us. It is our greatest national strength, as well as its neglect our most noticeable weakness, for it has been that document which has been at the heart of both the establishment and embellishment of justice. Both citizens and their representatives must continue to woo, appreciate and appease our Constitution, for our continuance as a nation is dependent upon it.

Notes

1. Friedrich Nietzsche, *Beyond Good and Evil*, trans. R. J. Hollingdale. 1990 reprint (New York: Penguin Books, 1973), 39.
2. Samuel Noah Kramer, *History begins at Sumer: Thirty-Nine Firsts in Recorded History* (Philadelphia: University of Pennsylvania Press, 1988), 52–5.
3. *The Code of Hammurabi* (Santa Cruz, CA: Evinity Publishing, Inc., 2011); at http://www.sacred-texts.com/ane/ham/ham06.htm. Accessed 28 August 2016.
4. Herodotus, *The Histories*, ed. John M. Marincola (New York: The Penguin Group, 1972), 22–5.
5. Aristotle, *The Constitution of the Athenians*, trans. Sir Frederick G. Kenyon; at The Internet Classics Archive; http://classics.mit.edu/Aristotle/athenian_const.mb.txt. Accessed 28 August 2016.
6. *Ibid.*, Section I, Part 3.
7. *Ibid.*, Section I, Part 6. Herodotus, *The Histories*, ed. John M. Maricola, Reprint of 1972 edition (New York: Penguin Books, 1996), 12.
8. *Constitution of the Athenians*, Section I, Part 9.
9. *Ibid.*, Section 1, Part 8.
10. Herodotus, 187.
11. *Ibid.*
12. *Ibid*, 188–9.
13. *The Constitution of the Athenians*, Section II, Part 29.

14. *Ibid.*, Section II, Part 42.
15. *Ibid.*, Section II, Part 31; Section II, Part 62.
16. *Ibid.*, Section II, Part 39.
17. *Ibid.*, Section III, Part 45.
18. *Ibid.*
19. *Ibid.*, Section III, Part 49.
20. H. F. Jolowicz, *Historical Introduction to the Study of Roman Law* (New York: Cambridge University Press, 1932), 108.
21. Cicero, *On the Good Life*, ed. Michael Grant (New York: Penguin Books, 1971), 257.
22. Paul du Plessis, *Borkowski's Textbook on Roman Law,* 4th edition (New York: Oxford University Press, 2010), 5–6.
23. Livy, *The Early History of Rome*, ed. Aubrey De Sélincourt (New York: Penguin Books, 1960), 247.
24. Edward Gibbon, *The Decline and Fall of the Roman Empire*, ed. J. B. Bury (New York: The George Macy Companies, Inc., 1946), II: 1470.
25. Michael Grant, *History of Rome* (New York: Charles Scribner's Sons, 1978), 102–5.
26. *Ibid.*, 106–7.
27. *Ibid.*, 188.
28. *Ibid.*
29. *Ibid.*, 323.
30. *Ibid.*, 380–2.
31. *Ibid.*, 382.
32. *Ibid.*
33. *Ibid.*, 378.
34. Frederic William Maitland, *The Constitutional History of England*; ed. H. A. L. Fisher, 1965 Reprint (Cambridge, England: Cambridge University Press, 1908), 11.
35. Thomas Lord Macaulay, *The History of England from the Accession to James II* (New York: Harper and Brothers, Publishers, 1849), I: 16.
36. David Hume, *The History of England from the Invasion of Julius Caesar to the Abdication of King James the Second, 1688*, 5 vols. (Boston: Phillips, Sampson and Company, 1849), I: 430.
37. *Magna Carta*, Clauses 39 and 52 (1215); at http://www.constitution.org/eng/magnacar.pdf. Accessed 28 August 2016. Cited by Frederick Pollard & Frederic William Maitland, *The History of English Law Before the Time of Edward I*, 2 vols. (Cambridge, England: Cambridge University Press, 1923) I: 171, 173.
38. Maitland, 93.
39. Pollard & Maitland, I: 172.
40. Maitland, 160.
41. Hume, I: 431.
42. Pollard & Maitland, I: 172.
43. Maitland, 293.

44. *The Petition of Right*, Section II (1628), 3 Car. 1 c 1. Maitland, 307. Macaulay, I: 79–80. Hume, V: 37.
45. Hume, V: 42.
46. Maitland, 323. Macaulay, 80.
47. *The Habeas Corpus Act* (1679) 31 Cha. 2 c. 2. Maitland, 313, 315. Macaulay, 80.
48. *An Act Declaring the Rights and Liberties of the Subject and Settling the Succession of the Crown* (1689) 1 William & Mary Sess 2 c 2. Maitland, 284.
49. *Act Declaring the Rights and Liberties.* Maitland, 288.
50. *Ibid.*, 296.
51. *Ibid.*, 306, 309.
52. *Act Declaring the Rights and Liberties.* Maitland, 313.
53. Niccolo Machiavelli, *The Prince*, eds. Quentin Skinner and Russell Price (New York: Cambridge University Press, 1988), 67.
54. *Ibid.*, 68.
55. *Ibid.*, 78.
56. *Ibid.*, 88.
57. Jean Bodin, *Six Books of the Commonwealth*, ed. M. J. Tooley (Oxford, England: Basil Blackwell, 1955), 133.
58. *Ibid.*
59. *Ibid.*, 137.
60. *Ibid.*, 138.
61. Thomas Hobbes, *Leviathan*, ed. Richard Tuck (New York: Cambridge University Press, 1996), 90.
62. *Ibid.*, 101.
63. *Ibid.*
64. *Ibid.*, 105.
65. *Ibid.*, 232.
66. Algernon Sidney, *Discourses Concerning Government*, ed. Thomas G. West (Indianapolis, IN: The Liberty Fund, 1996), 30–1.
67. *Ibid.*, 83.
68. *Ibid.*, 220.
69. *Ibid.*, 182.
70. *Ibid.*, 380–1; 436–7.
71. *Ibid.*, 339, 365.
72. *Ibid.*, 438, 460.
73. *Ibid.*, 522.
74. *Ibid.*, 522–3.
75. Hugo Grotius, *The Rights of War and Peace*, ed. Richard Tuck (Indianapolis, IN: The Liberty Fund, 2005), I: 94.
76. *Ibid.*
77. *Ibid.*, I: 142.

78. *Ibid.*, I: 143.
79. *Ibid.*, I: 146; 182.
80. *Ibid.*, I: 138; II: 886.
81. *Ibid.*, II: 951; 952.
82. *Ibid.*, II: 953.
83. *Ibid.*, II: 1005.
84. Samuel von Pufendorf, *Of the Law of Nature and Nations*, 8 vols., Reprint of 1712 edition, ed. Basil Kennet (Andover, Hampshire, England: Gale ECCO Print Editions, 2005), I: 2.
85. *Ibid.*
86. *Ibid.*, I: 4.
87. *Ibid.*, I: 6.
88. *Ibid.*, VIII: 3.
89. *Ibid.*
90. John Trenchard & Thomas Gordon, "Essay #10", 3 January 1720; in *Cato's Letters; or, Essays on Liberty, Civil and Religious, and Other Important Subjects*, ed. Ronald Hamowy (Indianapolis, IN: The Liberty Fund, 1995), I: 83.
91. *Ibid.*
92. John Trenchard & Thomas Gordon, "Essay #11", 7 January 1720; in *Ibid.*, 87.
93. John Trenchard & Thomas Gordon, "Essay #200", 11 March 1720; in *Ibid.*, 138.
94. John Trenchard & Thomas Gordon, "Essay #37", 15 July 1721; in *Ibid.*, 262–8.
95. Baron de Montesquieu, *Spirit of the Laws*, eds. Anne Cohler, Basia Miller, Harold Stone (New York: Cambridge University Press, 1989), 22.
96. *Ibid.*
97. *Ibid.*, 154–5.
98. *Ibid.*, 155.
99. Jean-Jacques Rousseau, "A Discourse on Political Economy", 1755; in, *The Social Contract and Other Later Political Writings*, ed. Victor Gourevitch (New York: Cambridge University Press, 1996), 6.
100. *Ibid.*, 7.
101. *Ibid.*, 10.
102. Jean-Jacques Rousseau, "Of the Social Contract (Geneva Manuscript)", 1762; in *Ibid.*, 160. *U.S. Constitution*, Preamble.
103. Cesare Beccaria, *On Crimes and Punishments and Other Writings*, ed. Richard Bellamy (New York: Cambridge University Press, 1995), 3.
104. *Ibid.*, 7.
105. *Ibid.*, 9.
106. *Ibid.*, 10.
107. *Ibid.*, 12–13.
108. *Ibid.*, 17.
109. *Ibid.*, 22–3, 31.

110. *Ibid.*, 25.
111. *Ibid.*, 76–7.
112. *Ibid.*, 39–44.
113. *Ibid.*, 76.
114. *Ibid.*, 35.
115. *Ibid.*
116. Voltaire, "Commentary on the book 'On Crimes and Punishments'", 1766; in *Political Writings*, ed. David Williams (New York: Cambridge University Press, 1994), 278–9.
117. Adam Smith, *An Inquiry Into the Wealth of Nations*, ed. Edwin Cannan, 1976 Reprint (Chicago, IL: The University of Chicago Press, 1904), V: 231.
118. *Ibid.*, 237.
119. *Ibid.*, 239.
120. *Ibid.*, 240, 339.
121. Maitland and Pollard, I: 19–20.
122. *Ibid.*, I: 20.
123. *Ibid.*
124. *Ibid.*, I: 74.
125. *Ibid.*, I: 112.
126. Maitland, 105.
127. *Ibid.*, 106.
128. *Ibid.*
129. *Ibid.*, 105.
130. *Ibid.*, 106.
131. *Ibid. U.S. Constitution*, Article III § 1 and 2.
132. Maitland, 106.
133. *Ibid.*, 106–7.
134. *Ibid.*, 108–9.
135. *Ibid.*, 114.
136. *Ibid.*, 106, 109.
137. *Ibid.*, 126.
138. *Ibid.*, 128.
139. *Ibid.*, 131.
140. *Ibid.*, 133, 134–5.
141. *Ibid.*, 204.
142. *Ibid.*, 211–2, 214.
143. *The Act of Settlement of 1701*, 12 and 13 Will. 3 c. 2.
144. Maitland, 312–3.
145. *Ibid.*
146. *The Habeas Corpus Act of 1679*, 31 Cha. 2 c. 2; *An Act Declaring the Rights and Liberties of the Subject and Settling the Succession of the Crown*, 1 William & Mary Sess 2 c. 2.

147. *R v Richardson* (1758) 97 ER 426. Maitland, 317–18.
148. Maitland, 318–20.
149. William Blackstone, *Commentaries on the Laws of England*, ed. William Draper Lewis, reprint of 1922 edition (Clark, NJ: The Lawbook Exchange, 2004), I: 141.
150. *Ibid.*, I: 130.
151. *Ibid.*, III: 1107.
152. IV: 1521. The italics are that of the author.
153. *Ibid.*, IV: 1577.
154. *U.S. Constitution*, Fifth Amendment.
155. Blackstone, IV: 1692.
156. *Ibid.*, IV: 1695–6.
157. *U.S. Constitution*, Fifth Amendment.
158. *U.S. Constitution*, Fifth Amendment. Blackstone, III: 1330.
159. *U.S. Constitution*, Sixth Amendment.
160. Blackstone, III: 1304–5.
161. Blackstone, III: 1312–13.
162. *Magna Carta*, Clause 39 (1215). Blackstone, IV: 1735.
163. Blackstone, 1313.
164. *U.S. Constitution*, Eighth Amendment. Blackstone, IV: 1430–31.
165. *Ibid.*, IV: 1431.
166. *Ibid.*
167. *Ibid.*, IV: 1432.
168. *Ibid.*, IV: 1435.
169. James Madison, *Notes of Debates in the Federal Constitution of 1787* (Athens, OH: Ohio University Press, 1966, 1985), 116.
170. *Ibid.*, 116–17.
171. *Ibid.*, 374.
172. *Ibid.*, 385, 393.
173. *Ibid.*, 486. The clause as later revised is found in Article I § 6.
174. *Ibid.*, 539. The clause as later revised is found in Article III § 2.
175. *Ibid.*, 49.
176. *Ibid.*, 56.
177. *Ibid.*, 116.
178. *Ibid.*, 139, 315. This procedure was later incorporated into Article I § 3.
179. *Ibid.*, 331.
180. *Ibid.*, 618. *U.S. Constitution*, Article I § 3.
181. Madison, 138.
182. *Ibid.*, 390.
183. *Ibid.*, 489. *Declaration What Offences Shall Be Adjudged Treason* (1351) 25 Edw 3 St. 5 c 2.
184. *Ibid.*, 489, 491.

185. *Ibid.*, 490.
186. *Ibid.*, 493.
187. *Ibid.*, 625. *U.S. Constitution*, Article I § 6; Article III § 3; and, Article IV § 2.
188. Madison, 510, 511.
189. *Ibid.*, 511.
190. *Ibid.*, 547. Blackstone, I: 46–7.
191. *Ibid.*, 640.
192. Madison, 605.
193. *U.S. Constitution*, Article I § 9.
194. Madison, 486.
195. *Ibid.*, 541.
196. *Ibid.*
197. *Ibid.*, 621. *U.S. Constitution*, Article I § 9.
198. James Madison, "Essay #51"; in *The Federalist,* The Gideon Edition, eds. George W. Carey and James McClellan (Indianapolis, IN: The Liberty Fund, 2001), 271.
199. James Madison, "Essay #10"; in *The Federalist,* 44.
200. Alexander Hamilton, "Essay #17"; in *The Federalist,* 80.
201. *Ibid.*, 81.
202. *Ibid.*
203. *Ibid.*, 82.
204. 'The State Soldier', "To the Good People of Virginia, on the new Federal Constitution, by an old State Soldier, in answer to the proposition for amendments"[Essay #2], 16 November 1787; in *Friends of the Constitution: Writings of the "Other" Federalists 1787–1788*, eds., Colleen A. Sheehan and Gary L. McDowell (Indianapolis, IN: The Liberty Fund; 1998), 124.
205. Tench Coxe (as 'An American Citizen'), "An Examination of the Constitution" [Essay #4] 21 October 1788; in *Friends*, 472.
206. 'The Federal Farmer', Essay #II, 9 October 1787; in *The Anti-Federalist: Writings by the Opponents of the Constitution*, ed. Herbert Storing (Chicago: University of Chicago Press, 1981), 39–43.
207. *Ibid.*
208. *Ibid.*
209. *Ibid.*, 41.
210. Brutus', "Essay #7", 3 January 1788; in *The Anti-Federalist*, 146.
211. *Ibid.*
212. 'Centinel', "Letter #1", 5 October 1787; in *The Anti-Federalists: Selected Writings and Speeches*, ed. Bruce Frohnen (Washington, DC: Regnery Publishing, Inc., 1999), 36.
213. *Ibid.*
214. *Ibid.*, 37.
215. *Ibid.*, 38.
216. *Ibid.*, 43.

217. 'An Old Whig', "Essays of an Old Whig [#7]", 28 November 1787; in *The Anti-Federalists*, 353.
218. *Ibid.*
219. *Ibid.*
220. *U.S. Constitution*, Article VI.
221. James Madison, "Essay #10"; in *The Federalist,* 44.
222. *Ibid.*, 46.
223. *Ibid.*
224. *Ibid.*, 48.
225. James Madison, "Essay #19"; in *The Federalist,* 94–5.
226. Alexander Hamilton, "Essay #69"; in *The Federalist,* 361.
227. 'The Federal Farmer', "Letter #4", 12 October, 1787; *The Anti-Federalist*, 58.
228. *Ibid.*
229. *U.S. Constitution*, Article I § 8.
230. *U.S. Constitution*, Article VI.
231. *U.S. Constitution*, Article II § 1.
232. *Calder v. Bull,* 3 U.S. 388 (1796).
233. *Calder v. Bull,* 3 U.S. 388 (1796). The italics are those of the original author.
234. Benjamin Nathan Cardozo, *The Growth of the Law* (New Haven, CT: Yale University Press, 1924), 133.

3

"Insure Domestic Tranquility"

A Unified Nation through a Balanced Government

Nothing ensures a nation's domestic tranquility more assuredly than the unity of its citizens. It was among the foremost goals of the Framers, and of such importance it was placed within the mission statement of the Constitution. In our time, we have thought it to mean keeping the peace through law and order, but those who constructed the document had an entirely different reasoning in mind. They had concluded a nation united under an equitable and firm charter of law was necessary to quell internal squabbles so as to not destroy the union of the sovereign states.

At the close of the American War for Independence the states bickered amongst themselves over western expansion: Due to this issue three separate sets of states had prepared for war against one another.[1] Then internal rebellions emerged which either interfered with the process of government, or shut it down completely, the most famous being Shays' Rebellion during the winter of 1786/7.[2] Something had to be done before the nation spiraled into anarchy and collapse. It remains one of the ironies of American history that the debate between Federalists and Anti-Federalists over 'domestic tranquility' was so divisive, as both parties agreed upon the premise of national unity. What separated them was the manner by which it was to be achieved.

In 1787 the United States of America was not so much a unified nation, but a collection of barely cohesive sovereign states. When the Framers began constructing the Constitution they looked towards historical models to uncover solutions. The Greek city-states, or the *polis*, were akin to self-contained medieval fiefdoms.[3] In Plato's work *The Republic* not only does Socrates offer his thoughts on the union of city-states, but also deduced several ways the system could be improved. As governments were of the construction of men, forged to serve the needs of the citizens of society, the morality of the *polis* reflected its founders.[4] Such states were not the intellectual product of humanity, but a gathering of like-minded individuals united by either tribal commonalities or shared purpose.[5] As human beings were incapable of complete self-sufficiency, the community flourished or died dependent upon how well they worked interdependently.[6] Justice was achieved when those at the lowest end of the economic scheme were not deprived of the necessities of life.[7] Socrates also stated the aim of a commonwealth was not to coddle one sector of the populace, but all of the people.[8] A written constitution was the instrument by which it was achieved.[9] Finally, the polis must not be allowed to grow beyond its capability to remain united.[10]

As evidenced within the *Constitution of the Athenians*, many of Socrates' assessments were obvious. The outlying communities lived under the same laws and political system as those within the city proper. Taxes placed upon residents were managed by the Athenian Council along with the magistrates, and they administered aid programs for the indigent and impoverished.[11] The commissioners who maintained local temples and building projects were elected by all of the residents.[12] These communities were also allowed to popularly elect their own representatives to serve as Arbitrators, as well as select their own commanding officers for the companies of soldiers they provided.[13] Thus, in every manner those who lived outside of the city of Athens held all the rights and privileges of citizens within the city.

Once the Romans had freed themselves from the domination of the Etruscans during the Fourth Century BCE, they began the process of constructing what became an empire.[14] Their methods of integrating defeated provinces not only stabilized the region, but provided a stake to its citizens in continuing Roman rule as semi-independent client-states, thus curtailing rebellion.[15] This governmental scheme remained in force for a century-and-a-half, when it was replaced by an imperial system under the rule of the Roman senate and later the emperors.[16]

In colonies founded by Rome every site chosen held the potential to be modified into a military base.[17] The governing and religious institutions of the conquered realms were assimilated into the Roman civil culture.[18] Land within these colonies was also given as a reward to career soldiers too old to serve, with former officers often presiding as governor.[19] Unfortunately, this policy was also the author of several impractical edicts implemented solely for personal gain.[20]

The third model was the British colonies. Though England had been under the rule of Rome for four centuries, as noted by legal historian Frederick Maitland, their civil law had but scant impact.[21] The British Constitution began with the Anglo-Saxon dooms, or edicts of the kings.[22] These statutes were collected under the authority of Henry II, who established a legal system under which they became precedent upon which future law and court decisions were based.[23] Under the laws of Henry III and Edward I the authority of the British government was the possession of the monarch by prerogative, rather than the aristocracy.[24] With the decree of Edward I, all law practiced and cited was exclusively English, which ended the then current fascination with Roman legal traditions.[25] The culmination of laws passed and legal precedent were made available to both judges and practitioners with the issuance of annual Year Books.[26]

Once England had organized colonies along the North Atlantic coastline, it did so in a manner to provide maximum benefit with minimal expenditure. There would three specific categories of colonies established under British rule: Crown, Proprietary and Charter. With the Crown, or Royal colony all political administration was centered in London under the authority of the British government with appointed officers.[27] The second was the proprietary colonies created under the authority of the monarch as self-governing used as a means of rewarding political allies, and which also allowed for private investment. The prime impetus of these colonies was to generate profit for the monarchy, the owners of the company which held the charter, and investors. The third type was the charter colonies established by royal proclamation which served as its legal charter of laws.[28]

England's colonies in North America were either ceded, or conquered countries with existing codes of law, thus the colonists were not proper English citizens.[29] As they had not formally joined with the English commonwealth, as Scotland had been by the *Act of Unification* in 1707,[30] they did not enjoy the same legal privileges of citizenship as other colonies did, as stated within the text of the law itself:

> [T]he common law of England, as such, has no allowance or authority there; they being no part of the mother-country, but distant, though dependent, dominions. They are subject, however, to the control of the parliament, unless particularly named.[31]

Though the colonies were legally obligated to establish the English common law at the onset, only the laws specifically applicable to their circumstances were enforced.[32]

Such were the legal perimeters under which George Lord Grenville, Chancellor of the Exchequer and administrator of colonial affairs, was presented with. In place upon his appointment was a policy of "salutary neglect" implemented by Prime Minister Robert Walpole over four decades earlier that allowed the American colonies to conduct business without the interference of excessive tax assessment or collection.[33] At the close of the Great War for Empire England, though victorious against the French, had incurred massive national debt in the effort.[34] To immediately raise revenues, Grenville pushed for both the enforcement of tax laws already on the books, as well as implementing other revenue-gathering schemes.[35] These policies proved to be disastrous as the colonists openly resisted paying the new levies. This action by Lord Grenville proved to be first political volley of the American Revolution.

Relations between central authorities and their satellites were based upon political reciprocity to promote national unity. Though the sovereign held the authority to enforce the laws, it was not conclusive such actions unified the citizens into an interconnected whole. For the populace to embrace a national identity they had to be participants in the realm's protection and fortuity. Their role was to elect those to speak for them, and to hold both their representatives and sovereign to the honorable administration of the nation's business serving their collective interests.

Jean Bodin contended it was the sovereign's most vital purpose to maintain unity within his realm.[36] In doing so, Bodin insisted a legitimate monarch respected natural law in the same manner he wished his subjects to regard his own edicts.[37] Within his three models of monarchy distinctions were made towards domestic tranquility. Despotic sovereignties were enduring due to their being the most authoritative.[38] Royal monarchies were the result of succession, though usurpers often evolved into true kings so long as they ruled with equity and mercy.[39] Tyrannical monarchy was the least stable, as it willfully violated natural law in its abuse of the citizens' liberty by enslaving them to his will.[40] Such a ruler, having used force to obtain power, was subjected to the vengeance of rivals by the same method.[41] Thus, the vital element in gaining or losing political power was the unity of the people governed by the sovereign.

Thomas Hobbes echoed Bodin in his assertion that because human beings existed in a constant state of war, the law of nature was to pursue amity and stasis.[42] This law applied to nations as it did to nature, for it was the sovereign's duty under the social contract to obtain both peace and stability for those under his charge.[43] Thus, without domestic tranquility civilization could not exist.

Hugo Grotius put forward a rationale for peace treaties which could be adapted towards an equitable relationship between a central government and its individual states. The element which made it possible was that amity was obtained through citizens living lives of contentment.[44] Provinces were to be kept by justice, not force.[45] Though admittedly a complicated process, it was necessary to consider both the outcomes of such agreements as well as the administrative authority held to maintain it.[46] It was the 'Sovereign Council' who possessed the authority to negotiate and enter into binding contracts of peace.[47] Such treaties should neither be made in perpetuity, nor constructed too narrowly not to allow flexibility, but within the confines of what a sovereign authority could reasonably sustain.[48]

The property and goods of the people were under the ownership of the state through eminent domain, especially in maintaining the peace.[49] Also, the possession of anything was a moot point if the viability of the state was in jeopardy.[50] No action taken by a sovereign was to be entered into arbitrarily, but at all times taken in the best interest of the peace and stability of the realm.[51] Allies were obligated to keep the peace and any action which threatened such an agreement was a legitimate cause for war.[52]

Algernon Sidney advocated domestic tranquility based upon active involvement of the citizens.[53] Using examples from Greek and Roman history, he warned placing the task of governing into the hands of an elected few, or one, without personal involvement in public affairs was a recipe for tyranny.[54] For a nation to survive the citizens must be engaged, for they were as responsible for the wellbeing of the realm as the sovereign.[55] It was the peoples' charge to hold their representatives accountable for their actions, and who also possessed the authority to remove incompetent officers from power before they wrought harm upon their communities and their nation.[56]

John Locke distinguished the principles at the heart of the social contract which bound the people and the sovereign together within society. He described the social contract as modeled after the family unit, as it was the first power structure most people were acquainted with.[57] As the family unit represented both safety and stability, people in societies looked to government in the same fashion, and accepted the premise monarchies were natural without ever considering more democratic models of governance.[58] To Locke, the similarities were striking: All governments appealed to law, depended upon judges to make decisions, as well as looking towards the sovereign to maintain order and restrict violence as much as was possible.[59] Furthermore, the citizens were obligated to believe this paradigm so the law could be effective.[60] Even when the people accepted the notion of representative democracy, they nonetheless allowed the sovereign to determine when such institutions would convene.[61] When the sovereign violated the public trust, and acted in a belligerent manner toward the people, it was the citizen's right under the social contract to withdraw their allegiance, and to prosecute the sovereign under the full terms of the law.[62]

Baron de Montesquieu maintained the imperative trait within the citizens of every community was virtue. With a reliance upon it, the community flourished, yet without it the opposite occurred. Whereas virtue was a necessary trait within a democratic government, once it was no longer viable corruption set in.[63] It should also be a vital element of any code of laws or constitution for it provided legitimacy for the execution of its edicts.[64] In despotic governments there was no virtue, only the fear of death as reprisal should one disobey the sovereign.[65] Montesquieu made no value judgments when he delineated the differences between large and small republics:

> In a large republic, the common good is sacrificed to a thousand considerations; it is subordinated to exceptions; it depends upon accidents. In a small one, the public good is better felt, better known, lies nearer to each citizen; abuses are less extensive there and consequently less protected.[66]

The sole advantage of a small republic was when the sovereign was held accountable by the citizens and ousted from power, the decision and action taken were final, but in a larger republic a war would result.[67]

Jean-Jacques Rousseau declared civilizations were composed of distinct human beings detached from one another in physicality and thought. The cohesiveness of society was an abstract idea among its constituents rather than a concrete reality.[68] The reason why functioning communities were rare was due to a common law to govern them being a nearly impossible task to realize.[69] The greatest good was the goal a society whose elements were freedom and equality.[70] If there were to be governments, they must consist of an executive working concurrent with a representative legislature, and the people's constant responsibility to choose the wisest among them to serve in both capacities.[71] Inevitably, because each citizen desired ends which suited their particular wants, parties developed which would thwart the 'general will'.[72]

As the relationship between the individual states became terse in the wake of independence, many held trepidations the *Articles of Confederation* did not possess the requisite power to hold the country together. As stated by Alexander Hamilton:

> We may indeed, with propriety, be said to have reached almost the last stage of national humiliation. There is scarcely any thing that can wound the pride, or degrade the character, of an independent people, which we do not experience.[73]

Due to the rampant disquiet within the country ensuring 'domestic tranquility' was not a pragmatic issue.

During the Constitutional Convention George Read of Delaware asserted that a united nation needed to end its high regard for state governments.[74] In voicing his support for a national legislature, Read maintained he was not against the existence of individual states, but for them to be subordinate to a sovereign government which unified them.[75] James Madison of Virginia answered Read that the new constitution was to derive its power from the States, for it would be they who chose the representatives.[76] To leave the bulk of political power with the individual States in a loose confederacy weakened any chance of national unity, for it failed to control the will of the individual states towards attaining further political power.[77] Roger Sherman of Connecticut was adamant a national legislature have sovereign power, for failing to do so would result in the state legislatures defying the authority of the federal government.[78]

At the center of the debate was the balance of federal and state authority. James Wilson of Pennsylvania maintained the liberty of action asserted by the individual States were akin to the personal freedom of individuals, and they were intent on not only maintaining what authority they already possessed, but also would interfere with any other body who sought to limit it.[79] As voiced by John Dickinson of Delaware, the *Articles* had created a relationship in which the States existed concurrently as both individual political entities, as well as collectively for their mutual benefit.[80] It was a principle most delegates sought to carry forward into the new federal constitution.[81] Dickinson put forward the repercussions of Shays' Rebellion had not been addressed, and if this issue were to be ignored, it would damage the peaceful interrelationship among the States.[82] His unease was that the majority would run roughshod over the minority creating an unresolvable conflict between them.[83]

The report of the Committee of detail issued on the 6th of August contained clauses which did much to address the lingering issues of individual states in a federal union:

1. No state was allowed to coin or print its own currency.
2. No state was allowed to enter into its own separate treaty with a foreign country.
3. The issuance of credit between the states must be approved by the Congress.

4. The citizens of the separate states were to enjoy the same rights and protections within the other states.
5. Any person charged with a crime in one state could not escape prosecution by fleeing to another.
6. Full faith and credit was given to all states equally.[84]

These proposals were agreed to by the convention on the 29th of August, and accepted as put forward in Article IV of the draft constitution on the 12th of September 1787.[85]

If only the construction of the national legislature had been formulated as easily. Should there be domestic tranquility among the separate sovereign states, they would have to be represented in a manner in which all had an equal voice, yet were also able to flex their political muscles due to the size of their population. This was the balancing-act to be achieved if a united nation was to be the end result. It proved to be an arduous piecemeal process.

The debate opened on 29 May 1787 with the first action being the construction of a national legislature and the agreement upon how it was to be structured akin to the *Articles of Confederation*.[86] Pierce Butler of South Carolina rejected it because all legislative power would be entrusted within a unicameral representative body, to which Elbridge Gerry of Massachusetts agreed.[87] Roger Sherman argued the contrary: The Congress under the *Articles* was dysfunctional due to it having been provided with scant power to govern.[88] Two days later Edmund Randolph of Virginia put forward that the national congress should consist of two branches and it was approved by a nearly unanimous vote—the single nay being Benjamin Franklin of Pennsylvania who favored a single body.[89]

Roger Sherman objected to the popular election of members to Congress, the reason being the people were often misled by the rhetoric of ambitious men, to which Elbridge Gerry agreed.[90] George Mason of Virginia proposed a compromise: Representatives to the larger of the two branches be elected by the people, and the smaller branch by the State legislatures, to which James Wilson concurred.[91] Pierce Butler voiced opposition to what he viewed as taking substantial power away from the State governments which would, in turn, marginalize their authority.[92] This resolution was voted down in committee.[93]

In the Committee of the Whole on the 6th of June, Charles Coatesworth Pinckney of South Carolina recommended the members of the 'first branch' of the national legislature be chosen by the state legislatures, rather than the people.[94] It was seconded by John Rutledge also of South Carolina.[95] George Mason pointed out Congress under the *Articles of Confederation* represented not the people, but the states, to which James Madison concurred.[96] Following heated debate, John Dickinson proposed one branch be directly elected by the people, while the other by the State legislatures.[97] The Committee voted against this measure as well, though James Wilson moved to reconsider it at a later time, and it was seconded by James Madison.[98] The following day Madison asked that Dickinson's suggestion to be reconsidered. He insisted proportional representation was not feasible due to the escalating numbers made mandatory by new states entering the Union.[99] The committee briefly debated the motion and voted in favor of the power of the State legislatures to appoint their Senate delegation.[100] They continued to debate issues concerning the right and perimeters of suffrage without reaching a compromise.[101]

Two days later a compromise motion was read aloud in committee that proposed the national legislature be divided into two separate bodies: One whose representation would be equal and representatives served a term of seven years, while the was other based upon population and representatives were elected for a term of three years.[102] John Lansing of New York argued against the proposal as it absorbed the authority of the states to act in purely local matters.[103] James Wilson was not convinced this plan guarded against the ascent of the legislature, the example being the host of laws enacted by the British parliament which led to the revolution.[104] John Lansing retorted the true question was whether this new constitution would be congruent with the idea of a confederation, or would it abandon that notion completely.[105] Edmund Randolph countered the confederacy had failed to unite the states, and that the public safety was endangered.[106] When the vote was taken on the 20th of June, the proposal was defeated, and the convention was at a standstill.[107]

Following the vote Charles Coatesworth Pinkney proposed the member of the first branch be elected in a manner specifically chosen by the state legislatures individually.[108] Alexander Hamilton of New York claimed the motion was a scheme to take power from the citizens and transfer it to the State legislatures, which increased the latter's power and influence.[109] Rufus King of Massachusetts chided such a plan was devious, as the State legislatures would select those who would pursue the state's interests, rather than those of the nation as a whole.[110] After a vote on the proposal which proved the delegation were still divided, Pinckney revised his scheme, and proposed its members be elected by the people in a manner the state legislatures would design.[111] It passed by a comfortable margin.

James Wilson brought up how the members of the second branch of the national legislature were to be elected. George Read thought it prudent that the States be eclipsed, and that a national legislature be as connected to the citizenry as much was possible.[112] Roger Sherman reiterated the question before them was not about the abstract idea of rights, but rather the structure of the national legislature who would protect those rights.[113] Oliver Ellsworth of Connecticut proposed the compromise: Congruent with Article II of the *Articles'* statement of mimetic equality within Congress, the Senate would be equal in representation, while the House of Representatives be determined, as agreed upon, by the number of citizens within the State itself.[114] The delegates agreed. William Richardson Davie of North Carolina commented as new states entered the union, the number of representatives in both houses of Congress would become unmanageable.[115] James Wilson thought it prudent to consider a population requirement, though he later relented for the sake of compromise.[116] On the 2nd of July, Ellsworth's compromise measure was voted down.[117]

Either a working compromise had to be reached, or the convention would end in failure. Hugh Williamson of North Carolina urged both sides to reconsider Ellsworth's compromise measure.[118] Edmund Randolph warned if such an agreement remained unattainable it would result in the increase of executive power.[119] James Wilson conceded a perfect plan was unachievable.[120] In the end, after heated debate, Ellsworth's compromise measure passed a committee vote on Saturday, the 14th of July.[121]

Three days later Gouverneur Morris of Pennsylvania asked the committee for a reconsideration of the Ellsworth compromise to explore the powers allocated toward each branch.[122] This motion opened up a hotbed of debate. Roger Sherman agreed with Morris, and asked for a modification in the language in favor of 'individual Legislatures' be added, to which James Wilson and Gunning Bedford of Delaware agreed.[123] Edmund Randolph voiced his opposition, as it would violate wholesale the authority of the States and their constitutions.[124] The amendment passed.[125] Again the notion of federal legislative power being granted to the general government was brought up by Morris, to which Luther Martin of Maryland, James Madison, and Charles Coatesworth Pinckney voiced their opposition.[126] Oliver Ellsworth restated the argument made previously by Edmund Randolph that should issues regarding the Congress be left unresolved, such power would naturally gravitate toward either the Executive or Judicial branches.[127] On the 26th of July, after much contention, the committee passed its report unanimously, and it was sent to the entire body of delegates for consideration.[128]

On the 6th of August John Rutledge delivered a printed copy of the committee's report to each member of the convention, and the next stage of the debate commenced.[129] The initial sticking point was the length of residency in the State prior and during service in Congress, with the proposed changes voted down.[130] Modifications to the equality of State representation in the Senate were also voted down.[131] Gouverneur Morris and James Madison offered a change of reference from 'each House' to the House of Representatives and the Senate which passed handily.[132] The Report of the Committee of Stile & arrangement issued its statement on Wednesday, the 12th of September that began with Article I, and defined the membership and powers of the Legislative branch of the federal government.[133] With its passage following over three months of debate and haggling, a successful conclusion was finally reached.

Among the most vexing issues was taxation as put forth in Article I § 8's Necessary-And-Proper Clause. This power was authored by William Paterson of New Jersey who proposed on 15th of June 1787 as powers 'proper & expedient'.[134] Within the report submitted to the entire group on 6th of August by the Committee of Detail, chaired by John Rutledge, the language provided for a general federal power of taxation under two conditions: 1) There would be no such levies placed upon interstate trade; and, 2) no capitulation tax be levied without a national census having been taken.[135] Sixteen days later Rutledge proposed a time limit on national debt and loan payments for an undecided period of years.[136] It was voted down, but later included in the report of the Committee of the Eleven, chaired by David Brearly of New Jersey, issued on 4th of September.[137] There were no objections to the language and it was adopted with the passage of the document in convention, and later with its ratification.

Once the document was constructed, the language finalized, and the delegates had approved it, every one of the issues which had proved a source of contention during the convention arose once more during the State ratification debates. What ensued was more than the approval of a new governing charter, but of how sovereign States could be united and governed under a central authority.

Federalist John Jay depicted the United States as always having been permanently one nation forged by the first colonists. They shared a common descent, spoke the same language, professed the same Christian religion, agreed upon the principles of self-government, and had fought together to establish the independence of their new nation.[138]

As such, throughout their short history Americans, though citizens of separate sovereign states, had forged a united political identity, and they had also created a national government which had recognized that political reality.[139] When government failed to unite them, the people of the states called a convention, sent their most intelligent and trusted men to represent them in crafting a new and better one.[140] For Jay the ratification of the Constitution was a national necessity, as it was more efficient for one national government to maintain the peace between thirteen sovereign states than for the individual sovereign states to do so separately.[141] Relations with foreign powers were more easily administrated under one centralized government.[142] Furthermore, a foreign government was unable to turn one state against another to gain favor.

James Madison referenced Hobbes in his explanation: Conflicts were the elements of a constant state of war amongst people, for they were biased towards their own interests.[143] Even religious leaders were incapable of excising unbiased judgments due to their partiality toward that which benefitted their faith and their church.[144] No one but an impartial authority could render just verdicts between conflicting factions.

Alexander Hamilton maintained a strong central government provided an effective bulwark against divergences between states which led to political aggression towards one another.[145] The leading function of the federal constitution was as an instrument for the continued merger of the sovereign states.[146] The states played a vital role in the protection of a republican form of government due to their sovereign status. Citing Montesquieu, Hamilton contended the idea of unification for common protection and security was not a new idea, but one which had been asserted for several centuries.[147] Without a national authority the Union would tear itself asunder through internal squabbles, or fall under the authority of a foreign power, as they were too fractured to engage in a united defense.[148] Also, in times of crisis men of dubious character rose to power.[149] From this circumstance individual states were no more immune than any other sovereign authority, as demonstrated through historical examples beginning with ancient Athens' defeat in the Peloponnesian War against Sparta, and later their falling under the authority of Rome.[150]

One of the leading concerns Hamilton addressed was how a well-regulated federal military force was essential for maintaining internal security. In matters of defense, he surmised under a federal Union, the states would have one another's military resources in a cohesive whole against an external threat.[151] Also, a series of fortifications were of vital importance to all of the states, as they provided protection for all at critical invasion points along the Eastern seaboard and the Western frontier.[152] Also, with internal rebellions, a federally controlled force would be more effective in ending them in a timely manner.[153] The state militias would not be dismantled, as they were vital in not only providing protection for their specific state, but also held a supporting role for a national military in the specific instance of attack.[154]

Hamilton discussed the issue of commercial trade. He contended there were compelling reasons why a united federal government was of greater value than trade with separate sovereign states. United they could effect changes to the hostile trading policies of other countries that were not possible if negotiated by the states separately, along with local markets that would be a strong source of revenue due to interconnected trade.[155] Furthermore, without a centralized government the individual states could not protect their goods from piracy, nor receive fair trade agreements, nor gain the respect of countries with whom a trading relationship already existed.[156] Finally, free and fair trade among the individual states would only serve to strengthen the bonds of Union between them, while creating further profits for every state in the country.[157]

Hamilton also discussed how unity under a national government generated revenue for all the states. Uniform tax laws promoted a higher level of trade between the states than a continuance of trade tariffs.[158] Anticipating the American System of Henry Clay by more than three decades, he claimed an interlocking structure of national trade—in which the economies of specific regions of the country were interdependent through government encouragement—would be the by-product of adopting a federal constitution.[159] A strong union between the states under a centralized government was more frugal for all parties involved.[160] Continuing under the *Articles of Confederation* meant every political task with a national interest needed to be filtered through several layers of state government before it was brought to the attention of a central government, which lacked the necessary authority to administer it correctly.[161]

The Anti-Federalists held it was the sovereign states united in the common cause that had procured independence from Great Britain, thus preserving the confederacy between them was the best manner by which domestic tranquility was insured. Their ideas centered upon two separate interlocking governments, each with their own set of responsibilities, operating simultaneously. They proposed no union of sovereign states was worth the liberty of their states and citizens, and questioned large grants of authority to the federal government which absorbed power from the states. In doing so, they also raised the specter of secession from the Union in their rhetoric.

'Brutus' acknowledged that the crisis between the states had threatened the burgeoning nation: "We have felt the feebleness of the ties by which these United States are held together"[162] He took umbrage in offering a new federal constitution which abandoned confederation government and queried as to whether the individual states could be properly represented within one national legislature, one national executive, and one national judicial body.[163] The author was suspicious of Article VI's assertion the Constitution was "the supreme law of the land" without any recourse for the states.[164] Taken together, these clauses confirmed the misgivings of the Anti-Federalists: Under the Constitution, the states lacked all authority to prevent any policy enacted by the Congress and signed into law by the president, which meant in time, state governments would be amalgamated into the federal government.[165]

'Brutus' also cited Montesquieu with the assertion republics were effective only in small territories, and if enacted within a large territory there would be men who would use their wealth and influence to gain control of the government.[166] He then attempted to uncover historical precedents to counter Montesquieu's assertion, but found not a single instance. Though both Greece and Rome had begun as republics, with acquisitions wrought from territorial conquests, they had both abandoned republicanism for empire.[167] He then concluded in the future public servants would forsake the best interest of the people in favor of agendas of beneficence to themselves.[168]

Patrick Henry bluntly stated there was no need in abandoning the confederation for a centralized government.[169] Henry portrayed the adoption of the Constitution as a revolution as radical as that which American had fought to gain their independence from Great Britain.[170] He pointed out there existed no statement on the rights of American citizens which were guaranteed by state constitutions. Furthermore, the overarching and unspecified powers of the federal government were enough to allow it to usurp the powers of the states to defend themselves.[171] Though Henry railed against the onslaught of centralized power, he also made sure to include the statement: "I mean not to breathe the spirit nor utter the language of secession."[172]

Throughout the course of his speeches at the New York State Ratifying Convention, Melancton Smith posed the question as to the worth of Union. Smith reproached the Federalists for conspiring to force the states to accept the Constitution.[173] With more than a hint of secession in his rhetoric, Smith forcefully stated there was no need to abandon the *Articles* in order to preserve the Union.[174] Smith accused the Federalists of producing a military threat against the Eastern states which did not exist, a tactic to influence the convention towards ratification. Though the Confederation government definitely had problems, Smith argued it was a more efficient form of government than a federal republic.[175]

Article IV § 1 made certain "Full Faith and Credit shall be given in each State to the public Acts, Records, and judicial Proceedings of every other State."[176] It was a guarantee laws made in one state remained enforceable within all of the states. James Madison framed the clause within the context of the individual states, and maintained that the consistency of the law made unifying the States easier, which was of benefit to all.[177] The Federalist author "The State Soldier" concurred, adding such a clause was the sole manner by which the states could be unified.[178] The writer reasoned if the country wanted to maintain its standing among its fellow nations of the world, its credit must be addressed and all of the member states needed to be held to their responsibilities.[179] As for the Anti-Federalists, they remained mute as to this specific clause.

Article IV § 2 mandated "[t]he Citizens of each State shall be entitled to all Privileges and Immunities of Citizens in the several States".[180] Not only did this clause allow for legal recognition and protection of national citizenship, but concurrently guaranteed the laws of one state were enforceable law in all the other states.[181] Alexander Hamilton explained that to provide an effective administration of the laws of one state, it was necessary for all of the States to do so for their counterparts.[182] 'The Federal Farmer' agreed with Hamilton's premise, but disagreed with the means as, in the author's view, the language of the clause had not been thoughtfully contemplated.[183] 'Brutus' opposed the clause on the grounds that the federal government would pass a multitude of laws which would be of benevolence to one state or region, but would be destructive to another.[184]

> But this was not to be the case regarding Article VI Paragraph 2, which read:
> This Constitution, and the Laws of the United States which shall be made in Pursuance thereof; and all Treaties made, or which shall be made, under the Authority of the United States, shall be the supreme Law of the Land; and the Judges in every State shall be bound thereby, any Thing in the Constitution or Laws of any State to the Contrary notwithstanding.[185]

'The Impartial Examiner' discussed what the author termed "a prefect solecism": The notion that two separate sovereign political entities could not coexist, as one would inevitably usurp the power of the other.[186] There could be only one final authority, and within the text of the constitution it was given to the central government.[187] "The Federal Farmer" argued if all laws made under the federal constitution were sovereign, it logically followed that over time federal laws would either undermine or abolish state laws.[188] Furthermore, when coupled with the authority of the Necessary-and-Proper Clause of Article I § 8, it provided the federal government with unlimited legislative power, and every other state laws and constitution must yield to its authority.[189]

'An Old Whig' queried whether placing such authority within the purview of a centralized government was prudent.[190] The author was concerned with the exclusive presidential power to negotiate treaties, as the product could produce results which would adversely affect the states without them having any recourse.[191] 'John DeWitt' questioned the Supremacy Clause, specifically what protections the sovereign states were provided to their citizens from the encroachment of their rights by the federal government, and the author's answer was none.[192]

To the Federalists the criticisms of the Supremacy Clause were a source of incredulity. Under Article II of the *Articles of Confederation* each individual state had retained its jurisdiction and sovereign rights, which meant the laws of those states were the supreme law of the land.[193] Hamilton claimed in all governments the laws of the realm must hold the mantle of authority in order to be effective.[194] The clause retained sovereign authority, but only within the realms of the power given to it by the constitution itself; furthermore, any law passed outside of the said legal perimeters would be the usurpation of its authority within the constitution itself.[195]

James Madison was in full agreement with his colleague. He stated it was not a novel concept that local authorities answered to the state governments, and the individual state governments exercised this power within their borders, as had the *Articles of Confederation* with a vote by the Congress.[196] Madison further explained such authority given to the federal government was in reality a protection for the states against the questionable actions of the states against one another.[197] With the checks-and-balances placed into the document itself, not only could the president veto unconstitutional legislation, but there was also the Supreme Court to review such laws and to nullify them, if necessary.[198]

There was one area of constitutional interpretation where the Federalists achieved their aim: It was during the 34 years John Marshall served as chief justice of the United States Supreme Court (1801–35). From his service as a delegate at the Virginia state ratifying convention through his tenure as the nation's foremost judge, Marshall never wavered in his support of federalism.[199] Many of the pivotal majority opinions of the Court's history bore his name as author, and were consistent with the jurisprudence of "judicial nationalism", the paradigm of binding a country together through its laws.[200]

The first important decision of the Marshall court was *Marbury v. Madison* (1803).[201] It was the majority opinion in this case which made all of the decisions that followed possible. Based upon the Empowerment Clause of Article III § 1, the U.S. Supreme Court was given supreme jurisdiction over all inferior courts in the land.[202] In a case involving a federal appointment—one of President John Adams' "midnight judges"—and Secretary of State James Madison's refusal to honor it, the Court speaking through Chief Justice John Marshall not only declared its authority to nullify laws inconsistent with the Constitution, but demonstrated its legal paradigm by nullifying the *Judiciary Act of 1789* which had, ironically, authorized the existence of the Court.[203] With this decision the

U.S. Supreme Court became an equal partner with both the presidency and the congress within a tripartite governmental system.[204]

Fletcher v. Peck (1810) held an application in the relationship between the federal government and the individual states.[205] The case involved questionable land grants in Georgia's Yazoo Valley and the state legislatures' legal interference. The Court ruled the state's interposition was in violation of the Contracts Clause of Article I § 10.[206] With this decision the Court established its right of judicial review over laws passed by the state legislatures.[207]

Martin v. Hunter's Lessee (1816) was a state government challenge to federal authority, specifically the U.S. Supreme Court's declared right of judicial review.[208] The case itself involved Loyalist lands confiscated by a statute passed by the Commonwealth of Virginia during the American Revolution. Complicating the matter were both Article V of the *Treaty of Paris* (1783) and the Explanatory Article of the *Treaty of Amity, Commerce and Navigation between His Brittanic Majesty and the United States of America* (1796)—known as "Jay's Treaty"—both of which contained provisions protecting the property of exiled Loyalists.[209] In the previous case of *Fairfax's Devisee v. Hunter's Lessee* (1813), the Court amplified the ire of the state governments when it ruled in favor of the plaintiff based upon the above precedents.[210] Afterwards, the Commonwealth of Virginia refiled the case. The Court, speaking through Associate Justice Joseph Story, and citing Article III §1 and § 2, sustained its right of judicial review.[211] Not only did the Court possess the power of judicial review over decisions made by the state courts, as they were inferior in authority to the federal judiciary, but also each individual state-or-commonwealth had the necessary obligation to abide by both the Constitution and the edicts of the U.S. Supreme Court.[212]

The Trustees of Dartmouth College v. Woodward (1819) involved a college charter enacted prior to American independence which was voided under the authority of the New Hampshire state legislature.[213] Once the old charter had been removed, the legislators issued a new one, appointed a fresh board of trustees, and modified Dartmouth as a university. Following their dismissal, the former trustees filed a suit which challenged the constitutionality of the legislative actions. The Court speaking through Chief Justice John Marshall legally defined the previous charter as a legitimate contract and could not be nullified or voided by any act of a state legislature.[214] The Court reiterated Article I § 10's Contracts Clause that any commonwealth or state had not been provided with the authority to enact any legislation which interfered with either legal commitments and/or terms of a legitimate contract. Thus, by reaffirming full federal jurisdiction in such matters, the body limited the regulatory power of the states.[215]

A month following its decision in the *Dartmouth College* case, the Court issued a statement of federal sovereignty over the states in *McCulloch v. Maryland* (1819).[216] At the close of the War of 1812, the complications in financing such a military action without a national bank were addressed by the creation of the Second Bank of the United States, which was chartered in 1816. The physical location of the institution was outside of the District of Columbia in the state of Maryland, a state whose representatives had opposed the bank as being "unconstitutional" and enacted a business tax upon it. When the Bank refused to pay the charge on the grounds state governments were not authorized to levy taxes against a federal institution, a law suit was launched. The Court again speaking through Chief Justice John Marshall reiterated the legitimacy of the Constitution and the supremacy of the federal government over the state entities.[217] The Court stated:

> [T]he government of the Union, though limited in its power, is supreme within its sphere of action. This would seem to result, necessarily, from its nature. It is the government of all; its powers are delegated by all; it represents all, and acts for all.[218]

The Court's decision in the *McCulloch* case was a landmark. In nullifying the Maryland state excise as unconstitutional, as well as declaring Congress did indeed possess the authority to establish the bank under the aegis of Article I § 8's Necessary-and-Proper Clause, the Court issued a definitive proclamation of federal sovereignty over state governments.[219]

Gibbons v. Ogden (1824) involved a state-granted steamboat monopoly.[220] Following Robert Fulton's invention of the steam-powered water vessel, financed by the powerful Livingston family, Fulton and Robert Livingston were granted a monopoly in steamboat navigation, against which there were mounted several legal challenges. One of these cases involving Aaron Ogden and Thomas Gibbons was heard by the U.S. Supreme Court. Again speaking through Chief Justice John Marshall, the Court reaffirmed the doctrine of federal government sovereignty over the states.[221] Though the Court recognized there were restrictions in the powers of the federal government, within those powers it was sovereign, which included innovations and advancements within its sphere of influence. This authority, found in the Necessary-and-Proper Clause of Article I § 8, was a mechanism designed by the Framers to allow the constitution to ebb and flow with the timbre of the times—a living legal instrument as well as fundamental law.[222]

In a tangible sense, the jurisprudence of the Supreme Court under the leadership of John Marshall bound the nation together, using the essential law of the land as its sinews. Each decision of the Court became the center of controversy for those who viewed it as an ever-increasing encroachment upon state authority. Marshall's successor, Roger Brooke Taney, steered a "dual-sovereignty" course, and in less than two decades he abandoned this legal philosophy, as it provoked so many cases as to overwhelm the entire judicial system. Taney returned to the full sovereignty of the federal government with the Court's majority opinion in *Ableman v. Booth* (1859) two decades later.[223] Though the intent of the Marshall Court decisions had been to ensure domestic tranquility through national unity, the backlash could not have been more intense, as each new controversy inspired a militant entrenchment.

The two-party system became engrained within American politics by 1800 with two clear ideologies. In the ratification debates the Federalists had predicted more internal unrest if the federal constitution was not ratified, while the Anti-Federalists predicted the rise of a tyrannical centralized government in which secession would the sole mechanism at the citizen's disposal with which to free themselves. Ultimately, the constitution was ratified, but as American history bears out, national unity was not the natural by-product of a centralized government. That would take the bloodiest war in American history conducted four generations later to decide.

At the heart of President John Kennedy's inaugural address was a concept the Framers themselves had placed within the Preamble of the Constitution: "And so my fellow Americans, ask not what your country can do for you, ask what you can do for your country."[224] During the constitutional convention it was a quandary which intrigued James Madison, who concluded protections against the encroaching power of both government and the wealthy class were necessary.[225] In the 1950s and 1960s Chief Justice Earl Warren, a conservative Republican by ideology, was accused of being a socialist when he enforced the Constitution as written, an intriguing irony on both counts.

There is a marked difference between tranquility and safety which has eluded most contemporary Americans. To be 'tranquil' is to be at peace, both with yourself and with those around you; while being 'safe' is merely a state in which you are protected from harm by an outside force. One bears no relation with the other, for one can be safe from harm, but it does not infer that somebody is tranquil. Therefore, how these two terms with diametrically opposed meanings are interchanged is incomprehensible. Domestic tranquility will never be preserved so long as we seek only safety for ourselves and ignore the loss of tranquility for others. But it also a trait of human beings to look after our own specific interests above those of others, often at our own peril.

Notes

1. Jack N. Rakove, "The Collapse of the Articles of Confederation", 1988; in, *The American Founding: Essays on the Formation of the Constitution*, eds. J. Jackson Barlow, Leonard W. Levy, and Ken Masugi (Santa Barbara, CA: Praeger Books, 1988), 225–45.
2. Jack N. Rakove, *Original Meanings: Politics and Ideas in the Making of the Constitution* (New York: Alfred A. Knopf, Inc., 1997), 33–4.
3. Ian Morris, "The Early Polis as City and State"; in *City and Country in the Ancient World*, eds. John Rich and Andrew Wallace-Hadrill (London: Routledge Books, 1992), 27–40.
4. Plato, *The Republic*, trans., Francis MacDonald Cornford (New York: Oxford University Press, 1941), 55.
5. *Ibid.*, 56.
6. *Ibid.*, 55.
7. *Ibid.*, 58–9.
8. *Ibid.*, 110.
9. *Ibid.*
10. *Ibid.*, 114.
11. Aristotle, *The Constitution of the Athenians*, trans. Sir Frederick G. Kenyon, Section III, Parts 47 and 49; at The Internet Classics Archive; http://classics.mit.edu/Aristotle/athenian_const.mb.txt. Accessed 27 June 2018.
12. *Ibid.*, Section III, Part 50.
13. *Ibid.*, Section III, Part 53; Section III, Part 63.
14. Michael Grant, *History of Rome* (New York: Charles Scribner's Sons, 1978), 60.
15. *Ibid.*, 60–1.
16. *Ibid.*, 56–7, 61.
17. *Ibid.*, 61.
18. *Ibid.*, 57–9.
19. *Ibid.*, 187, 233.
20. Grant, 338.
21. Frederick William Maitland, *The Constitutional History of England*; ed. H. A. L. Fisher, 1965 reprint (Cambridge, England: Cambridge University Press, 1908), 5.
22. *Ibid.*, 6.
23. *Ibid.*, 11.
24. William Blackstone, *Commentaries on the Laws of England*, ed. William Draper Lewis, reprint of 1922 edition (Clark, NJ: The Lawbook Exchange, 2004), II: 531.
25. Maitland, 21.
26. *Ibid.*, 22.

27. Edward Jenks, *The Government of the British Empire* (Boston, MA: Little, Brown, and Company, 1918), 70.
28. John C. Miller, *Origins of the American Revolution* (Boston, MA: Little, Brown and Company, 1943), 173–4.
29. Blackstone, I: 94.
30. *An Act for the Union of the Two Kingdoms of England and Scotland*, 1706 c. 11. *An Act Ratifying the Treaty of Union of the Two Kingdoms of Scotland and England*, 1707 c. 7.
31. *Ibid.*
32. Maitland, 337.
33. Miller, 37.
34. *Ibid.*, 70–1. The Great War for Empire is also referred to as either the French-and-Indian War or the Seven Years' War.
35. Miller, 181. John Richard Alden, *The American Revolution: 1775–1783* (New York: Harper and Brothers, Publishers, 1954), 4–7.
36. Jean Bodin, *Six Books of the Commonwealth*, ed. M. J. Tooley (Oxford, England: Basil Blackwell/The Alden Press, 1955), 63.
37. *Ibid.*, 59.
38. *Ibid.*
39. *Ibid.*, 60.
40. *Ibid.*, 61.
41. *Ibid.*
42. Thomas Hobbes, *Leviathan*, ed. Richard Tuck (New York: Cambridge University Press, 1996), 92.
43. *Ibid.*, 244.
44. Hugo Grotius, *The Rights of War and Peace*, ed. Richard Tuck (Indianapolis, IN: The Liberty Fund, 2005), III: 1504.
45. *Ibid.*
46. *Ibid.*, III: 1551.
47. *Ibid.*, III: 1553.
48. *Ibid.*, III: 1555.
49. *Ibid.*, III: 1556.
50. *Ibid.*
51. *Ibid.*, III: 1558, 1561, 1570–1.
52. *Ibid.*, III: 1570–1.
53. Algernon Sidney, *Discourses Concerning Government*, ed. Thomas G. West (Indianapolis, IN: The Liberty Fund, 1996), 271.
54. *Ibid.*, 274.
55. *Ibid.*
56. *Ibid.*, 276, 279.
57. John Locke, *Two Treatises of Government*, ed. Peter Laslett (New York: Cambridge University Press, 1960), II: 357.

58. *Ibid.*, II: 375.
59. *Ibid.*, II: 328.
60. *Ibid.*, II: 378.
61. *Ibid.*
62. *Ibid.*, II: 425–6.
63. Baron de Montesquieu, *Spirit of the Laws*, eds. Anne Cohler, Basia Miller, and Harold Stone (New York: Cambridge University Press, 1989), 23.
64. *Ibid.*, 24.
65. *Ibid.*, 27.
66. *Ibid.*, 124.
67. *Ibid.*
68. Jean-Jacques Rousseau, *The Social Contract and Other Later Political Writings*, ed. Victor Gourevitch (New York: Cambridge University Press, 1996), 155.
69. *Ibid.*, 78.
70. *Ibid.*
71. *Ibid.*, 93.
72. *Ibid.*, 105.
73. Alexander Hamilton, Essay #15; in *The Federalist*, The Gideon Edition, eds. George W. Carey and James McClellan (Indianapolis, IN: The Liberty Fund, 2001), 69.
74. James Madison, *Notes of Debates in the Federal Constitution of 1787* (Athens, OH: Ohio University Press, 1966, 1985), 78.
75. *Ibid.*, 104.
76. *Ibid.*, 140.
77. *Ibid.*, 142.
78. *Ibid.*, 160.
79. *Ibid.*, 90.
80. *Articles of Confederation and Perpetual Union*, Article III.
81. Madison, 143–4.
82. *Ibid.*, 144.
83. *Ibid.*
84. *Ibid.*, 394.
85. *Ibid.*, 546–7; 625. *U.S. Constitution*, Article IV § 1–4.
86. *Ibid.*, 31. *Articles of Confederation and Perpetual Union*, Article V.
87. *Ibid.*, 34–5.
88. *Ibid.*, 35.
89. *Ibid.*, 38–9.
90. *Ibid.*, 39.
91. *Ibid.*, 39–40.
92. *Ibid.*, 41.
93. *Ibid.*, 43.
94. *Ibid.*, 73.

95. *Ibid.*
96. *Ibid.*, 75. *Articles of Confederation and Perpetual Union*, Article XIII.
97. *Ibid.*, 77.
98. *Ibid.*, 79.
99. *Ibid.*, 83.
100. *Ibid.*, 87.
101. *Ibid.*, 94, 95, 97.
102. *Ibid.*, 115.
103. *Ibid.*, 121.
104. *Ibid.*, 127–8.
105. *Ibid.*, 155.
106. *Ibid.*
107. *Ibid.*, 162.
108. *Ibid.*, 166.
109. *Ibid.*, 166–7.
110. *Ibid.*, 167.
111. *Ibid.*, 168.
112. *Ibid.*, 195.
113. *Ibid.*, 208.
114. *Ibid.*, 208. *Articles of Confederation and Perpetual Union*, Article II.
115. *Ibid.*, 225–6.
116. *Ibid.*, 226.
117. *Ibid.*, 232.
118. *Ibid.*, 236.
119. *Ibid.*, 235.
120. *Ibid.*, 295.
121. *Ibid.*, 297.
122. *Ibid.*, 302.
123. *Ibid.*
124. *Ibid.*, 303.
125. *Ibid.*, 304.
126. *Ibid.*
127. *Ibid.*, 337–8.
128. *Ibid.*, 379, 384.
129. *Ibid.*, 385.
130. *Ibid.*, 406–8.
131. *Ibid.*, 414.
132. *Ibid.*, 423, 428.
133. *Ibid.*, 616–21.
134. *Ibid.*, 118–9.
135. *Ibid.*, 389, 390.

136. *Ibid.*, 509.
137. *Ibid.*, 547.
138. John Jay, Essay #2; in *The Federalist*, 6.
139. *Ibid.*, 6–7.
140. *Ibid.*, 5.
141. John Jay, Essay #3; in *The Federalist*, 9–10.
142. *Ibid.*, 11.
143. James Madison, Essay #10; in *The Federalist*, 43–4.
144. *Ibid.*, 46.
145. Alexander Hamilton, Essay #6; in *The Federalist*, 21.
146. Alexander Hamilton, Essay #9; in *The Federalist*, 37.
147. *Ibid.*, 38.
148. Alexander Hamilton, Essay #6; in *The Federalist*, 21.
149. *Ibid.*
150. *Ibid.*, 21–2.
151. Alexander Hamilton, Essay #8; in *The Federalist*, 33.
152. *Ibid.*, 32–3.
153. *Ibid.*, 35.
154. *Ibid.*
155. Alexander Hamilton, Essay #11; in *The Federalist*, 49–50.
156. *Ibid.*, 50–1.
157. *Ibid.*, 52.
158. Alexander Hamilton, Essay #12; in *The Federalist*, 56.
159. *Ibid.*, 58–9.
160. Alexander Hamilton, Essay #13; in *The Federalist*, 60.
161. *Ibid.*, 61.
162. Brutus, Letter #1, 18 October 1787; in *The Anti-Federalist: Writings by the Opponents of the Constitution*, ed. Herbert Storing (Chicago, IL: University of Chicago Press, 1981), 108.
163. *Ibid.*, 109.
164. *Ibid.*, *U.S. Constitution*, Article VI.
165. *Ibid.*, 111.
166. *Ibid.*, 113. The passage cited can be found in Montesquieu, *Spirit of the Laws*, 124.
167. *Ibid.*, 113–4.
168. *Ibid.*, 116.
169. Patrick Henry, Speech at the Virginia State Ratifying Convention, 4 June 1788; in *The Anti-Federalist*, 296–7.
170. Patrick Henry, Speech at the Virginia State Ratifying Convention, 5 June 1788; in *The Anti-Federalist*, 298.
171. *Ibid.*, 309.
172. *Ibid.*, 314.

173. Melancton Smith, "Speech by Melanction Smith Delivered in the Course of Debate by the Convention of the State of New York on the Adoption of the Federal Constitution", 20 June 1788; in, *The Anti-Federalist*, 333.
174. *Ibid.*
175. *Ibid.*
176. *U.S. Constitution*, Article IV § 1.
177. James Madison, Essay #42; in *The Federalist*, 220–1.
178. "The State Soldier", "An Address to the Good People of Virginia on the New Federal Constitution", 16 January 1788; in, *Friends of the Constitution: Writings of the "Other" Federalists*, eds. Colleen A. Sheehan and Gary L. McDowell (Indianapolis, IN: The Liberty Fund, 1998), 115.
179. *Ibid.*, 116.
180. *U.S. Constitution*, Article IV § 2.
181. James Madison, Essay #42; in *The Federalist,* 220–1.
182. Alexander Hamilton, Essay #80; in *The Federalist*, 413.
183. 'The Federal Farmer', "Letter #6", 25 December 1787; *The Anti-Federalists*, 192.
184. 'Brutus', "Essay #12", 14 February 1788; *The Anti-Federalists*, 458.
185. *U.S. Constitution*, Article VI clause 3.
186. "The Impartial Examiner", Essay #1, 20 February 1788; in, *The Anti-Federalist*, 281.
187. *Ibid.*
188. "The Federal Farmer", Letter #4, 12 October 1787; in, *The Anti-Federalists*, 173.
189. *Ibid.*, 174.
190. "The Old Whig", Essay #3, 20 October 1787; in *The Anti-Federalists*, 328.
191. *Ibid.*
192. "John DeWitt", Essay #3, 5 November 1787; in *The Anti-Federalists*, 506.
193. *The Articles of Confederation*, Article II.
194. Alexander Hamilton, Essay #33; in *The Federalist,* 161.
195. *Ibid.*
196. James Madison, Essay #39; in *The Federalist,* 198.
197. James Madison, Essay #44; in *The Federalist*, 235.
198. *Ibid.*, 236.
199. Albert Beveridge, *The Life of John Marshall*, 4. Vols. (Boston and New York: Houghton Mifflin Company, 1916) I: 475–7. Jean Edward Smith, *John Marshall: Definer of a Nation* (New York: Henry Holt & Company, Inc., 1996), 142–3.
200. Beveridge, II: 441.
201. *Marbury v. Madison*, 5. U.S. 137 (1803).
202. *U.S. Constitution*, Article III § 2.
203. *Marbury v. Madison*, 5. U.S. 137, 180 (1803). Discussions of the *Marbury* decision can also be found in Beveridge, III: 138–42; and, Smith, 319–23.
204. Discussions of the *Marbury* decision can also be found in Beveridge, III: 138–42; and, Smith, 319–23.

205. *Fletcher v. Peck*, 10 U.S. 87 (1810).
206. "No State shall…pass any Bill of Attainder, ex post facto Law, or Law impairing the Obligation of Contracts". *U.S. Constitution*, Article I § 10. *Fletcher v. Peck*, 10 U.S. 87, 139 (1810). Discussions of the *Fletcher* decision can also be found in Beveridge, III: 586–90; and, in Smith, 388–94.
207. Discussions of the *Fletcher* decision can also be found in Beveridge, III: 586–90; and, in Smith, 388–94.
208. *Martin v. Hunter's Lessee*, 14 U.S. 304 (1816).
209. *The Treaty of Paris*, Article V, 3 September 1783; at http://avalon.law.yale.edu/18th_century/paris.asp. *The Treaty of Amity, Commerce and Navigation between His Brittanic Majesty and the United States of America*, 4 May 1796; at http://www.tuscaroras.com/index.php/1796-jay-treaty-of-amity-commerce-and-navigation. Both accessed 8 June 2018.
210. *Fairfax's Devisee v. Hunter's Lessee*, 11 U.S. 603 (1813).
211. *Martin v. Hunter's Lessee*, 14 U.S. 304, 328 (1816).
212. Discussions of the *Martin* decision can be found in Beveridge, IV: 161–3.
213. *Trustees of Dartmouth College v. Woodward*, 17 U.S. 518 (1819).
214. *Trustees of Dartmouth College v. Woodward*, 17 U.S. 518, 653–4 (1819).
215. *U.S. Constitution*, Article I § 10. Discussions of the *Dartmouth College* decision can also be found in Beveridge, IV: 261–73; and, Smith, 435–9.
216. *McCulloch v. Maryland*, 17 U.S. 316 (1819).
217. *McCulloch v. Maryland*, 17 U.S. 316, 404–5 (1819).
218. *McCulloch v. Maryland*, 17 U.S. 316, 405 (1819).
219. Discussions of the *McCulloch* decision can also be found in Beveridge, IV: 289–308; and, Smith, 440–6.
220. *Gibbons v. Ogden*, 22 U.S. 1 (1824).
221. *Gibbons v. Ogden*, 22 U.S. 1, 210–11 (1824).
222. *Gibbons v. Ogden*, 22 U.S. 1, 199–200 (1824). Discussions of the *McCulloch* decision can also be found in Beveridge, IV: 429–33; and, Smith, 477–80.
223. *Ableman v. Booth*; *United States v. Booth*, 62 U.S. 506 (1859).
224. John F. Kennedy, "Presidential Inaugural Address", 20 January 1961; at http://www.jfklibrary.org/Asset-Viewer/BqXIEM9F4024ntFl7SVAjA.aspx?gclid=CjwKEAiA3IKmBRDFx-P_rLyt6QUSJACqiAN8OWbOyWedE58cjcbJ5D9iYPWMQn505si7GPpfwp5KzBoCnCDw_wcB. Accessed 8 June 2018.
225. James Madison, Essay #51; in *The Federalist,* 269.

4

"Provide for the Common Defense"

Protecting a New Nation under the Constitution

The most effective national defense is demonstrated not by the size or strength of its armed forces, but through the degree of genuine respect it holds among its fellow countries throughout the world. It has been proven throughout the pages of history when empires rise based solely upon its military strength, they inevitably self-destruct. In his 1986 book *The Rise and Fall of the Great Powers*, historian Paul Kennedy reasoned all modern imperial nations fell not due to external threats, but through internal economic crisis. Kennedy explained nations who engaged in empire-building caused their own ruin by allocating such a large degree of their domestic fiscal resources towards its military, their national economy collapsed due to incurred debt.[1] This situation also increased political instability amongst neighboring nations, as their relationship with an empire is based upon force, rather than by mutual advantage.[2]

This was a situation the Framers knew well. They had not only studied the ancient Greek and Roman histories from the antiquated works of Thucydides, Appian and others, but they also had lived under the authority of the British Empire. As long as the Empire abided by its trading policy of salutary neglect, the colonies remained loyal to England.[3] But following a nine-year conflict with France the British government had accrued a huge debt which left them little choice but to rescind it.[4] This act was the opening of a series of calculated missteps which over the next dozen years led to the American war for independence.

A study of ancient Greek and Roman history makes apparent how swiftly the common defense evolves into empire building. The Greco-Persian War, a conflagration between the Greek states and the Persian Empire which lasted five centuries, was ignited with the Persian invasion of Naxos.[5] At the behest of King Darius, the Greek city-states of Macedon, Thrace, Eretria and the island nation of Cyclades fell under the invaders control.[6] When the Persians attempted to conquer Athens they were defeated at the Battle of Marathon.[7] It was Darius' son Xerxes who led the second invasion of Greece and successfully routed the Greeks at the Battle of Thermopylae.[8] Rather than surrendering to the Persians, the Greek states rallied and won crucial battles at Salamis, Plataea, and Mycale.[9] These victories directly led to the formation of the Delian League in 478 BCE, a group of over 150 Greek city-states led by Athens and dedicated to the final defeat of Persia.[10]

Within a few years Athens dominated the league. After the final defeat of Persia the Athenian leader Pericles moved the league from its established center at the island of Delos to Athens.[11] The rising power of Athens led the leaders of Sparta to prepare for war.[12] Following several battles in which the two inflicted great numbers of casualties, both sides agreed to uneasy peace at Nicias in March 421 BCE which lasted six years.[13] Hostilities began anew when Sicily, an ally of Athens, was attacked by Syracuse, allies of Sparta. At the close of extensive naval operations, the Athenians were defeated, their large navy was crushed, and its soldiers were sold into slavery.[14] Renewal of hostilities began again when the Ionian states rebelled and rejoined sides with Athens, but the Athenians were disastrously defeated at the Battle of Aegospotomi, and surrendered to the Spartans led by Lysander.[15] With the fall of the Athenian city-state came the destruction of what was among the most enlightened civilizations the world had known. As an Athenian commander who had witnessed the first half of the conflagration, the historian Thucydides concluded:

> The Peloponnesian War…not only lasted for a long time, but throughout its course brought with it unprecedented suffering for Hellas. Never before had so many cities had been captured and then destroyed, whether by foreign armies or by the Hellenic powers themselves…never had there been so many exiles; never such loss of life—both in the actual warfare and in internal revolutions.[16]

The lessons of ancient Greek history were not lost with the Framers. John Jay specifically noted the Greek leader Pericles had authored a destructive war in a political effort to curry favor with the people of Athens.[17] He also noted that Sparta, Athens, Rome and Carthage were all republics who were engaged in constant wars of conquest.[18] Patrick Henry reiterated these same points, and added the people lost their civil liberties in the process.[19] James Madison maintained had the ancient Greeks been as wise in their political decisions as in their courage, they would have seen the benefits of peaceful coexistence with their neighboring city-states.[20] Alexander Hamilton reiterated this same warning, and urged his colleagues to learn from history.[21]

Rome began in the mid-eighth century BCE as a small indigenous settlement on the Tiber River in the lowlands of Italy's Po Valley.[22] During its initial six-centuries Rome was ruled by the Etruscans, a situation which ended with the fall of King Sextus Tarquinius in the final years of the sixth century.[23] The historian Livy asserted the Romans rebelled against a military tax which had financed the Etruscan military.[24] To ensure its independence, the Latin League was formed in the 490s BCE.[25] For 150 years it remained an effective organization in the defense of its members. Then Rome asserted its dominance, and absorbed the league's member states.[26] By the close of the Third Punic War, the Roman Empire was forged with the final defeat of its most formidable rival, Carthage.[27] When Rome began its own empire building, revenues gathered for military endeavors were collected from landed citizens.[28]

The key events which led to international influence of Rome were its ultimate victory against Carthage in the three Punic Wars, which occurred beginning in 264 BCE due to the two expanding empires fighting over the same territory—Sicily. It started with a regional conflict between King Hiero II of Syracuse and the Marmertines of Messina, the latter of whom possessed alliances with Rome.[29] Once the initial invasion of Messina had occurred, the Romans dispatched a legion to assist as per their alliance, and which triggered alarm with Carthage.[30] With the devastating defeat of their land troops at the Battle of Agrigentum in 262 BCE, the Carthaginians adopted a purely naval strategy against the Romans.[31] It proved a sound one for at the Battle of the Lipari Islands two years later, the Carthaginian navy defeated the fledgling Roman fleet. But the Romans recognized their flaws, took the necessary steps to effectively correct them, and amassed a large naval force.[32] What followed was a plethora of Roman naval victories, after which Carthage signed a peace agreement in which they evacuated Sicily, and paid a large repatriation for a decade.[33]

The Second Punic War between Rome and Carthage lasted 17 years and began at the Iberian city of Saguntum. Hannibal was given orders by his uncle Hasdrubal to launch a military campaign of conquest against Rome.[34] The

Carthaginian commander commenced his crossing of the Alps which afterward contributed strategically to his defeat of the Romans at Trebbia, Lake Trasimene, and Cannae.[35] These defeats forced Rome to rethink war strategy in which taking cities by siege was preferable to facing Hannibal on the battlefield, a tactic proven correct with Hannibal's defeat and Hasdrubal's death at Metaurus.[36] The Roman commander Publius Cornelius Scipio initiated an offensive campaign on the Iberian Peninsula which culminated at the successful battles of Ilipa and Zama.[37] Those victories led to a bitter peace in which Carthage ceded her imperial territories to Rome.[38] The Third Punic War was commenced at the behest of Rome and ended with the extermination of Carthage and the assumption of the rest of its territories, after which it indisputably was the foremost military power in the Mediterranean.

With empire came a tremendous financial burden which over time imploded Rome. To pay for military operations during the Second Punic War, a heavy and unpopular property tax was levied by the Senate against the wealthy class of Romans which remained in place for over three centuries.[39] As Rome's holdings grew larger during the reign of Augustus, the first empire-wide census was implemented to gauge the availability of tax revenues, from which resulted a higher rate on property taxes, accompanied by a poll tax.[40] Augustus also undertook a reformation of military policy which mandated specific periods of service, a bounty to be paid upon its completion, and a pension to veterans, all of which were funded by additional taxes.[41]

As the empire grew further the need for funds became more acute with each passing year. Caligula ordered his tax-collectors to implement outrageous new taxes, including one on the institution of marriage.[42] Nero instituted a 4% tax upon those who sold human chattel.[43] The outcry of the Roman people against high levies were so vocal Nero considered abolishing indirect taxes, but when he consulted the Senate they conveyed to him the Empire could not afford it.[44] Vespasian placed a tax upon the use of the city urinals.[45]

Of the early emperors only Tiberius was cautious. When confronted by the governors of the provinces to institute new levies, the emperor stated: "A good shepherd shears his flock; he does not flay them."[46] He instead implemented a 1% auction tax.[47] By the end of the second century CE, the gulf between citizens of wealth and those who existed in poverty caused dissent within citizenry.[48] This situation was the result of Emperor Severus' dramatic increase in the number of legions for the security of the empire.[49] His successors sought every means of raising revenue to maintain Rome's military organization, which meant further hikes in tax rates.[50] By the reign of Diocletian the amount of Romans soldiers was over a half-million, which the ruler did nothing to reform.[51]

The fourth century saw a series of grievous missteps in taxation which made the fall of the empire inevitable. On top of the exorbitant tax rates necessary to fund Roman military operations, Galerius implemented a detailed study as to the property holdings of his subjects.[52] What came out of it was a new law which dictated that when a Roman bought a plot of land, the purchaser assumed the tax debts held by the previous owner.[53] Valentinian I implemented tax relief through reducing required tribute from the eastern provinces by one-fourth, which caused tax rates to incrementally rise for over four decades until they had doubled.[54] In 383 Theodosius I decreed that no one within the empire who owned property was exempt from taxes.[55] There was also mandatory service in the army whether as a soldier, or rendering vital goods and services in beneficence.[56] This move inspired an epidemic of tax evasion to avoid destitution, as well as looting.[57] Historian Edward Gibbon contended Rome drove itself into destitution due to its obsession with imperial power, and as demonstrated by the historical record, his assessment was proven correct.[58]

The lessons of imperial Rome were not lost upon the Framers. James Madison observed Rome had sacrificed the civil liberties of its citizens to its imperial aspirations.[59] Alexander Hamilton revealed how the lack of compromise in the Roman Senate had led to the assumption of power by military leaders.[60] 'Brutus' contended the departure from a republican system had led to an imperial monarchy which, in turn, had caused Rome to become the most tyrannical power in history.[61]

The history of England as a continuously inhabited land can be traced back over 13,000 years. Throughout that time the island has been invaded by a host of hostile nations. During the last two millennia there have been three significant military conquests, each had a lasting impact upon the English people: The Romans, the Danes and the Normans. The historical memory of these events exercised a profound influence upon the island nation as an imperial power.

Britain fell to the authority of the Romans in 43 CE under the direction of the Emperor Claudius. The English historian Bede noted that following the invasion of Julius Caesar, Romans did not attempt to conquer Britain, but when Claudius landed on the island it fell without bloodshed within just a few days.[62] During the Roman occupation this foreign dominance was accepted by the natives.[63] Nearly four centuries later Rome itself faced invasion and abandoned their English dominions.[64] As political power abhors a vacuum, following a period of plunder and violence, the land was first governed by the Britons, then by the Germanic Saxons.[65]

In the two centuries following the unification of England under King Alfred, the country endured turmoil within the royal succession. It was in this political atmosphere that in 1016 the Danes, led by Canute, invaded and conquered England.[66] Unlike the Romans, the Danes not only adopted the customs of the Saxons, they intermarried and assumed their Christian faith.[67] Ruling in a vigorous, but wise manner for 19 years, Canute obtained stability in his reign only after executing several of the Saxon nobility.[68] Prior to his death, the king made a peace treaty with Richard, the Duke of Normandy, which settled the crown upon his son Harold Hardicanute, who took the name of Canute III upon his coronation.[69] When he died unexpectedly in 1042, the youngest son of the penultimate Saxon king Æthelred—known as Edward the Confessor—ascended the English throne.[70]

King Edward inherited a weakened crown for his barons remained loyal to his Scandinavian predecessors.[71] A conflict with Earl Godwin of Wessex in 1051–2 further weakened the king's power.[72] Until this time King Edward had hoped an heir would be born from his wife Edith, but afterwards he abandoned her, and remained coy as to who would succeed him.[73] During Godwin's exile Duke William of Normandy had paid a visit to King Edward and it was during this visit the succession was offered to him.[74] When the king succumbed on 5 January 1066 Harold Godwinson, the son of the Earl of Wessex and brother of the Queen, was proclaimed king.[75] The new monarch's reign was muddled by a series of political crises, which culminated with an invasion of over 3,000 soldiers launched by Duke William.[76] King Harold was killed at the Battle of Hastings on 14 October 1066, and William became the unchallenged ruler of England.[77]

For a people proud of their history these invasions were a source of humiliation. Add to this an inconclusive century-long confrontation with their traditional enemy France, along with a divisive civil war which was resolved only with the execution of an anointed king, and what is left is a nationalistic recipe for empire. And when the opportunity to colonize a "new world" arose, the English leaped at it to spread their national influence, as well as increase its wealth. There were also legal rationales given for empire.

In his *Commentaries on the Laws of England*, Sir William Blackstone referenced the social contract theory of Thomas Hobbes in his argument on defense.[78] The 'law of nations' had been established among the civilized countries, and in diplomatic relations all concerned were obligated to declare and enforce it as their own, and fall within the purview of the courts.[79] If one violated such laws, it was to declare war against the ruler and his realm, and a justification for military retaliation in the common defense.[80] For government to maintain control of its armed forces, the military must be authorized by an act of parliament, be strictly controlled, and limited in its course and duration.[81]

In example, King James I viewed Spain has having terminated the law of nations and was looking towards successful American colonization as the means to check Spanish imperial ambitions.[82] According to a papal bull issued by Pope Alexander IV, the "new world" had been divided exclusively between Spain and Portugal.[83] Within a century England was economically benefitting from its colonies not only on the Atlantic coast, but in India and the Caribbean as well.[84] By the mid-18th century Great Britain was the foremost of European powers.[85] It had bested France in the Seven Years War and was ceded that nation's colonies in Canada, as well as holding dominion over India, portions of Africa, and Australia.

Britain's colonies on the Atlantic seaboard remained loyal through all of the mother country's internal chaos and external struggles, and fought willingly in her defense. Yet within the dozen years between the 1763 Treaty of Paris and the military confrontations between British troops and colonial militia at Lexington and Concord on 19 April 1775, something had occurred to dramatically alter that relationship. It was seen by the rest of the world as folly for the American colonies to engage in a war for independence. Historian John C. Miller noted Britain possessed a system of war manufacturing that dwarfed the capabilities of her colonies.[86] As recounted by Mercy Otis Warren, several privateers profited significantly from the Revolution, to the point where members of the Continental Congress, when the war had been successfully concluded, debated whether legal measures should be taken to limit, if not end such exploitation.[87] Though the Continental forces were often ill-trained, under-equipped and ill-led, they overcame their paucities and provided Great Britain another defeat in their quest for empire. Yet this setback did not deter Great Britain from further imperial efforts. Prior to the dismantling of its empire following World War Two, and the institution of the Commonwealth of Nations, it was a popular adage that the sun never set upon British Empire.

There has always been an inherent conflict between civil liberties and military involvement. In times of war the former is often sacrificed in aid to the latter. In this trade off Thomas Hobbes reasoned if the sovereign granted liberty to his subjects, he weakened his ability to provide for their safety.[88] The social contract was dependent upon the sovereign's ability to protect his subjects from harm.[89] He warned against maintaining a standing army as it inevitably produced political instability within the community, and influenced the sovereign toward an "insatiable appetite, or *Bulimia*, of enlarging Dominion".[90] Failure to uphold this basic premise of the social contract nullified it, and again imperiled its constituents.[91] John Locke agreed with Hobbes, but added that all decisions of war and peace must be made by the citizenry, for only they hold the legitimate power to do so.[92] In tandem, Niccolo Machiavelli argued the sole secured government authority was what he termed principalities such as the Vatican, for they neither directly governed their subjects, nor deprived them of any of their property by legal edict.[93] Therefore, to preserve his regime, and the loyalty of the people, a shrewd prince ensured that his subjects, not matter the circumstance, were dependent on his government.[94]

Hugo Grotius bluntly stated: "We do not include *Justice* in the Definition of War".[95] For war to be just it had to serve a just cause, and should the case be erroneous, there was no obligation from the citizens to engage in it.[96] He argued regardless of the nature of power and how it was attained, if a ruler had conquered a land or province, he had rightful authority over it.[97] In a conquered state it was the conqueror who determined all rights and privileges, if any, a vanquished people were allowed.[98] Once a state was conquered it ceased to exist by being added to the territory of the conqueror.[99] Under such circumstances the possessions of the conquered people no longer belonged to them.[100] Yet a vanquisher who demonstrated mercy towards the people, in his examples of Alexander of Macedonia and Julius Caesar, did much to foster loyalty among them.[101] The relationship between a conquered people and their conqueror, Grotius contended, mirrored one between master and slave.

Grotius also posed a vital query as to whether it was illegal for a captive of war to escape from internment.[102] He also pondered whether the children of conquered peoples were obligated to obey a ruler's edicts, and to what degree.[103] This inquiry led to a discussion of the amount of justice possible in the attainment of empire. As in all human relationships there were limits on the authority of the conqueror. Appealing to the exultations of the Greek philosopher Aristotle and the Roman historian and politician Sallust, Grotius asserted for a conqueror to show generousness towards a vanquished people was both prudent and laudable, as it did much to soothe tensions between them.[104] Furthermore, citing the example of Rome, it was also best to integrate the bested into the realm than to segregate them unto themselves, for it allowed them a stake in their new political reality.[105]

Baron Von Pufendorf specified that peace was an act of nature, whereas war was exclusively an act of men.[106] Consistent with Hobbes' assertions regarding the foundations of civilization, Pufendorf argued human beings sought safety in their everyday lives, as well as civility.[107] What was ethical did not stimulate the nationalistic appetites of the citizens without just cause and, thus war was the product of a lack of conception of what was good.[108] It was also the reason mankind could not long exist without the presence of laws.[109] The threat of war was constant, as well as the potential for carnage, and barbarous Nations were not expected to act within the confines of natural law, thus a defense against such a threat was natural to confront, for self-preservation warranted it.[110]

Voltaire found war to be a blight upon humanity.[111] Human beings were not peaceful creatures, for they had been acculturated into a war mentality.[112] Every society at peace was susceptible to attack by a more aggressive polity for such a situation. The prime reason for such an act was that a neighboring society was always planning for violence, and the citizen-soldiers were protecting other citizens from death and pillage through offense. Once this was accomplished, there were but two choices for the conquered: Either kill themselves, or serve the conqueror.[113] Under such a circumstance, any peace was unjust, as the vanquished were the slaves of the vanquisher.[114] The sole logical conclusion in the security of a society was in the constant confrontation with those who sought to conquer, thus war was an ever-present scourge upon humanity.[115]

Baron de Montesquieu observed small republics were conquered by larger ones, but large republics fell to internal depravity.[116] Governments with separated powers were better equipped to survive an internal attack, but for an external attack a defense constructed through small community based forces organized from within provided the best protection, such a force may survive an attack from many, but not from all. For this tactic to be effective, power had to be divided amongst smaller semi-independent republics.[117] This notion for a national defense was also advocated by Algernon Sidney, who supported citizen-militias in which every male was both armed and expertly trained.[118] Sidney claimed a virtuous society was one in which its citizens earned their freedom, as well as actively maintained a vigilance against tyranny.[119]

On the darker side of the defense equation, Montesquieu argued all despotic governments undertook the same pattern. The sole difference between them was semi-independent republics fought for the common cause, while the despotic state was willing to temporarily sacrifice a portion of its territory for ultimate gain.[120] To accomplish this, a force must construct a reputation of being unassailable.[121] A nation must refrain from attacking a polity in decline, thus hastening it, as it will unite the people of the polity under attack, as well as further empower its leader.[122]

John Trenchard and Thomas Gordon were succinct in their views on national defense, along with the ultimate cost of war to their own country. The authors argued military conflict was destructive to both the people and the government, and the preservation of empire would economically bankrupt Great Britain, and destroy its trade with neighboring nations.[123] As further conquests were made so was the necessity for further troop deployments which could end up numbering in the millions.[124] As other nations became circumspect of England's national motives, the island country would be forced to build a massive fleet on its own to benefit their conquests, while serving to sever trade with traditional allies. It would also deplete forces used to protect the homeland to the point where an effective invasion from an enemy was not only possible, but probable.[125] Lastly, extreme patriotism would not be enough to sustain a successful war effort.[126] As a general rule, the best defense was to stay clear of wars altogether.[127]

Economist Adam Smith asserted war was to be avoided as was possible. He claimed once a municipality built a wall for defense against neighboring communities, they were obligated to expend capital to maintain it, as revenues most assuredly were to be harvested from the citizens.[128] Such military endeavors were costly in more ways than mere expenditure.[129] Smith contended a further element of military operations were the maintenance of conquests which demanded a tremendous outlay of capital: 1) For large scores of troops deployed to both strengthen and maintain authority; 2) The marked decrease in homeland productivity and the constriction of money circulating within the municipality; and, 3) The excess of paper money exceeded the amount of precious metals at hand to support its worth, thus causing inflation in the homeland.[130] Finally, military conflict between nations discouraged trade with its allies as they were leery of being drawn into the fray.[131] Thus, conflicts between countries were best dealt with through commerce, rather than violence, as the former was economically productive, and the latter unreservedly destructive.[132]

The Federalists agreed the central government had the authority to establish a national military force, though it could not be called into action for any reason other than defense during war.[133] They also asserted American forces should not be involved in the crises of countries abroad.[134] Additionally, these Framers thought it prudent the military be placed under vigilant government scrutiny for, according to Federalist Tench Coxe, the military was always the tool of ambitious men who perverted current events in the pursuit of power.[135] Though they were cautious in their support of a standing army, they also viewed it as a necessity, and supported the power of congress to borrow money to support it.[136] But James Madison of Virginia reminded the convention large armies were the surest sign of a belligerent nation, as evidenced in the Punic Wars between Carthage and Rome that had led to the destruction of the former, and the rise of the latter; between

Austria and France in the Thirty Years War, which had completely devastated Europe; and, between England and France in the Great War for Empire, which had crushed the latter's own imperial ambitions in North America.[137]

Another group of delegates were leery that this unfortunate episode would be used as a means to a frightful end. "The people do not want virtue," exclaimed Elbridge Gerry of Massachusetts, "but are the dupes of pretended patriots."[138] In agreement, Oliver Ellsworth of Connecticut contended if the new constitution was derisory with regards to the individual states, it would not be able to secure the needs of the nation as a whole.[139] Alexander Hamilton of New York had foreseen dreadful repercussions in the uprising in Massachusetts: That with the United States in such a political disarray, a foreign power could easily invade and conquer the country.[140] But the most trying question before the delegates was posed by Rufus King of Massachusetts: What role the states would play in protecting one another?[141]

On the 18th of July Edmund Randolph offered a resolution to provide the central government with the authority to subdue domestic insurrections, which was seconded by James McClurg of Virginia.[142] Daniel Carroll of Maryland voiced his agreement, as the *Articles* had proven impotent in situations of this sort.[143] John Rutledge of South Carolina argued such a proposal was a moot point, as it was assumed such power belonged to the central government, and he was concerned whether or not it would work in tandem with the state militias.[144] James Wilson of Pennsylvania suggested the Constitution guarantee a republic, and with it an umbrella of protection against either foreign or domestic violence.[145] Edmund Randolph proffered a motion which forbade the states from establishing and/or maintaining forces under their own authority, and all officers were subject to approval by the U.S. military.[146] On the 6th of August the Committee of Detail presented to the convention its report, in which the national legislature was given the exclusive power to declare war.[147]

Toward the end of the convention James Madison declared "the greatest danger to liberty is from large standing armies."[148] Elbridge Gerry voiced his concerns there was no check against the federal military forces during periods of peace.[149] He proposed a peace time force of but one thousand troops be sustained during times of armistice.[150] Jonathan Dayton of New Jersey pointed out the essential preparations for war were often wrought during peacetime.[151] Oliver Ellsworth offered a compromise in which the state militias possessed the identical weapons as a federal army, as well as operated under identical regulations when in service to the country.[152] Among the final criticisms put forward by Gerry was the financial controls—specifically the reauthorization of budget allocations towards the military—were not stringent enough, and argued their authorization from Congress should be changed from two years to one.[153]

There was also the inevitability of war to ponder. Rufus King argued as the states were answerable to the central government, they did not possess the authority to declare war in their own right, yet were obligated to answer the call should the national legislature pass a declaration of war.[154] Luther Martin of Maryland disagreed as this plan held the possibility of the smaller states being militarily beholden to the three largest states.[155] James Wilson refuted Martin by pointing out when the *Declaration of Independence* was adopted by the states' representatives, the thirteen sovereign colonies had declared its separation from Great Britain not separately, but together as one nation.[156] Thus came the conclusion: If the country was declared to be at war, the states were also at war together, as the threat was common to all. Later, Edmund Randolph proposed the declaration of war should be made in the House of Representatives.[157] Charles Coatesworth Pinckney of South Carolina disagreed with this proposal, as the Congress met but once a year and the membership of the House of Representatives would prove too large to reach a consensus.[158] His support was for such a declaration emanating from the Senate where all the states were equally represented.[159] In the end, it was Randolph's proposal which garnered the majority of the committee's votes.

Next was how a declared war was to be executed and peace achieved. On the 14th of June William Paterson of New Jersey suggested it be the president who, in his capacity of chief executive of the nation, possessed the sole power of administering the military during times of war.[160] Though Charles Coatesworth Pinckney voiced his full support of a strong president, he nonetheless argued without strong checks on his powers over the command of the military, it created a situation which provided the executive with dictatorial powers.[161] It was then Pinckney proposed a separate cabinet post of Secretary of War be established to assist the president in administering the nation's defenses.[162] John Rutledge agreed the president should have a strong hand in administering the laws of the country, but was not comfortable in providing the office with such blanket authority.[163] Later, Roger Sherman of Connecticut argued because the states were part of a unified war effort, the president should be provided with the executive power over the state militias.[164] Additionally, the Committee of Detail not only accepted Pinckney's suggestion for a position of Secretary of War, but also defined its function and authority.[165] The language of the Constitution's Article II, which detailed the executive powers and authority, was approved in the full convention on 11th of August.[166]

Next came the definition of treason. The Constitution's Article III § 3 defined the charge of treason as "levying War against them [the United States], or in adhering to their Enemies, giving them Aid and Comfort."[167] James Madison thought the language too specific in its definition and incongruent with the English legal tradition established by King Edward III.[168] In the *Treason Act of 1351*, which was specifically cited by Madison, the monarch had declared the criterion of the crime as follows:

1. Threatened or imagined the death of the reigning monarch, the royal family, or "companion";
2. Conducted war against the monarch and his realm;
3. Adhered to the enemies of the monarch and his realm, providing them with aid and comfort;
4. Counterfeited either the Great Seal, Privy Seal, coinage or currency of the realm;
5. Murdered any of the monarch's ministers or judges in the commission of their duties.[169]

Madison also suggested more authority be provided to the national legislature, to which his colleague George Mason of Virginia agreed.[170] William Samuel Johnson of Connecticut voiced his incongruity that the language as proposed possessed a more encompassing meaning, as one against the sovereignty of either one or more of the individual states, or the central government, or both.[171] It was Edmund Randolph who put forward the proposition though the president was provided with the authority to pardon, it was restricted in that one could not be issued for those convicted of treason.[172] This language was approved by the full convention on the 6th of August.[173] Later, Luther Martin asked for the phrase "or, on confession in open court" be added, which was also agreed to.[174] With the above efforts the definition of treason was placed within Article III of the Constitution.

At the conclusion of the constitutional convention the Framers were convinced, as far as the issue of a national military force was concerned, they had placed stringent controls against its abuse. Any federal army could not be created until circumstances warranted, but only if Congress had approved and for a term no longer than two years. The president acted as commander-in-chief, initiating and changing military strategy and tactics as was needed, but only within the perimeters prescribed by the Congress, and his actions being within the original jurisdiction of the Supreme Court.

In the ratification debates many of the controversies which were argued during the constitutional convention became serious bones of contention. The first was the nature of the union of states to national defense. John Jay argued a united American army was necessary to maintain its amity with the other nations of the world.[175] He insisted a national military force would not be an aggressor in times of war, but be the entity which provided the strength to keep the peace.[176] James Madison reasoned a united force would be more effective than a conglomeration of those under the authority of the separate states.[177] In addition, the sole manner by which a full-time military would be needed was if the United States were assured potential enemies would do likewise.[178]

Of the Federalists, Alexander Hamilton contributed the greatest volume of writings on the subject. Firstly, he voiced his agreement with Jay, and added a national military force was instrumental in maintaining fraternal relationships between the individual states.[179] In answering the criticism the new nation did not need a full-time military, Hamilton maintained to do so in this manner would be to sentence the United States to a worldwide reputation of insignificance.[180] It was his opinion during its first few years as an independent nation, the United States had emerged as a significant force in international trade, which was reason alone for a national naval force.[181] The military would not act in the manner of a *posse comitatus*, using it as an agency of law enforcement upon American citizens.[182]

But the Federalists were not all of one mindset. Though his strategies had proven victorious over the better trained and equipped British army during the Revolution, George Washington was not convinced a federal standing army was required for the effective defense of the United States. In his 1783 *Circular to the States*, the former commander argued it was better to focus the country's military power within the state militias.[183] James Wilson disagreed with Washington, as it was important for a burgeoning nation to maintain the appearance of military strength.[184]

The Anti-Federalists advocated federally subsidized state armies which united in the defense of the nation, a structure which had proven itself effective during the Revolution. As voiced by Thomas Jefferson in the year prior to the Constitutional Convention, a national military held the potential to engage in a successful mutiny against the central government, the end result being the demise of the country.[185] 'Brutus' agreed with Jefferson and contended the country should never be allowed to possess a standing army.[186] The individual states must play a decisive role in any decision to go to war.[187] In his view, a national force under the authority of the relatively few representatives in Congress diminished the role of the states and allowed the federal government to, indeed, operate as a *Posse*

Comitatus.[188] Furthermore, the federal government did not possess the authority to establish or maintain any permanent standing army.[189]

'The Federal Farmer' took a philosophical approach.[190] Government was a necessary evil, but if it must exist people should obey its laws due to their loyalty, and not be forced to obey at the behest of an army.[191] If this were to come to pass it would inevitably lead to revolution.[192] 'The Impartial Examiner' further explored this adage with the contention the wealth of the nation would prove to be enticing to corrupt representatives, and they would utilize their authority over a standing army to overthrow the federal government, and institute a monarchy.[193] Patrick Henry voiced the same concerns, adding once such a force was established, the people would prove themselves impotent to exert authority.[194]

In Article I § 8, the Congress had been provided the exclusive authority to declare war, to authorize a military force and to provide funds for the duration of the conflict, or for no longer than two years, whichever came first.[195] Alexander Hamilton argued though such a force had not been authorized, its provisions were made necessary by the continual conflicts between the individual states, as well as popular insurgences such as Shays' Rebellion, for if the nation could not protect itself from internal strife, it was clear it would be less able to do so against an external threat.[196] The individual states were in neither a financial position, nor in an encouraging fraternal relationship necessary to provide for a military force capable of a defense against a foreign enemy.[197] Such a disposition between the independent states would not only jeopardize the independence of the country, as well as the freedom of its citizens, but also incapacitate the nation in its duty to defend itself.[198] Hamilton upheld the supervision of the Congress over a federal armed force as being a mechanism for the popular sovereignty of the people which would allow them a say in military policy.[199]

'Brutus' argued Congress, exploiting the authority of the Necessary and Proper Clause, could not only raise a federal military force, but also impress members of the state militias into service, thus rendering them impotent.[200] Utilizing the historical examples of both the Roman and the British empires, he reasoned such a standing military would influence less than honorable leaders to assume ultimate political power through force, the best historical examples being Julius Caesar and Oliver Cromwell.[201] Finally, the maintenance of a standing army during peacetime would in actuality have the opposite effect of that which Hamilton predicted, and be the instrument of despotism and tyranny.[202]

This same clause also authorized Congress "to provide and maintain a Navy", as well as "To make Rules for the Government and Regulation of the land and naval Forces".[203] Alexander Hamilton upheld the notion a naval force in time of war was decisive in the protection of the country, as a guarantee for the viability of military supply lines, and to maintain the security of commercial interests.[204] 'The State Soldier' not only reiterated Hamilton's points, but also discussed how naval power was of remarkable value to the individual states.[205] A further power invested in the Congress concerning the common defense was:

> To provide for calling forth the Militia to execute the Laws of the Union, suppress Insurrections and repel Invasions; To provide for organizing, arming, and disciplining, the Militia, and for governing such Part of them as may be employed in the Service of the United States, reserving to the States respectively, the Appointment of the Officers, and the Authority of training the Militia according to the discipline prescribed by Congress.[206]

Hamilton pointed out under the above provision, with the exception of general procedures dictated by the federal government, the militias were the charge of the states.[207] The militias were a necessary bulwark in the nation's defense, as they were in a better position to take action against an invasion by an enemy.[208] 'The Federal Farmer' disagreed and claimed under such a system the states were defenseless against a federal force of their own authorization. Furthermore, under the federal aegis of organizing their own state militias for national defense purposes, the larger states would be made to provide the bulwark of protection for the smaller states.[209] Echoing the sentiments of Algernon Sidney and Baron de Montesquieu, the author reasoned only mandatory service in the state militias, rather than the authorization of a federal force, could maintain the security of both the country and the individual states.[210] Under these auspices, the protection of the country was placed in a personally involved populace, rather than a detached national government.[211]

Within the Constitution it was the responsibility of the Executive Branch to administer the law, so it was that the president was provided with the duty to oversee the nation's military.[212] Alexander Hamilton pointed out historically the military had been placed within the authority of a 'chief magistrate', as the structure of command was designed to be directed by an 'executive authority'.[213] Patrick Henry viewed such a power as a potential threat to the continued independence of the nation.[214] In the same example as to how Caesar had conquered Rome, Henry cautioned a president could do the same in a federal Union, for there was no substantive check upon his constitutional power.[215] Under such circumstances the president would become either a monarch or a dictator.

A further power granted under Article II § 2 was the "Power, by and with the Advice and Consent of the Senate, to make Treaties, provided two thirds of the Senators present concur".[216] All of the powers listed had previously been assumed by the national executive under Article VI of the *Articles of Confederation*, therefore it seemed natural to the delegates they remain so under the authority of a federal constitution.[217] 'The Federal Farmer' argued it was inappropriate to involve the senate in the negotiation of treaties.[218] He suggested due to the nature of trade, as it affected the individual states, all treaties should be ratified by the separate state legislatures.[219] To James Madison such involvement by the states was absurd.[220] John Jay went further, claiming such power was concurrent with those previously granted to the state governors, which held the full force of law, and placing such a power with the chief executive was obvious.[221]

The judicial branch was also given a role in this charge: The power of review. The Constitution's Article III § 2 indicated authority was given to the Supreme Court to determine whether treaties negotiated by the executive branch and approved by the Senate were consistent with the Constitution.[222] Alexander Hamilton provided four vital reasons for such a mandate: 1) There had to be one branch of government whose primary responsibility was to restate constitutional principles when necessary; 2) As the judicial branch was charged with interpreting the law, it was logical the purview of such review be rendered there; 3) Legal disputes involving either the nation or its citizens were already, by tradition, within the jurisdiction of the court system; and, 4) The system of checks-and-balances depended upon a proportionate distribution of power, not sole authority being settled within one branch, or officer.[223]

The Anti-Federalists were not persuaded. 'The Federal Farmer' opined such authority as structured was a large amount of power presented to a feeble tribunal who would use it to enhance their own prestige.[224] The military must be maintained with strict civilian control, and must be kept out of the hands of government officials.[225] Further restrictions regarding who could serve in such a national militia—from those without property and towards those with a vast amount of property—were necessary to keep the military from becoming an instrument of tyranny.[226] The author objected to federal judicial oversight of the military in any fashion, as in its duty to interpret the laws passed by Congress, the body already had broad influence.[227] Due to the vague language of Article III, it was impossible to affix any real restrictions upon the Court's power; thus, the nation was forced to rely upon the integrity of the sitting justices who, in the face of the authority given them, would be capable of misconduct.[228] Oversight of the military in any capacity was a recipe for a usurpation of federal authority for personal gain.[229] 'Brutus' also warned of the danger to liberty posed by a federal judiciary not held accountable by either the Congress or the people.[230] Moreover, due to the nature of the Supreme Court, there was an inherent bias in their decisions.[231] The inference was that if the federal judiciary were to be involved in matters of defense, it was a foregone conclusion the Court would undoubtedly rule in favor of the federal government over the states without any consideration of whether the state's argument was the strongest.[232]

Finally, treason was defined in Article III § 3 as "levying War against them, or in adhering to their Enemies, giving them Aid and Comfort".[233] In his case in favor of this clause, Alexander Hamilton stated cases of treason would not be excused under the powers of pardon granted to the president under Article II § 2.[234] The sole criticism leveled at this clause by the Anti-Federalists was given by 'Brutus', who pointed out members of the federal judiciary could only be removed by being found guilty of high crimes and misdemeanors, of which only treason and bribery were the only charges specifically included.[235]

The Framers' concern over control of the military were also of concern to the Supreme Court. In nearly every case presented to them in which the military played a crucial role, from the initial Court through the American Civil War, the resulting adjudication strongly reiterated constitutional principle in restricting the powers and conduct of the military.

In *Bas v. Tingy* (1800), a case concerning the recapture of an American ship from the French, the Court considered the disposition of war under the authority of Article I § 8.[236] Speaking through Associate Justice Bushrod Washington, the Court surmised there were two legitimate definitions of armed conflict: The first was "a perfect war" in which the Congress had issued a declaration of hostilities, and the other "an imperfect war" as one in which the legislative branch had neither taken action, nor had interfered when hostilities had occurred.[237] Thus, the outcome was the legal definition of war as either declared or undeclared, as well as the affirmation of the constitutionality of both classifications.

With *Little v. Barreme* (1804), the Court denied to the president of the United States the "inherent" authority to ignore any act passed by the legislative branch.[238] Also, the constitutional doctrine of separated powers was reiterated. The Court speaking through Chief Justice John Marshall specified that the military was obligated to operate within the strict perimeters of federal law.[239] As the boundaries of military authority were set within the Constitution to be regulated by the legislative branch, the military must pay heed to them, even if ordered to act in a manner as to violate them by their commander-in-chief. Thus, the Court upheld the constitutional principle that no person or entity was above the law, which included the military.

The constitutional definition of treason was at the center of *Ex Parte Bollman* (1807).[240] At the close of his single term as vice-president, Aaron Burr had embarked upon a sojourn westward. During that time he supposedly entered into a plot, later disproven, with James Wilkinson to detach the western lands from the United States and construct a new country in which he would be the acknowledged leader.[241] Two civilians implicated in this plot were Erick Bollman and Samuel Swartwout, as they had actively recruited others to participate in the theoretical Burr-Wilkinson Plot. In its majority opinion the Court made the distinction between that which was advocated and actions in the participation of treason. It also stated the former was not a prosecutable offense, whereas the latter was.[242] The Court decided in the prosecution of an individual for treason, there must have been a treasonable act committed, not merely the intent to do so.

In *Houston v. Moore* (1820), the Court examined whether the states possessed jurisdiction over their militias, and if this was a specific power granted under the Constitution.[243] This legal action involved disciplinary actions taken by the state of Pennsylvania towards absent members of the state militia. The Court referred to the Hobbesian doctrine of negative freedom when it affirmed the authority of the states in the absence of federal law.[244] Citing the Second Amendment, the Court speaking through Associate Justice Joseph Story confirmed the federal government retained the authority to press the state militias into service if the situation necessitated it.[245] Seven years after its decision in the *Houston* case, the Court reaffirmed the president's authority under Article II § 2, in his capacity as commander-in-chief, to call upon state militias in time of national crisis in its majority opinion in *Martin v. Mott* (1827).[246]

With its decision in *Ex Parte Milligan* (1866), the Court declared unconstitutional the use of military tribunals against private citizens at a time when civilian courts were in operation.[247] A group of five American citizens who were Confederate sympathizers, of which the defendant Lambdin Milligan was a member, had sought to liberate Union prisoner-of-war camps located in Indiana, Ohio and Michigan, afterwards using the freed detainees to take control of their respective state governments. When the plot was discovered all five were arrested, tried by a military court, found guilty, and were sentenced to execution by hanging in 1864. The sentence was not carried out until May 1865, by which time civilian courts were in full operation.[248] Though the Court upheld President Abraham Lincoln's suspension of the right of habeas corpus, it contended the military possessed only the authority to hold a civilian prisoner without charge, not to try, convict or execute them. The Court, speaking through Associate Justice David Davis stated:

> By the protection of the law human rights are secured; withdraw that protection, and they are at the mercy of wicked rulers, or the clamor of an excited people. If there was law

> to justify this military trial, it is not our province to interfere; if there was not, it is our duty to declare the nullity of the whole proceedings.[249]

Moreover, the Court specifically defined the perimeters of military jurisdiction: 1) That which is "exercised both in peace and war"; 2) That which is "exercised in time of foreign war without the boundaries of the United States, or in time of rebellion and civil war within states or districts occupied by rebels treated as belligerents"; and, 3) That which is "exercised in time of invasion or insurrection within the limits of the United States, or during rebellion within the limits of states maintaining adhesion to the National Government, when the public danger requires its exercise."[250] Thus, the Court was not to operate as an autonomous entity, but one which was bound by the authority of the Constitution.

Each of the above cited U.S. Supreme Court decisions either limited or defined the power of the military in a manner consistent with both the Framers' intentions and the Constitution itself. The justices were familiar with both the history of the law and of human events, and saw fit to tightly control the federal government in matters of 'the common defense'.

The Preamble of the U.S. Constitution stated as one of its goals to "provide for the common defense". Yet if the United States must wage continuous war not for its internal security, but for national economic viability, is such a practice consistent with the Constitution?

Upon reading the debates during the 1787 constitutional convention, it is clear neither the Federalists, nor the Anti-Federalists wanted a standing army. Their idea was to mobilize a national force, and once the conflict had concluded, it was to be demobilized. This was the pattern of the American military until the close of the Second World War. And when it comes the common defense used as the premise for empire building, we have seen this phenomena before.

At the close of the Franco-Prussian War, the countries of Western Europe actively involved themselves in both colonization and a permanent arms industry. These manufacturing concerns became so vital to their nation's economic wellbeing, military conflicts were manufactured as justification for further requisitions of arms and war materiel. Such concurrent developments led to the First World War and the economic destruction of all European nations involved. After the Second World War, which was caused by the rearming of Germany under Chancellor Adolf Hitler with the collapse of the Weimar Republic, the European Economic Union was formed out of necessity to rebuild the continent with minimal assistance from the United States.

Therefore, as this country involves itself in several military conflicts at once we, as concerned citizens, must ask our elected representatives whether we are truly providing for our 'common defense', or merely propping up a failing national economy for the profit of others through the maintenance of empire. It begs a serious question: Is the attainment of profit worth the price of the blood spilled by our young men and women? In their serious contemplation of history, philosophy and law, and their thoughtful debates with one another at both the constitutional and state ratifying conventions, the Framers answered that question over two centuries ago with a resounding "no".

Notes

1. Paul Kennedy, *The Rise and fall of the Great Powers: Economic Change and Military Conflict from 1500 to 2000* (New York: Random House, Inc., 1986), xv–xvi.
2. *Ibid.*
3. John C. Miller, *Origins of the American Revolution* (New York: Little, Brown and Company, 1943), 37.
4. *Ibid.*, 48–9.
5. Herodotus, *The Histories*, ed. Aubrey De Sélincourt; trans, John Marincola (New York: Penguin Books, 1996), 289–1. Victor Ehrenberg, *From Solon to Socrates: Greek History and Civilization during the 6th and 5th Centuries B.C.*, Third Edition (Abington, England: Routledge Books, 2011), 99–100.
6. Herodotus, 339.
7. *Ibid.*, 362. Herodotus' account of the battle itself is found in pages 360–3.
8. *Ibid.*, 440–5.
9. *Ibid.*, 319–22, 517–25, 531–7.
10. *Ibid.*, 531, 534.
11. Thucydides, *History of the Peloponnesian War*, trans., Rex Warner (New York: Penguin Books, 1972), 92–3.
12. *Ibid.*, 96.
13. *Ibid.*, 356–63.
14. *Ibid.*, 414–30.
15. Polybius, *The Rise of the Roman Empire*, trans., Ian Scott-Kilvert (New York: Penguin Books, 1979), 42, 46.
16. Thucydides, 48.
17. John Jay, Essay #6; in *The Federalist,* The Gideon Edition, eds. George W. Carey and James McClellan (Indianapolis, IN: The Liberty Fund, 2001), 22.
18. *Ibid.*, 23–4.

19. Patrick Henry, "Speech at the Virginia Ratifying Convention", 4 June 1788; in *The Anti-Federalist: Writings by the Opponents of the Constitution*, ed. Herbert Storing (Chicago, IL: University of Chicago Press, 1981), 299.
20. James Madison, Essay #18; in *The Federalist*, 86.
21. Alexander Hamilton, Essay #28; in *The Federalist*, 209.
22. Michael Grant, *History of Rome* (New York: Charles Scribner's Sons, 1978), 5–6.
23. *Ibid.*, 19, 36–8. Livy, *The Early History of Rome*, Trans., Aubrey DeSélincourt, 1971 reprint (New York: Penguin Books, 1960), 98–9.
24. Livy, 115.
25. Grant, 45.
26. *Ibid.*, 56–7.
27. *Ibid.*, 143–5. Polybius, 535–6.
28. Grant, 59.
29. *Ibid.*, 48.
30. *Ibid.*, 50–1.
31. *Ibid.*, 88–9.
32. *Ibid.*, 68.
33. *Ibid.*, 108–9.
34. Livy, *The War with Hannibal*, Trans., Aubrey DeSélincourt, 1972 reprint (New York: Penguin Books, 1965), 26–7.
35. Polybius, 236–44 (Trebbia); 249–52 (Trasimene); and, 267–75 (Cannae). Livy, *Hannibal*, 38–9 (Trebia); 100–1 (Trasimene Lake); and, 158–60 (Cannae).
36. Polybius, 424–7. Livy, *Hannibal*, 491.
37. Polybius, 468–79. Livy, *Hannibal*, 513; 659–73.
38. Livy, *Hannibal*, 665–6.
39. Grant, 157.
40. *Ibid.*, 247, 261.
41. Suetonius, *The Twelve Caesars*, trans. Robert Graves, reprint of 1957 edition (New York: Penguin Books, 1989), 83.
42. Suetonius, 174.
43. Tacitus, *The Annals of Imperial Rome*, trans, Michael Grant. Reprint of 1956 edition (New York: Penguin Books 1971), 298.
44. *Ibid.*, 308–9.
45. Suetonius, 290.
46. *Ibid.*, 131.
47. Tacitus, 76.
48. Grant, 156.
49. *Ibid.*, 359.
50. *Ibid.*, 375.
51. *Ibid.*, 398.

52. Edward Gibbon, *The History of the Decline and Fall of the Roman Empire*, ed. J. B. Bury, 3 vols. (New York: The Heritage Press, 1946), I: 313.
53. *Ibid.*, I: 489.
54. *Ibid.*, I: 755.
55. Grant, 441.
56. *Ibid.*
57. *Ibid.*, 441, 443.
58. Gibbon, I: 488.
59. James Madison, Essay #41; in *The Federalist*, 86.
60. Alexander Hamilton, Essay #70; in *The Federalist*, 363–4.
61. 'Brutus', "Essay #1", 18 October 1787; in *Ibid.*, 113.
62. Bede, *Ecclesiastical History of the English People*, trans., Leo Shirley-Price, 1990 edition (New York: Penguin Group, Inc., 1955), 48.
63. David Hume, *The History of England From the Invasion of Julius Caesar to the Abdication of James II* (Boston: Phillips, Sampson, and Company, 1854), I: 8.
64. *Ibid.*, 57. Grant, 434–6.
65. Bede, 57–8. Hume, I: 10–16.
66. Hume, I: 114–5. Thomas Lord Macaulay, *The History of England* (New York: Harper and Brothers, Publishers, 1849), I: 9.
67. Macaulay, I: 10.
68. Hume, I: 115.
69. *Ibid.*, I: 119.
70. *Ibid.*, I: 122–4.
71. *Ibid.*, I: 123.
72. *Ibid.*, I: 128–9.
73. Stephen Baxter, "Edward the Confessor and the Succession Question": in *Edward the Confessor: The Man and the Legend*, ed. Richard Mortimer (Woodbridge, Suffolk, England: The Boydell Press, 2009), 77–118.
74. *Ibid.*
75. *Ibid.*, Hume, I: 138–9.
76. Hume, I: 144–51.
77. *Ibid.*, I: 150–1.
78. William Blackstone, *Commentaries on the Laws of England*, ed. William Draper Lewis, reprint of 1922 edition (Clark, NJ: The Lawbook Exchange, 2004), I: 33.
79. *Ibid.*, I: 229; IV: 1474.
80. *Ibid.*, IV: 1485.
81. *Ibid.*, I: 373.
82. Hume, IV: 449.
83. *Ibid.*
84. *Ibid.*, IV: 518–9.

85. John Richard Alden, *The American Revolution 1775–1783* (New York: Harper & Brothers, Publishers, 1954), 1.
86. John C. Miller, *Triumph of Freedom 1775–1783* (Boston: Little, Brown & Company, 1948), 2.
87. Mercy Otis Warren, *History of the Rise, Progress and Termination of the American Revolution*, ed. Lester H. Cohen, 2 vols. (Indianapolis, IN: The Liberty Fund, 1994), I: 199.
88. Thomas Hobbes, *Leviathan*, ed. Richard Tuck (New York: Cambridge University Press, 1996), 153.
89. *Ibid.*
90. *Ibid.*, 230.
91. *Ibid.*
92. John Locke, *Two Treatises of Government*, ed. Peter Laslett (New York: Cambridge University Press, 1960), 238. This point is reiterated in the *Second Treatise on Government*. *Ibid.*, 324–5.
93. Niccolo Machiavelli, *The Prince*, eds. Quentin Skinner and Russell Price (New York: Cambridge University Press, 1988), 39–40.
94. *Ibid.*, 37.
95. Hugo Grotius, *The Rights of War and Peace*, ed. Richard Tuck (Indianapolis, IN: The Liberty Fund, 2005), I: 136. The italics are that of the author.
96. *Ibid.*, I: 101.
97. *Ibid.*, I: 288.
98. *Ibid.*, III: 1374.
99. *Ibid.*, III: 1377.
100. *Ibid.*, III: 1378.
101. *Ibid.*, III: 1380.
102. *Ibid.*, III: 1495.
103. *Ibid.*
104. *Ibid.*, III: 1499.
105. *Ibid.*, III: 1500, 1506.
106. Samuel von Pufendorf, *Of the Law of Nature and Nations*, 8 vols., Reprint of 1712 edition, ed. Basil Kennet (Andover, Hampshire, England: Gale ECCO Print Editions, 2005), I: 6.
107. *Ibid.*, I: 27.
108. *Ibid.*, I: 36.
109. *Ibid.*, II: 96.
110. *Ibid.*, II: 115, 183.
111. Voltaire, "Etats, governments, Quel est le meilleur?" ("States, Governments, Which is the Best?"), 1771; in *Political Writings*, ed. David Williams (New York: Cambridge University Press, 1994), 9.
112. Voltaire, "Dialogues Between A B C", 1768; in *Political Writings*, 107.

113. *Ibid.*, 151.
114. *Ibid.*, 152–3.
115. *Ibid.*, 158. "Etats", 11.
116. Baron de Montesquieu, *Spirit of the Laws*, eds. Anne Cohler, Basia Miller, and Harold Stone (New York: Cambridge University Press, 1989), 131.
117. *Ibid.*, 132.
118. Algernon Sidney, *Discourses Concerning Government*, ed. Thomas G. West (Indianapolis, IN: The Liberty Fund, 1996), 199.
119. *Ibid.*
120. Montesquieu, 134.
121. *Ibid.*, 135.
122. *Ibid.*
123. John Trenchard and Thomas Gordon, "Essay #86", 21 July 1722; in *Cato's Letters; or, Essays on Liberty, Civil and Religious, and Other Important Subjects*, ed. Ronald Hamowy (Indianapolis, IN: The Liberty Fund, 1995), II: 618–9.
124. *Ibid.*
125. *Ibid.*, II: 620.
126. *Ibid.*, II: 621.
127. *Ibid.*, II: 625.
128. Adam Smith, *An Inquiry Into the Wealth of Nations*, ed. Edwin Cannan, 1976 Reprint (Chicago, IL: The University of Chicago Press, 1904), III: 423.
129. *Ibid.*, II: 319.
130. *Ibid.*, IV: 463.
131. *Ibid.*, III: 445.
132. *Ibid.*, IV: 456.
133. "A Foreign Spectator" [Nicholas Collin], "An Essay on the Means of Promoting Federal Sentiments in the United States", 18, 21 and 28 September 1787; in, *Friends of the Constitution: Writings of the "Other" Federalists*, eds. Colleen A. Sheehan and Gary L. McDowell (Indianapolis, IN: The Liberty Fund, 1998), 50.
134. "A Citizen of Philadelphia" [Pelitiah Webster], "The Weakness of Brutus Exposed", 1787; in *Friends of the Constitution*; 185.
135. "An American Citizen" [Tench Coxe], "An Examination of the Constitution of the United States", 26–29 September 1788; in *Friends of the Constitution*; 473.
136. James Wilson, "Speech", 4 December 1787; in *Friends of the Constitution*; 246.
137. James Madison, "Speech at the Constitutional Convention", 28 June 1787; in James Madison, *Notes of Debates in the Federal Constitution of 1787* (Athens, OH: Ohio University Press, 1966, 1985), 206.
138. Elbridge Gerry, quoted in *Ibid.*, 39.
139. *Ibid.*, 190.
140. *Ibid.*, 131.
141. *Ibid.*, 409–10.

142. *Ibid.*, 321.
143. *Ibid.*
144. *Ibid.*, 322.
145. *Ibid.* Wilson's language during this session was the foundation for Article IV § 4. *U.S. Constitution*, Article IV § 4.
146. Madison, 139.
147. *Ibid.*, 389. *U.S. Constitution*, Article I § 8.
148. Madison, 516.
149. *Ibid.*, 481, 482.
150. *Ibid.*, 482.
151. *Ibid.*
152. *Ibid.*, 483.
153. *Ibid.*, 580.
154. *Ibid.*, 152.
155. *Ibid.*, 153.
156. *Ibid.*
157. *Ibid.*, 448.
158. *Ibid.*, 475.
159. *Ibid.*, 475–6.
160. *Ibid.*, 120.
161. *Ibid.*, 45.
162. *Ibid.*, 80.
163. *Ibid.*, 46.
164. *Ibid.*, 535.
165. *Ibid.*, 487.
166. *Ibid.*, 503, 510.
167. *U.S. Constitution*, Article III § 3.
168. Madison, 489.
169. *Ibid.*, 489. 25 Edw 3 St 5 c 2.
170. Madison, 489.
171. *Ibid.*, 490.
172. *Ibid.*, 138.
173. *Ibid.*, 390.
174. *Ibid.*, 493.
175. John Jay, Essay #3, in *The Federalist,* 10.
176. John Jay, Essay #4, in *The Federalist*, 14.
177. James Madison, Essay #45; in *The Federalist*, 241.
178. James Madison, Essay #41; in *The Federalist*, 209.
179. Alexander Hamilton, Essay #8; in *The Federalist*, 32–3. Hamilton reiterated this point in Essay #34. *Ibid.*, 163.
180. Alexander Hamilton, Essay #25; in *The Federalist*, 123.

181. Alexander Hamilton, Essay #11; in *The Federalist*, 51.
182. Alexander Hamilton, Essay #29; in *The Federalist*, 141.
183. George Washington, "Circular to the States", 14 June 1783; in *Friends of the Constitution*; 20.
184. James Wilson, "Speech", 6 October 1787; in *Friends of the Constitution*; 104.
185. Thomas Jefferson, "Answers and Observations for Démeunier's Article on the United States in the Encyclopedie Methodique", 24 January 1786; in *Thomas Jefferson: Writings*, ed. Merrill D. Peterson (New York: Library Classics of the United States, 1984).
186. Brutus, Essay #I, 18 October 1787; in *The Anti-Federalist*, 115.
187. *Ibid.*, 116.
188. Brutus, Essay #IV, 29 November 1787; in *Ibid.*, 131.
189. Brutus, Essay #IX, 17 January 1788; in *The Anti-Federalist*, 156.
190. The Federal Farmer, Letter #VII, 14 December 1787; in *The Anti-Federalist*, 43.
191. *Ibid.*, 74.
192. The Federal Farmer, Letter #2, 9 October 1787; in *The Anti-Federalist*, 73.
193. The Impartial Examiner, "To the Free People of Virginia", 5 March 1788; in *The Anti-Federalist*, 291.
194. Patrick Henry, "Speech at the Virginia Ratifying Convention", 5 June 1788; in *The Anti-Federalist*, 303.
195. U.S. Constitution, Article I § 8.
196. Alexander Hamilton, Essay #8; in *The Federalist*, 33. Hamilton reiterated this point in Essay #23. Alexander Hamilton, Essay #23; in *Ibid.*, 113.
197. Alexander Hamilton, Essay #25; in *The Federalist*, 122.
198. *Ibid.*, 123–4.
199. Alexander Hamilton, Essay #26; in *The Federalist*, 127.
200. Brutus, Essay #8, 10 January 1788; in *The Anti-Federalist*, 151.
201. Brutus, Essay #10, 24 January 1788; in *The Anti-Federalist*, 158.
202. Brutus, Essay #9, 17 January 1788; in *The Anti-Federalist*, 155.
203. U.S. Constitution, Article I § 8.
204. Alexander Hamilton, Essay #11; in *The Federalist*, 51.
205. The State Soldier, "Essay #5"; in *Friends of the Constitution*, 133.
206. U.S. Constitution, Article I § 8.
207. Alexander Hamilton, Essay #29; in *The Federalist*, 140.
208. *Ibid.*, 145.
209. The Federal Farmer, Letter #3, 10 October 1787; in *The Anti-Federalist*, 51.
210. The Federal Farmer, Letter #18, 25 January 1788; in *The Anti-Federalists: Selected Writings and Speeches*, ed. Bruce Frohnen (Washington, DC: Regnery Publishing, Inc., 1999), 304.
211. *Ibid.*, 305.
212. *U.S. Constitution*, Article II § 2.
213. Alexander Hamilton, Essay #74; in *The Federalist*, 384–5.

214. Patrick Henry, "Speech at the Virginia Ratifying Convention", 5 June 1788; in *The Anti-Federalist*, 311.
215. *Ibid.*
216. U.S. Constitution, Article II § 2.
217. *Articles of Confederation*, Article VI.
218. The Federal Farmer, Letter #11, 10 January 1788; in *The Anti-Federalists*, 237.
219. *Ibid.*, 237–8.
220. James Madison, Essay #42; in *The Federalist*, 215.
221. John Jay, Essay #44; in *The Federalist*, 335.
222. *U.S. Constitution*, Article III § 2.
223. Alexander Hamilton, Essay #80; in *The Federalist*, 411–12.
224. The Federal Farmer, Letter #18, 25 January 1788; in *The Anti-Federalists*, 303.
225. *Ibid.*, 304.
226. *Ibid.*, 305.
227. The Federal Farmer, Letter #15, 18 January 1788; in *The Anti-Federalists*, 269.
228. *Ibid.*
229. *Ibid.*
230. Brutus, Essay #11, 31 January 1788; in *The Anti-Federalists*, 448.
231. *Ibid.*, 452–3.
232. Brutus, Essay #12, 7 February 1788; in *The Anti-Federalists*, 457.
233. U.S. Constitution, Article III § 3.
234. Alexander Hamilton, Essay #69; in *The Federalist*, 358.
235. Brutus, Essay #15, 20 March 1788; in *The Anti-Federalists*, 479–80.
236. *Bas v. Tingy*, 4 U.S. 37 (1800).
237. *Ibid.*, 40–2.
238. *Little v. Barreme*, 6 U.S. 170 (1804).
239. *Ibid.*, 177.
240. *Ex Parte Bollman*; *Ex Parte Swartwart*, 8 U.S. 75 (1807).
241. Case Summary, *Ibid.*, 75–93.
242. *Ibid.*, 126.
243. *Houston v. Moore*, 18 U.S. 1 (1820).
244. *Ibid.*, 52–3.
245. *Ibid.*, 53.
246. *Martin v. Mott*, 25 U.S. 19 (1827).
247. *Ex Parte Milligan*, 71 U.S. 2 (1866).
248. Case Summary, *Ibid.*, 2–107.
249. *Ibid.*, 119.
250. *Ibid.*, 141–2.

5

"Promote the General Welfare"

The Federal Government and the Public Good

The magnitude of a person is not demonstrated through exceptional achievements: It is revealed in how they respect those who live lives of lesser fortune. They give of themselves towards the betterment of the human condition, and in doing so make known the depth of their character through their actions. They seek not power for its own sake, nor for their own benefit, but to make their community a more equitable place for all. In the same manner as an individual, a compassionate government shall always be held in higher esteem, as well as earning the sincere loyalty of its citizens, than one which purveys its benefits towards a few at the expense of the many.

In late-1775, when asked by Richard Henry Lee how the burgeoning American nation could rule itself, John Adams reasoned the most crucial concern of government was the greatest good for the greatest number.[1] Adams queried of what intrinsic value was a government that did not look after the interests of its people? As an answer, his construct of governance was not centered upon efficiency, but equity and the public good. So rapt by Adams' work, Lee anonymously printed it as a pamphlet, and it was widely circulated throughout the colonies, much to its author's amazement.[2] Such were the power of Adams' ideas that eleven years later they were the primary source referenced in the construction of the federal constitution.[3]

Thus contrary to the arguments of contemporary politicians, the general welfare was of deep concern to the Framers. So much, in fact, that it became one of the tenets of the Preamble of the Constitution.[4] They wanted to place within the document not only the charge, but the means by which changes could be fashioned. There are also the prototypes of the general welfare to consider provided by the ancient Greeks and Romans which were vibrant demonstrations of government assistance to citizens of lesser means. Yet under feudal systems forged in the outgrowth of the dominance of the Roman Catholic Church, the poor are left to fend for themselves in a narcissistic political system based upon individual effort and personal beneficence.

The Athenians were deeply concerned as to the plight of the poor. As a people they did so because scarcity was a potent source of social and political anxiety due to its demeaning effects upon the human spirit. As Aristotle noted in *The Politics*, poverty was the author of social discontent.[5] Socrates maintained it was more profitable in the long term for human beings to act in a just manner towards others.[6] Doing the most good for the greatest number was more effective when acted upon by the community, rather than by every individual.[7] Aristotle proposed "the duty of the true democrat is to see that the population is not destitute; for destitution is the cause of a corrupt democracy."[8]

In *The Histories*, the historian Herodotus observed the direst human condition was to possess wisdom without the means to act upon it.[9] Pericles, within his funeral oration, put forward three specific mentions as to the plight of the poor in Athenian society. In the first instance, Pericles asserted for Athenians to live within an enlightened civilization, leadership should be defined by the talents of each individual, not by their accumulated wealth.[10] Another was that no one need feel shame for a lack of means, only for the lack of initiative towards lifting themselves out of it.[11] Lastly, the mettle of Athenian troops was not the differences between them due to class, but in that they together, rich and poor, strove together to defeat the realm's enemies.[12]

Such rhetoric would have been a moot point if not for clauses within *The Constitution of the Athenians* which legally mandated programs to assist the destitute.[13] With no account paid to either wealth or status, every man was required to provide their service to the government of Athens.[14] The constitution stipulated the relief of paupers unable to work due to debilitating illness, along with a governing Counsel charged with examining each one who applied for aid.[15] There was also in place not only laws to protect orphans, but also one that mandated their care within the realm under the auspices of the Archon.[16]

In the Roman world, social standing was determined not by the money one possessed, but their standing within the political realm.[17] This was evidenced by Plutarch in his comparison between the Roman politicians Aristides and Cato the Elder, where he concluded those who provided the everyday services to the Empire were of greater worth than those who lived in extravagance.[18] This adage was apparent in the actions and words of Julius Caesar, a man who held a lifelong concern for those in poverty.[19] Caesar, as quoted by Plutarch, stated that honors be given to the strong, but the necessities of life were to be provided to the weak.[20] He made it mandatory that the richer among his troops use their wealth to provide for those of lesser means.[21] His heir Augustus instituted a policy of paying his soldiers a fixed salary to keep them from poverty.[22]

Poverty within Rome itself was aggravated by two factors: 1) The rise of immigration due to the expansion of the empire; and, 2) The destruction of established social networks which in the past had provided relief from poverty.[23] The Emperor Claudius engaged in several public works projects which addressed this condition, such as an aqueduct to provide ample water for a thriving city, and deepening the harbor at Ostia to secure a year-round supply of grain.[24] According to Suetonius, Claudius himself often distributed food and clothing to the poor.[25] He also made mandatory official guardians for orphans.[26] When it was brought to his attention chattel owners had exiled their sick and dying slaves to keep from treating them, Claudius granted the slaves their freedom, and when some had died he had their masters charged and tried for murder.[27] When the Roman senator Helvidius Priscus accused the emperor's exchequer of the over-rigorous confiscation and sale of property belonging to the poor, Nero transferred such authority to commissioners under the authority of the Senate to rectify the situation.[28]

Vespasian held a deep concern for those in poverty: "I must always ensure that the working classes can earn enough money to buy themselves food."[29] He established regular salaries for teachers and a fund for artists and poets.[30] Suetonius recounted how the Emperor Titus, faced with the natural disasters of both the eruption of Mount Vesuvius in 79 CE, along with a city-wide fire which devastated Rome a year later, pooled all government resources for relief and rebuilding efforts.[31] Not only did the emperor call upon the Senate to provide all necessary relief, he auctioned off his own belongings to contribute. Though Titus gained the admiration of the Roman people for his noble efforts, he himself was left financially ruined.[32] Trajan instituted a poll-tax specifically allocated to pay for poverty relief programs.[33] Thus, due to concentrated efforts made by Roman emperors, politicians, and citizens, poverty as a whole was less of a political issue as it is in contemporary times.[34]

In his work *Feudal Society* Marc Bloch contended European feudalism occurred with the fragmentation of political authority following the destruction of the Western Roman Empire in which sovereign power was localized within the nobility.[35] Its foremost characteristic was "the rigorous economic subjugation of a host of humble folk to a few powerful men."[36] This system left the peasantry in a permanent state of debt, while those who operated farms or businesses outside of it were not guaranteed the protection of the realm.[37] Without an independent source of wealth there were no secure rights to real property for anyone except the nobility.[38] This was the established political system throughout all of Europe for over a millennium, and discussed in detail by historians from Geoffrey of Tours and Bede to Machiavelli and Guicciardini.

England was no exception. Much of the parliamentary legislation passed during the medieval period penalized the poor. An example was the *Vagabonds and Beggars Act of 1495*, passed during the reign of Henry VII, that mandated all vagrants be placed in stocks for three days and nights.[39] In his *Commentaries on the Laws of England*, Sir William Blackstone specifically cited the *Justices Commitment Act of 1743* which divided the poor into three classes—the idle and disorderly; rogues and vagabonds; and, incorrigible rogues—and allowed the courts to sentence those found guilty of being any one of the three to prison time.[40] When such laws are placed side-by-side with other legal precedent, it demonstrated a discordant attitude towards the poor.

During the reign of King Edward VI, parliament passed the *Poor Act of 1551* which allowed churches "to collect charitable contributions" in relief for those in poverty.[41] It also empowered bishops to file a law suit against those approached for a donation and either outright refused the request, or influenced others to do the same.[42] The first comprehensive law specifically centered upon the relief of the poor was not passed until 1597, during the final years of Queen Elizabeth I's reign.[43] *The Poor Act of 1597* established limited relief for those recognized by overseers as being among the "deserving poor", defined legally as those who engaged in "proper industry".[44]

As to the legal comportment of the poor, it was the duty of either the opulent or religious organizations to provide relief, not the responsibility of government.[45] It was the passage of *Queen Anne's Bounty Act of 1714*, which mandated a collection of a specific percentage of farm yields for the beneficence of the poor, that the above legal paradigm began to change.[46] As for public assistance, the reigning monarch was the controller of all charities within the borders of the country, but also possessed the authority to appoint a lord chancellor to oversee such responsibility.[47] It was this subordinate who investigated both the legitimacy of charitable donations, as well as abuses.[48] Personal bankruptcy cases also fell under the jurisdiction of the Lord Chancellor to judge as to their legitimacy.[49]

Under English law all debts incurred were mandated to be paid, as it was a tenet of the Hobbesian social contract.[50] Thus, under process of exigent statue, failure to rectify debt allowed the party owed to file a suit and, if a guilty verdict was rendered, the debtor faced a term in prison until the debt was satisfied.[51] If one imprisoned for debt died during incarceration, the plaintiff possessed the right to bring suit against the deceased's estate, depriving their family of any inheritance.[52]

The 'general welfare' is defined as the greatest good for the largest number of citizens. This concept of 'the public good' had been discussed at length by the Enlightenment political philosophers. Jean Bodin proposed the public good was found in the unwritten law that all sovereigns were obligated to act in accordance.[53] A ruler could not interfere with the process of justice within the realm, nor deny such a right to any citizen.[54] Yet Bodin's concern was the inevitable uneven distribution of riches within the commonwealth, and how a ruler should address such an issue. Bodin observed inequality was the source of envy and prejudice. It was a mutually toxic relationship in which the wealthy demanded respect from those they believed to be of a lesser class than themselves, and in return those who suffered from poverty placed the blame of their plight upon those with means.[55] The most destructive condition to a commonwealth occurred when citizens who have suffered from the ills of poverty come into means, for the influence gained from such wealth would be used to procure further wealth, thus making the entire populace the poorer.[56] Should this occur, it allowed the possessor to circumvent any government allegiance or responsibility.[57]

Algernon Sidney consistently referenced what he termed "the public good", which he defined as: "[W]hen the good of every particular man is comprehended in the publick prosperity, and the success of their achievements is improved to the general advantage."[58] People originally had gathered together into communities for a better more stable existence.[59] As these communities became organized, they adopted rules and structures of government to protect the expected equality of each of its members.[60] Societies existed within a duality in which governments can either be just or tyrannical.[61] In every society there were some citizens who were more adept, but the goal of their labor must not be for their own recompense, but for the maintenance of 'the public good'.[62] As governments were created by the citizens themselves, it was up to them to hold their leaders and one another accountable to act in a civilized manner.[63]

John Locke demarcated the public good by vigilantly guarding against the usurpation of power by those who would use it to their own advantage.[64] Foremost was the protection of a citizen's property.[65] Education was a right no less vital, for learning was a debt society owed to its children.[66] Utilizing the relationship between parent and child as a metaphor for the relationship between government and citizen, there was a practical justification for teaching children. Though they were born with the ability to reason, they would be incapable of discovering and protecting their rights without an education in concepts of society, rights and property.[67] Locke then questioned as to how a child could exercise a freedom it knew nothing of.[68] Without a proper education, the author contended, human beings would inevitably drift backward into the state of nature.[69]

Baron de Montesquieu defined the public good as a society protected under the aegis of civil law.[70] So long as citizens obey the laws, they would not be confronted with the penalties conferred by the people of the said community.[71] Public learning was vital to the public good and it was society's duty to acculturate its citizens to its traditions and its laws.[72] The education of the masses was also the best defense against the rise of despots.[73] It was the responsibility of the previous generation to provide a systematic program of schooling for their children.[74] The arts, especially music, was a highly recommended course of study.[75] Montesquieu scorned education for profit, stating that money should be purged from the duty of education.[76]

Jean-Jacques Rousseau stated the foremost purpose of government was to establish and maintain the public good.[77] It was education which provided acculturation and loyalty for the child towards the society in which it resides.[78] Under these terms, a system of national education was both suitable and necessary, as well as a unified curriculum for all children whether rich or poor.[79]

John Trenchard and Thomas Gordon argued the public good was best served by a frugal and responsible government.[80] Those who betrayed the public trust should be prosecuted to the fullest extent of the law, for to be lenient was to foster ever larger crimes.[81] It was the citizen's duty to be ever mindful of political corruption, as well as to oust such offenders from power.[82] Trenchard and Gordon contended the greatest protection for the liberty of the people was their education, and they supported a public system for that charge.[83] Yet they were leery of schools operated by private charities, as children were susceptible to the influence of the clergy who would "load their heads with airy chimeras and fairy distinctions", rather than to provide an education in the Classical mode.[84] It was the government's charge to provide a system of learning for the children as the means to educate them to be productive members of society.[85]

In his *A Dissertation on the Canon and Feudal Law*, John Adams argued the most formidable ally of inequality was the lack of education for the masses, as well as it was also the primary tool despots used to keep subjects under their rule. Therefore, a system of public education was needed, paid for by a tax levied upon the wealthiest citizens of the realm, of which he was one.[86] Only education allowed citizens to realize their full potentials in a manner such governmental systems could not.[87] A classical education in the ancient Greek and Roman models was a popular defense against tyranny.[88] "[T]he preservation of the means of knowledge among the lowest ranks," Adams wrote, "is of more importance to the public than all the property of all the rich men in the country."[89]

No single person of the framing generation either wrote, or acted upon public education as extensively as Thomas Jefferson. His personal and private correspondence attest to his devotion to public education, and for many of the same reasons as John Adams. As governor of the Commonwealth of Virginia, Jefferson had written and enacted a public education bill financed by a raise in tax rates,[90] and later, from his position as American minister to France, he pushed for the introduction of such a bill in the Confederation congress which was "by far the most important bill in our own code".[91] In his sixth State of the Union address to Congress, Jefferson became the first American president to propose the establishment of a national system of public education.[92] A dozen years later, he compellingly advocated the education of women on an equal basis with their male counterparts.[93]

At the start of the constitutional convention, Roger Sherman of Connecticut placed the 'General Welfare' within the purview of national stability and reasoned a separate set of constitutional procedures, as well as a funding mechanism, was necessary to meet this charge.[94] He saw this issue being entwined in an interrelationship between the individual States and the central government.[95] George Mason of Virginia held a similar position, and put forward the States must not be forced into enacting policies through laws which either coerced or punished.[96] Gouverneur Morris of Pennsylvania was adamant there needed to be a central authority to set national priorities.[97] James Wilson, also of Pennsylvania, echoed Morris' assertion and maintained in this issue the federal government should not hold the monopoly of power.[98] Charles Coatesworth Pinckney of South Carolina further defined the goal of the public good consistent with Wilson, and bemoaned that within the country there were so few with so much, yet so many with so little.[99] But this tenet of the Constitution also opened up a topic many wished had remained mute.

It was within the context of 'the General Welfare' the provocative subject of human chattel slavery was pertinent for discussion. From its inception the United States of America was a nation with an identity crisis: The majority of those who framed its constitution, whose goal was to promote the 'general welfare' and to "secure the Blessings of Liberty to ourselves and our Posterity," were plantation owners with a considerable cadre of slaves.[100] Historian Bernard Bailyn noted these conflicting notions were the product of the Enlightenment, of new interpretations of sovereignty and republicanism with which America's founding generation were intrigued.[101] Intellectual historian Sue Davis claimed what appealed to these men was the creation of a uniform society in which citizens worked together toward the public good, and in doing so achieved self-satisfaction—the closest we in our time can arrive at a definition of the 'General Welfare' as the Framers themselves viewed it.[102] The historical issue was how these abstract philosophical ideas culminated into a constitutional definition of a 'person', especially as it applied to slaves.

It begins with the rancorous debates in the Second Continental Congress on the nature of taxation and representation. As noted by Thomas Jefferson in his *Autobiography*, Samuel Chase of Maryland proposed only white inhabitants be responsible for taxes, as they were the only ones who were citizens.[103] When contention broke out, rendered at the behest of John Adams of Massachusetts and James Wilson of Pennsylvania, Benjamin Harrison of Virginia proposed that two slaves be counted as one freedman.[104] Thus, what Harrison recommended was that people of color were only half-human in comparison to their Caucasian counterparts in his legal delineation of personhood. The majority of the delegates who participated in the debate were in agreement: Though the 'negroes' were persons in some abstract sense, the political reality was they were not equal to the 'citizens' who owned them. These debates legally defined the legitimacy of Locke's theory of qualitative rights, and set a disquieting precedent for future conventions to follow.[105]

At the Constitutional Convention eleven years afterwards, there several delegates who never meant for any person of color to be recognized as anything other than property. William Paterson of New Jersey made this adage clear: Slaves were property and nothing else.[106] Pierce Butler of South Carolina contended it was crucial the Constitution protect the right of Southerners to own slaves, which he recognized specific members as having labored to abolish.[107] Among those who sought to eradicate slavery was James Wilson, who not only maintained those held in slavery were people, but also argued they were due all the rights and privileges of all American citizens.[108] James Madison of Virginia argued for the eventual abatement of the slave trade but not the end of slavery itself, while his mentor George Mason made a forceful plea to put an end to the practice:

> Every master of slaves is born a petty tyrant. They bring the judgment of heaven on a country. As nations cannot be rewarded or punished in the next world they must be in this. By an inevitable chain of causes and effects providence punished national sins by national calamities. I hold it essential to every point of view that the General Government should have the power to prevent the increase of slavery.[109]

Other members such as John Jay of New York and Benjamin Franklin of Pennsylvania argued for comprehensive abolition.[110] Charles Coatesworth Pinckney objected to all efforts towards abolition and cited several historical instances of societies which had allowed slavery.[111] Furthermore, Pinckney declared there had never been a time when one was not the slave to another.[112] John Dickinson of Delaware retorted that Athens and Rome had experienced much grief due to the comportment of their slaves.[113]

The Framers were faced with the dilemma of whether they should pursue the eradication of slavery, and with it the defection of the southern States; or, if the price of Union was worth allowing a million people to exist in chains? The threat of the southern states abandoning the Union was real, for during the debate over the ratification of the *Declaration of Independence* southern representatives had walked out with the intent of voting against the measure due to a clause which criticized the British crown for having encouraged the practice. To retain southern support for the cause of independence from Great Britain it had been necessary to remove the clause from the *Declaration*.[114] Thus, when given the choice between the freedom of the slaves and the reclamation of the Union, the delegates chose the latter.

A heated debate among the delegates was the delineation of representation for people of color. Gouverneur Morris and Alexander Hamilton of New York argued active participation had to be narrowed to ensure political stability. Morris believed in the Lockean notion only those who held a stake in the community through the ownership of property possessed the voting franchise.[115] He was hostile to the democratic concept every citizen should be allowed suffrage, for to provide such a right to the poor was to give an extra vote to the rich.[116] John Dickinson agreed, adding to give the right of voting to those who did not own property allowed such property to be taken away from those who possessed it, and ceded it to those who were without means.[117] This led to a dispute over the constitutional criterion of 'citizen' and 'person.' The question was posed to the convention by William Paterson that if slaves were merely property, why would they warrant the right to vote.[118] Afterwards, the disputes caused further animosity until even Rufus King of Massachusetts, an opponent of slavery who repeatedly proposed abolition, became disgusted with the entire convention.[119]

The Three-Fifths Clause of Article I § 2 was introduced on 11th of June by Charles Coatesworth Pinkney during a meeting of the Committee of the Whole, and which stated:

> Representatives and direct Taxes shall be apportioned among the several states which may be included within this Union, according to their respective Numbers, which shall be determined by adding to the whole Number of free Persons, including those bound to service for a Term of Years, and excluding Indians not taxed, three fifths of all other Persons.[120]

It prompted further disputes over how representation would be determined. The concern was Southern issues would not be adequately addressed without suitable representation, but to rely upon chattel property to guarantee such a vote was circumspect. Northerners did not want the South to possess power by circumventing constitutional mechanisms. The proposal was objected to by Elbridge Gerry of Massachusetts.[121] During a meeting of the full convention on the 30th of June, James Madison argued representation had to take into account the varied interests of the individual States which did not necessarily have anything to do with size, but whether or not one owned slaves.[122] He pointed out in some States the slave population was more numerous than freedmen by a ratio of five-to-three.[123] Roger Sherman retorted Congress was not responsible for the faults and fallacies of the individual States.[124] Later Pinckney backtracked from his proposal, and then articulated people of color should be equal to Whites, but would agree with any delineation made by Congress.[125] His reason was straightforward: Their labor added wealth to the entire country.[126] The motion of equal representation was voted down.[127] When Gouverneur Morris offered the idea of equal representation for persons of color for further consideration, James Madison railed against it, for if slaves were counted as equal persons to their owners, it would unbalance representation in the congress to favor the Southern States, as well as the legislation which would be produced from it.[128] Furthermore, the suffrage of Black Americans would not make a marked difference in the comportment of the slaves themselves.[129]

Next there was the controversy regarding the importation of slaves. Gouverneur Morris argued he could not agree with any scheme to prolong the slave trade, as it would not only affect how the Southern States were represented in Congress, but he also was convinced the South would never support the Constitution if it abolished slavery.[130] Rufus King proposed a choice between ether exports being taxed, or the slaves not be represented.[131] Roger Sherman agreed with King that slavery was immoral, but was against the revisitation of the representation debate.[132] Morris was adamant states who were opposed to slavery should not be obligated to fight in wars for the benefit of slaves.[133] Sherman clarified it was Southern freedmen who paid taxes on their chattel property.[134]

Luther Martin of Maryland later proposed either prohibit the slave trade or institute a tax on the importation of slaves, for not to do so encouraged further importation of human chattel.[135] Sherman countered it was best to apply only a minimum amount of restriction at this time, as it would imperil the ratification of the Constitution in the Southern States.[136] He added as several States were in the process of prohibiting it, and if left alone the practice would eventually end of its own volition.[137] Southern delegates Pinckney, Butler, and John Rutledge stated their firm opposition to a slave trade prohibition, as well their intent to vote against the Constitution if the clause passed and was added to the final language of the document.[138] Oliver Ellsworth of Connecticut reasoned it was financially advantageous for the Southern States to foster a native crop of slaves rather than to further import them.[139] The slave trade ban for twenty years was added late to the debate as a compromise. James Madison objected, and predicted the next two decades would provoke all types of legal mischief involving the further importation of slaves.[140]

It was also Pinckney and Butler who offered a restrictive fugitive slave clause.[141] James Wilson objected as it obligated governors to provide public funds to administer this policy.[142] As slaves had been decreed to be property within the working language of the Constitution, Roger Sherman maintained if there was not a constitutional definition of slaves as people, there was no difference between delivering up a runaway slave and an escaped horse.[143] Butler withdrew the scheme, but later offered a new fugitive slave proposal in language nearly identical to that found in the Constitution's Article IV § 2.[144] James Madison was against it for it degraded any new State in its enforcement, to which Roger Sherman agreed.[145] Others voiced their opposition not in the principle of the clause, but for its implications towards immigration into the Western States.[146] John Langdon of New Hampshire and Hugh Williamson of North Carolina voiced their support for the measure.[147] Butler's motion passed nearly unanimously.[148]

Yet in the end these efforts made little difference in the lives of those it was meant for, as the Constitution's definition provided a legal discrimination toward slaves, freed Blacks, and mulattoes. Even abolitionist delegate Rufus King conceded defeat in that to include 'Blacks' as either citizens or persons with suffrage would have defeated the new constitution during the ratification process.[149] By 1836, the year Chief Justice Roger Brooke Taney was confirmed to the U.S. Supreme Court, all of the Framers had passed into history. In rendering the majority opinion in

Scott v. Sandford (1857), the only accurate assessment based upon the Constitution itself was that slaves in the United States of America were to remain as property, not as persons. It was truly a bondage in liberty, and a contradiction to the adage of promoting 'the General Welfare'.

James Madison defined what constituted 'the general welfare'. In a passage which echoed the sentiments previously made by John Adams in *Thoughts on Government*, he asserted the people themselves would hold the Union together based upon the condition of their lives, not governments.[150] The premise of all governments was to assure the greatest good for the greatest number of citizens. He bemoaned the specific role political parties would play in the construction of public policy.[151] In his estimation, this paradigm had been proven, for many delegates from several states holding specific political ideas had come together and achieved a just instrument of government.[152]

Alexander Hamilton maintained the general welfare was best served by the unity of the nation.[153] Without a strong centralized authority not only would the cohesion of the States disentangle, but each state would enfeeble themselves in matters involving the individual state governments, as well as their relations with foreign nations.[154] It made the individual states susceptible to government by charlatans who would control the government for their own interests.[155] The federal constitution, Hamilton reassured, had been structured to provide Congress with the authority necessary to both 'provide for the common defense', as well as 'promote the general welfare'.[156] The federal government was calculated to promote the public good be done by representatives elected by the people.[157]

Noah Webster, writing under the pseudonym 'A Citizen of America', reinforced this assessment, adding the states were not losing their power to a centralized government: They were sharing such authority and enhanced the good of their citizens in doing so.[158] Dr. Benjamin Rush, a signer of the *Declaration of Independence*, saw it as the duty of the federal government to promote public education.[159] The curriculum Rush advocated was all-encompassing, ranging from training in the law, to military tactics, with graduates returning to their home states to become the next generation of republican leaders.[160] Webster also supported such an education plan, for it was crucial for citizens to learn the doctrines of constitutional government, as well as encroachments upon the rights of the people.[161]

The Reverend Nicholas Collin, a Swedish clergyman and friend of Thomas Jefferson, writing under the pen name of 'A Foreign Spectator', expanded upon the idea of a public education program sponsored by the new federal government. The most effective way to bind the nation together was through public education.[162] Such a plan would prove useful in preparing all people for a myriad of interests, as well as promoting one to lead a productive, passionate and imaginative life.[163] Educating the masses also offered a potent defense against demagogues who sought to finesse the public for their own gain[164]:

> When the public education shall distinguish many by political abilities and a polite taste; and enable great numbers to esteem these qualities; the most eminent characters will be chosen for the legislature, civil administration, and military command—consequently the government will not only in reality be much better, but acquire that love and respect from the people, so necessary for its efficacy.[165]

'Brutus' was disturbed by the legislative powers granted to Congress in Article I § 8 to "make all laws which shall be necessary and proper".[166] He surmised the influence of this clause would find its way into every aspect of America life, as it would lead to a plethora of taxes and a bevy of new regulations.[167] 'The Federal Farmer' was in full agreement: Though it could be used correctly for the benefit of the people, it also would be used by ambitious politicians to curry favor with the electorate.[168] 'Centinel' warned that Congress would inevitably construe this clause to allow them the leeway to do whatever they wanted when they wanted, and pay for it with new and inventive taxes.[169] To the Anti-Federalists, the power represented by Article I § 8's Necessary-and-Proper Clause was both comprehensive and lacking boundaries to check it. Yet, when it came to programs such as national public education, the Anti-Federalists did not object. 'Brutus' praised the Russian Czar Peter the Great not for his military prowess, but for his institution of a public education system in his country.[170] In the opening of his initial essay, 'John DeWitt' claimed one of America's foremost virtues was its efforts to educate its children.[171]

The Necessary-and-Proper Clause of Article I § 8 was an elastic measure which granted the legislative branch the authority to craft the laws required in the administration of modern issues. Six days following the ratification of the Constitution by the delegates of the Pennsylvania state convention on 12 December 1787, the Anti-Federalist minority published a full account of the reasons for their 'nay' vote: The foremost was the inclusion of the Necessary-and-Proper Clause which, in their view, provided the federal government with the power to levy any tax it saw fit.[172] "The Federal Farmer" criticized the clause as being both too vague in its language, as well as a grant of power too large to put into check.[173]

Echoing the words of 'The Federal Farmer', 'Brutus' was deeply concerned this clause—vaguely worded yet possessing great power—would lead to abuse by less virtuous representatives.[174] It allowed the federal legislature to pass laws without any explanation or specificity so long as it was deemed by the members to be either necessary, or proper, or both.[175] Moreover, it either intruded upon, or usurped entirely the power of states to legislate for their specific needs in the name of the central government.[176] Allowing an ill-defined power would render any state objections "nugatory".[177] 'Brutus' posed the question: How could a central government 'promote the general welfare', if it also possessed the power to destroy the state governmental structures?[178] His simple answer was it could not.

Alexander Hamilton argued the general fear levied against the Necessary-and-Proper Clause was unjustified and criticisms against it as ridiculous.[179] It was an application clause which allowed the Congress to engage in the business for which it had been authorized and as it was justified for the individual state governments to exercise their legislative authority in crafting needed legislation, the federal congress should possess the same power.[180] Hamilton stated it was the right of all governments to implement taxes, as without revenue every government would cease to exist.[181] Why then, the author queried, would it be proper for the individual states to exercise such an authority, but not a centralized government?[182] James Madison declared: "Without the *substance* of this power, the whole Constitution would be a dead letter."[183] He affirmed had the delegates enumerated every legal situation they had considered necessary and proper, it would have resulted in a collection of legislation too huge to contemplate.[184]

'The Federal Farmer' replied the constitutional authority of the legislative branch to authorize and collect taxes was of vital importance.[185] Through the use of both external and internal taxes, the federal government ultimately controlled all forms of national commerce without restraint.[186] In the collection of such revenue a bevy of new regulatory legislation, in tandem with a sizeable staff, would be required.[187] As such, it would not take long before state laws were circumvented in favor of the federal government.[188] The author stated with all tax authority placed within the purview of federal authority, the state governments possessed no legitimate political power of their own to do likewise.[189] Though this plan would be the prime funding mechanism for the federal government, it was not necessarily the sole manner by which operational funds could be collected.[190]

'Brutus' was blunt as to why he did not support the ratification of the federal constitution: It possessed uncontainable power.[191] This conclusion was based upon the premise if the legislature possessed the power to pass any law it wanted as authorized under the Necessary-and-Proper Clause of Article I § 8;[192] and, when passed and signed by the president, that bill became the essential law under the sanction of Article VI's Supreme Law Clause,[193] the government and laws of the sovereign states would be nullified.[194] The legislative power to levy taxes was without confines.[195] In addition, once the constitution was ratified, there would be no necessary reason for the states to have any political relations with one another.[196] As such, only the federal government would hold the authority to direct tax policy without any input from the states.[197] The defense of the country—the prime reason for taxation—should not be left solely to the federal government.[198] If the federal government was to retain the power of taxation, it must be made applicable under specific circumstances.[199]

'John DeWitt' criticized the Taxation Clause of Article I § 8. He urged his fellow citizens to use extreme caution in considering the adoption of the federal constitution, as it was an overarching system given every power imaginable.[200] By its design it was meant to minimalize the influence and power of the state governments.[201] As the clause itself lacked specificity, the Congress could tax at will; apply such taxes in an unequal manner; and, yet, find all the funds raised to not be enough to cover its expenses in collecting revenues.[202] Additionally, there was no bill of rights to guard against further usurpation of power from the states by the federal government.[203] Thus, in DeWitt's assessment, anyone who supported the ratification of the Constitution was a traitor.[204] It was these contentions which provided the ideological foundation of essays by 'An Old Whig' and 'Agrippa', as well as speeches by Patrick Henry at the Virginia Ratifying Convention, and by Melancton Smith at the New York Ratifying Convention.[205]

James Madison queried whether any tax could be implemented in a fair manner, especially if they were counter to the laws of the individual state governments.[206] He argued the power of taxation was essential for the operations of any government at any level and the authority to levy taxes given to the federal legislature was necessary.[207] In answering the Anti-Federalist criticism the clause would lead to an unlimited exercise of power, Madison merely ridiculed it as a fallacy.[208] He was dismayed at how they could deride the constitutional authority to act in the public good as a tax fraud scheme.[209] As for the critique federal taxes would necessitate the employ of innumerable collectors, Madison replied the number of collectors would be no more than those employed by the separate state governments.[210] In expending funds collected through taxes for the public good required good judgment and restraint, for such legislation was also an opportunity for the dominate political party to use it to gain popular sentiment in their favor, and in doing so perpetrate injustice.[211]

Alexander Hamilton was more aggressive in debunking the Anti-Federalist critiques. Echoing Thomas Hobbes, Hamilton argued as governments were the necessary outgrowth of the social contract, it had the undisputed right to exist.[212] In response to criticisms that taxes implemented by a central government would not be executed in a fair manner, he pondered how taxes should be levied without doing harm to vital constituencies; and, concluded such a tax on any level was not possible.[213] But, for every country to survive, it had to have a funding mechanism.[214] If there was no fair tax, then what sort of levy would be both acceptable to the public, and would generate the necessary revenue? Hamilton also proposed it was a citizen's duty to consider the plight of citizens with little income, and to assist.[215]

The Federalists and Anti-Federalists were concurrent with the importance of property rights, commerce issues, the significance of trade, and slavery. At the forefront of Anti-Federalist ideology was political liberty, specifically the ability of communities to dictate the course of their affairs without the encroachment of any governing authority outside of the state. To the advocates of confederation and limited government, none of the individual rights they championed applied to anyone held in bondage or indenturement. Slaves were property and, therefore, exempt from governmental protections and rights.

This point was made by 'Brutus'. He argued that if slaves were to be counted under the new constitution as 'all other persons', then in some states livestock ought to also be represented.[216] If traders in foreign slaves were allowed to import human chattel unabated for two decades, it would artificially inflate the representation of some states at the expense of others, much to the detriment of the democratic ideal.[217] For Melancton Smith in granting to slaves even partial recognition as persons was ludicrous, for it was pointless to grant the power of citizenship to those who no idea how to use it.[218] Slaves were of greater value as commodities for trade than as persons deserving citizenship rights. Free trade between free countries generated revenues of beneficence to all involved parties; therefore, if the slave trade, whether foreign or domestic, was profitable for the individual, the community, and the state, it was to be protected as valuable for the survival of all involved. The 3/5ths Clause of Article I § 2 took on an added significance in that it guaranteed that the transition of the former to the latter was impossible without a specific amendment and the rights of the southerners to own chattel property was secure.

The Constitution is an integrated governing document in which each clause was meant to add clarity and definition to another. As in a patchwork quilt, each idea was reinforced throughout every other article and clause. Many of the overarching concepts were undermined by the contradictory language of specific protections scattered throughout the document procuring both natural limits and abstract grants of power.

Human chattel slavery was not exempt from this paradigm, for not only were there clauses specifically designed to protect the practice, but when coupled with other seemingly unrelated passages, it was impossible to abolish except by amendment. For representation purposes, slaves comprised three-fifths of their actual number, effectively recognizing them as being not quite whole persons.[219] The slave trade was legally allowed to continue unabated for twenty years.[220] Finally, the document provided for the return of fugitive slaves—"persons held to Service or Labour"—from territories which had outlawed such bondage through legislative acts of their state governments.[221]

Once the debate over promoting 'the general welfare' became centered upon taxes it became a political brawl over government and money. The locus of the greatest good for the greatest number turned into a brouhaha over who ultimately paid the bill. More importantly, it reveals a political paradigm that remains in place in our time: Americans desire the full beneficence of government without having to pay for it.

The Framers conceptualized what are now known as social welfare programs, especially those involving government-sponsored public education, and provided for future generations the means by which to address them within a Constitutional framework. As the level of taxation became an issue, the individual state ratification conventions became the axis of debate between the two sides, and the tet-a-tet between them was the foundation of the nation's two-party political system.

But in consideration of human chattel slavery and "the General Welfare", the contradictions were glaring. In his 1853 work *What to the Slave is the Fourth of July*, abolitionist Frederick Douglass argued if the Constitution was on the side of liberty rather than slavery, it was feasible to seek moral and social reform through political means within the existing system. Specifically, as the document guaranteed the right of citizens to be secure in their persons, it was more consistent with the constitution to abolish slavery than to protect it.[222] Likewise within his book *Lincoln's Rise to the Presidency* historian William C. Harris presented the 16th president's most powerful political concept was that the Framers had meant for slavery's demise by establishing the legal means to constrict its growth. With an emphasis on the word "liberty," coupled with the *Declaration of Independence*, Lincoln argued the U.S. Supreme Court's majority opinion in *Scott v. Sandford* (1857) had obliterated the pro-slavery intent of those who had forged the nation.[223]

Unfortunately their interpretations could not have been more erroneous. Douglass and Lincoln made the mistake many of their contemporaries had of assuming the Constitution was based upon one passage or word without taking into consideration the entire document and its inherent interconnectedness. If one were to dwell on upon the word 'liberty' it would be a foregone conclusion the Framers meant for all under its authority to enjoy its freedom and protection. But when the specific clauses concerning slavery are coupled with those relating to property rights, commercial trade, along with the Full Faith and Credit and Fugitive clauses, those in a position of forced servitude were meant to remain within the confines of their bondage.

So what is to be understood concerning 'the public good' and promoting 'the general welfare'?

On 11 January 1944 President Franklin Delano Roosevelt asked the nation how a people could be free if they could not work at a job that paid a livable wage, nor have access to a home of their own, nor a quality education, or have the means by which to maintain their health.[224] In our time we have not only neglected to answer President Roosevelt's questions, but we have dismissed the notion as being "un-American". With fiscal inequity rampant, Americans have allowed their elected representatives to delineate rights on the basis of gender, color, religion, sexual preference fostering discontent and increasing the advent of a popular revolt.

The notion of 'promote the general welfare' remains a radical idea, as it demands we take into consideration *all* the people. The Framers placed constitutional mechanisms for the government which allowed it to address contemporary issues of social conscience and justice, as exampled by President Roosevelt's *Second Bill of Rights*. It remains the most contentious legacy of our founding document, as well as the one we have been the most reluctant to embrace.

To meet this constitutional charge, this country should spend its money to feed, clothe and shelter the poor; educate the next generation of citizens; build roads, bridges, and libraries; and, explore space; and, not coddle the wealthy and their insatiable lust for more ephemeral and expensive material goods. As they have made vast fortunes from the generosity of this nation, so should they give some of it back to aid the less fortunate. Tradition is unacceptable when it does damage to human beings and their right to a decent standard of living. In the same manner we mature and abandon childhood notions of Santa Claus, so must we abandon the ideas of "the-way-things-ought-to-be" merely because they have always been. The future is fluid and wrought with change, if we so chose to embrace it. And with regards to promoting 'the general welfare' there were flaws in their reasons—especially where human chattel slavery was involved—the Framers' still held an edge over Americans in our time, for they acknowledged the plight of those of lesser means, and placed within the Constitution both the charge and the procedures to address it.

Notes

1. John Adams, "Thoughts on Government: Applicable to the Present State of the American Colonies", 1776; in *The Revolutionary Writings of John Adams*, ed. C. Bradley Thompson (Indianapolis, IN: The Liberty Fund, 2000), 287. Page Smith, *John Adams, Volume One 1732–1784* (Garden City, NJ: Doubleday & Company, Inc., 1962), I: 245–8.
2. Smith, I; 247.
3. Jack Rakove, *Original Meanings: Politics and Ideas in the Making of the Constitution* (New York: Alfred A, Knopf, Inc., 1996), 97, 203, 251–2.
4. *U.S. Constitution*, Preamble.
5. Aristotle, *The Politics*, trans. T. A. Sinclair, Reprint of 1962 edition (New York: Penguin Books, 1992), 124.
6. Plato, *The Republic*, ed. Francis Cornford (New York: Oxford University Press, 1941), 37, 143.
7. *Ibid.*, 55.
8. Aristotle, *The Politics*, 375.
9. Herodotus, *The Histories*, trans. Aubrey DeSélincourt. 1996 Reprint. (New York: Penguin Books, 1954), 504.
10. Thucydides, *History of the Peloponnesian War*, Trans. Rex Werner (New York: Penguin Books, 1954), 145.
11. *Ibid.*, 147.
12. *Ibid.*, 149.
13. Aristotle, *The Constitution of the Athenians*, trans. Sir Frederick G. Kenyon; at The Internet Classics Archive; http://classics.mit.edu/Aristotle/athenian_const.mb.txt. Accessed 28 June 2018.
14. *Ibid.*, Article III § 47.
15. *Ibid.*, Article III § 49.
16. *Ibid.*, Article III § 56.
17. Robin Osborne, "Roman Poverty in Context", In *Poverty in the Roman World*, eds. Margaret Atkins and Robin Osborne (Cambridge, England: Cambridge University Press, 2006), 6.
18. Plutarch, *The Complete Collection of Plutarch's Parallel Lives*, trans. John Dryden (CreateSpace Independent Publishing Platform from Outskirts Press, 2014), 3.
19. Suetonius, *The Twelve Caesars*, trans. Robert Graves, reprint of 1957 edition (New York: Penguin Books, 1989), 25.

20. Plutarch, *Fall of the Roman Republic*, ed. Rex Warner, Reprint of 1958 edition (New York: Penguin Books, 1972), 261.
21. Suetonius, 42–3.
22. *Ibid.*, 83.
23. Neville Morely, "The Poor in the City of Rome", in *Poverty in the Roman World*, 38.
24. Suetonius, 197.
25. *Ibid.*, 198.
26. *Ibid.*, 200.
27. *Ibid.*, 201.
28. Tacitus, *The Annals of Imperial Rome*, trans. Michael Grant, 1996 Reprint (New York: Penguin Books, 1956), 297.
29. Suetonius, 288.
30. *Ibid.*
31. *Ibid.*, 296.
32. *Ibid.*
33. Michael J. Vickers, *The Ancient Romans* (Oxford, England: Stamford Press, Ltd, 1992), 30.
34. Dominic Rathbone, "Poverty and Population in Ancient Egypt"; in *Poverty in the Roman World*, 101.
35. Marc Bloch, *Feudal Society, Volume II: Social Classes and Political Organization*, trans. L. A. Manyon (Chicago, IL: Phoenix Books, University of Chicago Press, 1961), 441.
36. *Ibid.*, 443.
37. *Ibid.*, 444.
38. *Ibid.*, 445.
39. 11 Hen. 7. c. 2.
40. 17 Geo. II c. 5. William Blackstone, *Commentaries on the Laws of England*, ed. William Draper Lewis, Reprint of 1922 edition (Clark, NJ: The Lawbook Exchange, 2004), IV: 1571.
41. 5 and 6 Edw. VI. c. 2. David Hume, *The History of England From the Invasion of Julius Caesar to the Abdication of James II* (Boston: Phillips, Sampson, and Company, 1854), III: 376–7.
42. *Ibid.*, 377.
43. 39 Eliz. 1 c. 3. Hume, IV: 370.
44. 39 Eliz. 1 c. 3. Blackstone, IV: 1790. This law was not amended until 1834, when new legislation placed all poverty relief programs under the control of three Poor Law commissioners. Frederick William Maitland, *The Constitutional History of England* (Cambridge, England: Cambridge University Press, 1965), 412.
45. Blackstone, I: 120.
46. 1 Geo, 1. St. 2. Blackstone, I: 255.
47. Blackstone, III: 1385.

48. *Ibid.*
49. *Ibid.*, III: 1386.
50. Blackstone, III: 1152.
51. *The Process of Exigent Act*, 25 Edw. III c. 17 (1351). Blackstone, III: 1370–1.
52. *The Limitations Act*, 21 Jac. I. c. 24 (1623). Blackstone, III: 1371.
53. Jean Bodin, *Six Books of the Commonwealth*, ed. M. J. Tooley (Oxford, England: Basil Blackwell, 1955), 30.
54. *Ibid.*, 45–6.
55. *Ibid.*
56. *Ibid.*, 160.
57. *Ibid.*, 160–1.
58. Algernon Sidney, *Discourses Concerning Government*, ed. Thomas G. West (Indianapolis, IN: The Liberty Fund, 1996), 272.
59. *Ibid.*, 35.
60. *Ibid.*
61. *Ibid.*, 49.
62. *Ibid.*
63. *Ibid.*, 92.
64. John Locke, *Two Treatises of Government*, ed. Peter Laslett (New York: Cambridge University Press, 1960), 398–9. The italics are that of the author.
65. *Ibid.*, 399.
66. *Ibid.*, 208. It is an obligation Locke reiterates in the *Second Treatise* § 56. *Ibid.*, 305.
67. *Ibid.*, 308.
68. *Ibid.*, 308–9.
69. *Ibid.*, 381.
70. Baron de Montesquieu, *Spirit of the Laws*, eds. Anne Cohler, Basia Miller, and Harold Stone (New York: Cambridge University Press, 1989), 514.
71. *Ibid.*, 515.
72. *Ibid.*, 31.
73. *Ibid.*, 35, 36.
74. *Ibid.*, 36.
75. *Ibid.*, 41.
76. *Ibid.*, 38.
77. Jean-Jacques Rousseau, "On the Social Contract", 1762; in, *The Social Contract and Other Later Political Writings*, ed. Victor Gourevitch (New York: Cambridge University Press, 1996), 57, 121.
78. Jean-Jacques Rousseau, "Considerations on the Government of Poland and on its Projected Reformation", 1772; in, *Ibid.*, 189.
79. *Ibid.*, 190.
80. John Trenchard and Thomas Gordon, "Cato's Letter No. 10", 3 January 1720; in *Cato's Letters*, ed. Ronald Hamoury (Indianapolis, IN: The Liberty Fund, 1995), I:83.

81. John Trenchard and Thomas Gordon, "Cato's Letter No. 133", 11 March 1720; in *Ibid.*, I:142.
82. *Ibid.*, I:145–6.
83. *Ibid.*, I:145. John Trenchard and Thomas Gordon, "Cato's Letter No. 20", 15 June 1723; in *Ibid.*, II:918.
84. *Ibid.*, II:919.
85. *Ibid.*, II:924.
86. John Adams, "A Dissertation on the Canon and Feudal Law", 1765; in *The Revolutionary Writings of John Adams*, ed. C. Bradley Thompson (Indianapolis, IN: The Liberty Fund, 2000), 28.
87. *Ibid.*, 34.
88. *Ibid.*, 33.
89. *Ibid.*, 29.
90. Thomas Jefferson, "A Bill for the More General Diffusion of Knowledge"; in, *Thomas Jefferson: Writings*, ed. Merrill D. Peterson (New York: Literary Classics of the United States, Inc., 1984), 365–73.
91. Thomas Jefferson, Letter to George Wythe, 13 August 1786; in, *Ibid.*, 859.
92. Thomas Jefferson, "Sixth Annual Message", 2 December 1806; in *Ibid.*, 530.
93. Thomas Jefferson, Letter to Nathaniel Burwell, 14 March 1818; in, *Ibid.*, 1411–3.
94. James Madison, *Notes of Debates in the Federal Constitution of 1787*, 1985 Reprint. (Athens, OH: Ohio University Press, 1966), 35.
95. *Ibid.*
96. *Ibid.*
97. *Ibid.*
98. *Ibid.*, 74.
99. *Ibid.*, 184.
100. *U.S. Constitution*, Preamble.
101. Bernard Bailyn, *The Ideological Origins of the American Revolution* (Cambridge, MA: The Belknap Press of Harvard University Press, 1967), 27.
102. Sue Davis, *American Political Thought: Four Hundred Years of Ideas and Ideologies* (Englewood Cliffs, NJ: Prentice Hall, Inc., 1996), 47.
103. Thomas Jefferson, quoted in *The Founder's Constitution*, eds. Philip B. Kurland and Ralph Lerner (Indianapolis, IN: The Liberty Fund, 1996), II: 87.
104. *Ibid.*
105. Locke, 335.
106. Madison, 259.
107. *Ibid.*, 286.
108. *Ibid.*, 287.
109. George Mason, quoted in Madison, 504.
110. *The Anti-Federalist: Writings by the Opponents of the Constitution*, ed. Herbert Storing (Chicago, IL: University of Chicago Press, 1981), 100 n. 20.

111. Madison, 505.
112. *Ibid.*
113. *Ibid.*, 506.
114. Pauline Maier, *American Scripture: Making the Declaration of Independence* (New York: Alfred A. Knopf, Inc., 1997), 45.
115. Locke, 367.
116. Gouverneur Morris, quoted in M. E. Bradford, *Founding Fathers: Brief Lives of the Framers of the United States Constitution*, 1994 Reprint. (Lawrence: University of Kansas Press, 1981), 76.
117. Gordon S. Wood, *The Creation of the American Republic, 1776–1787* (Chapel Hill, NC: The University of North Carolina Press, 1969), 529.
118. Wood, 100.
119. Madison, 409.
120. *U.S. Constitution*, Article I §2.
121. Madison, 103.
122. *Ibid.*, 224.
123. *Ibid.*, 225.
124. *Ibid.*
125. *Ibid.*, 248.
126. *Ibid.*, 281.
127. *Ibid.*
128. *Ibid.*, 294–5.
129. *Ibid.*, 327.
130. *Ibid.*, 276.
131. *Ibid.*, 410.
132. *Ibid.*
133. *Ibid.*, 411–12.
134. *Ibid.*, 412.
135. *Ibid.*, 502.
136. *Ibid.*, 503.
137. *Ibid.*
138. *Ibid.*, 506–7.
139. *Ibid.*, 504.
140. *Ibid.*, 530.
141. *Ibid.*, 545.
142. *Ibid.*
143. *Ibid.*, 546.
144. *U.S. Constitution*, Article IV § 2.
145. Madison, 552.
146. *Ibid.*
147. *Ibid.*, 553.

148. *Ibid.*
149. Rufus King, quoted in Wood, 105.
150. James Madison, "Essay #45"; in *The Federalist,* The Gideon Edition, eds. George W. Carey and James McClellan (Indianapolis, IN: The Liberty Fund, 2001), 238.
151. James Madison, "Essay #10"; in *Ibid.*, 44.
152. James Madison, "Essay #37"; in *Ibid.*, 185.
153. Alexander Hamilton, "Essay #13"; in *Ibid.*, 61.
154. *Ibid.*
155. Alexander Hamilton, "Essay #22"; in *Ibid.*, 108.
156. Alexander Hamilton, "Essay #23"; in *Ibid.*, 114.
157. Alexander Hamilton, "Essay #73"; in *Ibid.*, 382.
158. "A Citizen of America" [Noah Webster], "An Examination into the Leading Principles of the Federal Constitution", 17 October 1787; in *Friends of the Constitution: Writings of the "Other" Federalists*, eds. Colleen A. Sheehan and Gary L. McDowell (Indianapolis, IN: The Liberty Fund, 1998), 393.
159. Benjamin Rush, "Address to the People of the United States", January 1787; in *Friends*, 3–4.
160. *Ibid.*, 4.
161. *Friends*, 402.
162. 'A Foreign Spectator' [Nicholas Collin], "An Essay on the Means of Promoting Federal Sentiments in the United States", 6 August 1787; in *Friends*, 409.
163. *Ibid.*, 411–12.
164. *Ibid.*, 414.
165. *Ibid.*, 435.
166. *Ibid.*, 110. *U.S. Constitution*, Article I § 8.
167. 'Brutus', Essay #VI, 27 December 1787; in *The Anti-Federalist*, 141–3.
168. 'The Federal Farmer', Letter #3, 10 October 1787; in *The Anti-Federalists: Selected Writings and Speeches*, ed. Bruce Frohnen (Washington, DC: Regnery Publishing, Inc., 1999), 157.
169. 'Centinel', Letter #1, 5 October 1787; "Centinel" Letter #5, 4 December 1787; in *The Anti-Federalists*, 39; 79.
170. 'Brutus', "Essay #7", 3 January 1788; in *The Anti-Federalist*, 146–7.
171. 'John DeWitt', "Essay #1", 22 October 1787; *The Anti-Federalists*, 490.
172. "The Address and Reasons of Dissent of the Minority of the Convention of Pennsylvania To Their Constituents", *Pennsylvania Packet and Daily Advertiser*, 18 December 1787; in *The Anti-Federalist*, 218.
173. The Federal Farmer, Letter #4, 12 October 1787; in *The Anti-Federalists*, 174.
174. "Brutus", Letter #12, 14 February 1788; in *The Anti-Federalist*, 171.
175. "Brutus", Letter #11, 31 January 1788; in *The Anti-Federalist*, 166.
176. "Brutus", Letter #5, 13 December 1787; in *The Anti-Federalist*, 134–6.
177. "Brutus", Letter #8, 10 January 1788; in *The Anti-Federalist*, 150.

178. "Brutus", Letter #1, 18 October 1787; in *The Anti-Federalist*, 112.
179. Alexander Hamilton, Essay #29; in *The Federalist,* 141.
180. Alexander Hamilton, Essay #31; in *The Federalist,* 152.
181. *Ibid.*, 159.
182. *Ibid.*, 160.
183. James Madison, Essay #44; in *The Federalist,* 233. Italic is that of the author.
184. *Ibid.*, 234.
185. 'The Federal Farmer', "Letter #3", 10 October 1787; in *The Anti-Federalist*, 48.
186. *Ibid.*
187. *Ibid.*, 48–9.
188. *Ibid.*, 49.
189. 'The Federal Farmer', "Letter #17", 23 January 1788; in *The Anti-Federalist*, 88.
190. *Ibid.*, 90.
191. 'Brutus', "Essay #1", 18 October 1787; in *The Anti-Federalist*, 110.
192. *U.S. Constitution*, Article I § 8.
193. *U.S. Constitution*, Article VI.
194. *Ibid.*
195. *Ibid.*
196. *Ibid.*, 111.
197. *Ibid.*
198. 'Brutus', "Essay #7", 3 January 1788; in *The Anti-Federalist*, 146.
199. *Ibid.*, 149.
200. 'John DeWitt', "Essay #1", 22 October 1787; *The Anti-Federalists*, 492.
201. *Ibid.*, 500.
202. 'John DeWitt', "Essay #4", 19 November 1787; *The Anti-Federalists*, 512.
203. 'John DeWitt', "Essay #2", 29 October 1787; *The Anti-Federalists*, 496.
204. 'John DeWitt', "Essay #1", 22 October 1787; *The Anti-Federalists*, 493.
205. 'An Old Whig', "Letter #6", 24 November 1787; *The Anti-Federalists*, 345–51; 'Agrippa', "Letter #9", 28 December 1787; in *The Anti-Federalist*, 244; Patrick Henry, "Speech at the Virginia Ratifying Convention", 5 June 1788; in *The Anti-Federalist*, 303; 309; and, Melancton Smith; "Speech at New York Ratifying Convention", 27 June 1788; in *The Anti-Federalist*, 352–6.
206. James Madison, "Essay #53"; in *The Federalist*, 279.
207. James Madison, "Essay #41"; in *The Federalist*, 213.
208. *Ibid.*, 214.
209. *Ibid.*
210. James Madison, "Essay #45"; in *The Federalist*, 240.
211. James Madison, "Essay #10"; in, *The Federalist*, 45.
212. Alexander Hamilton, "Essay #21"; in *The Federalist*, 99–100.
213. Alexander Hamilton, "Essay #12"; in *The Federalist*, 57.
214. *Ibid.*, 59.

215. Alexander Hamilton, "Essay #36"; in *The Federalist*, 177.
216. Brutus, "To the Citizens of the State of New York," 15 November 1787; in Storing, 123.
217. Summary culled from *Ibid.*, 124.
218. Melanction Smith, Speech at the New York State Ratifying Convention, 20 June 1788; in *The Anti-Federalist*, 336.
219. *U. S. Constitution*, Art. I § 2.
220. *U. S. Constitution*, Art. I § 9.
221. *U. S. Constitution*, Art. IV § 2.
222. Summary of Douglass' pamphlet in William S. McFeely, *Frederick Douglass* (New York: W. W. Norton & Company, Inc., 1991), 173. *U.S. Constitution*, Fourth Amendment.
223. William C. Harris, *Lincoln's Rise to the Presidency* (Lawrence: The University Press of Kansas, 2007), 69, 135, 168, 188.
224. Nathan Miller, *F.D.R.: An Intimate History* (Garden City, NY: Doubleday and Company, Inc., 1983), 498.

6

"To Secure the Blessings of Liberty"

The Protection of Personal Rights in the Constitution

The measure of a free society is not demonstrated by its citizens bearing no chains, but by the autonomy of their intellect to abide by their personal convictions without the interference of their government. Likewise, the progressive evolution of a civilization is secured by its ability to embrace new ideas wrought from citizens whose understanding and determination bear no limits. Due to factors ranging from outward experience to innermost reflection, every individual possesses a unique perspective upon the events they have endured. A government which actively promotes intellectual exploration and the free exchange of such viewpoints is one which survives all challenges to its sovereignty.

Among Americans the concept of freedom is at the heart of their nationalism. They cherish it as well as fight for it. Yet they have no real clue as to what it is, with each holding a separate idea of what constitutes "liberty". In its most ordinary state "freedom" is anarchy, what philosopher Thomas Hobbes called the state of nature, in which there is nothing to control the passions and actions of human beings. Within such a state the idea of property ownership was moot, for only force dictated who owns what and who ruled the pack. Human existence at this point state was, as Hobbes himself lamented, "solitary, poor, nasty, brutish and short".[1] What set us free from this anarchy was the will to come together and form civilization. In doing so we gave up a portion of our natural liberty to obtain a measure of safety. This was accomplished by not only the set of laws we agreed to adhere to, but also our allegiance to a sovereign power—all of it bound together by a social contract.

Rights and liberty are entwined within the notion of civic duty. In the Greek model with protection afforded by citizenship came responsibilities. From the initiation of their constitution until the conclusion of the Peloponnesian War, the Athenians were adamant in their adherence to popular democracy. They had adopted this form of government to free themselves from the grip of a wealthy oligarchy which had brought the rest of the population to the brink of economic destruction through debt enslavement.[2]

A citizen was one who took part in the essential business of the city. Any citizen who conspired against the state, lost their citizenship rights.[3] All persons above the age of thirty years were qualified to serve as jurors.[4] Ostracized citizens were mandated to live outside of the city limits, or they would lose their citizenship rights permanently.[5] Every citizen who remained loyal to Athens during times of strife and wished to leave the city were permitted to do so, and retained the full beneficence of a self-governing democracy, along with the rights to property ownership.[6] Such was its importance within Athenian society that its constitution mandated it.

Plato asserted constitutions were the creation of human intellect, drawn from the traditions and expectations of the communities they were designed to govern.[7] The determining factor as to the degree of liberty within society was dependent upon the levels of justice and injustice concurrent in the citizens' condition wrought from them.[8] Yet the quality of the leadership which arose within such a system was suspect, as liberty promoted men to power who possessed a reticence towards change.[9] Over time, they become so enamored by the wealth and authority that is wrought from a democracy, their personal avarice and greed would take precedence from acting in the best interest of the community.[10]

In *The Politics*, Aristotle maintained government consisted of an amalgamation of the people who subsisted within it, whose intent was to allow citizens under its authority to live contented lives.[11] A 'proper' citizen was defined by his role as one who held official office and rendered judgments, as per their elected charge.[12] There were inherent differences where equal treatment under law, the foundational supposition for the concept of political rights, was based upon the perception of the citizens as to what was just and unjust.[13] Thus, as far as any political right was concerned, freedom was dependent upon the ownership of property, for it was the reason people had sought refuge under the state and its laws in the first place.[14] However, the goal of the state was not one that applied to just those who owned property, but which concerned all who lived under its edicts.[15] In turn, the duty of its citizens was to maintain the state and its dedication to the greatest good for the greatest among them.[16]

Aristotle maintained the foremost element of democratic government was liberty.[17] Under such a government, justice was rendered by a vote of the majority, rather than fairness founded upon virtue.[18] It was up to the citizens themselves to define the perimeters of justice within their community.[19] The demarcation of liberty was to enjoy life as one wishes, for to do so was the function of being free.[20] In this sense, Aristotle was the first to define liberty as individual freedom.

Writing in the early fifth century BCE, the historian Herodotus contemplated ideas of democracy and liberty. Within *The Histories* he recounted a dialogue between King Darius of Persia and his aides Otanes and Megabyzus upon the most effective forms of government.[21] As stated by Otanes, monarchy was not an effective form of government for human beings were flawed, and prone to give into their violent and selfish nature.[22] It was under such an aberration kings either circumvented or desecrated at will tradition and the law.[23] This was the reason Athens had done away with monarchy and in its place had established a democracy.[24] In his defense of oligarchy, Megabyzus observed such a popular sovereignty was prone to ignorance, irresponsibility and violence due to those who were motivated enough to vote.[25] Due to the proclivity of the masses to act upon emotion, they made one bad decision after another based upon how they felt, rather than how they thought.[26] King Darius defended hereditary monarchy as the most effective form of government, for there was one source of power and decision-making.[27]

In reviewing Herodotus' account certain ideas become apparent. First, in the three forms of government discussed—democracy, oligarchy, and monarchy—it was within the democratic regime the responsibility for the maintenance of liberty fell to the people themselves. Secondly, the safety of the citizens was never of concern within any of the three political forms. Lastly, whereas government by the people was a messy affair, the rule of the one unquestioned monarch was efficient and effective. Yet, in his account of the Ionian revolt against the Persians, Herodotus noted the Athenians had lived under a constitutional democracy, and they were not going to return to the despotism inherent within monarchy.[28]

In his *History of the Peloponnesian War* Thucydides made several edifying statements regarding the interrelationship between democracy and liberty, and the courage required to maintain them. One example was revealed in the historian's account of Sparta's debate over its impending war with Athens.[29] In his funeral oration, the Athenian leader Pericles contrasted the rights and virtues of those living within its democracy, and how they took immense pride in making their own political decisions, and rendering them with the participation of all the people, in contrast to those living in Sparta.[30] During the Mytilenian debate over the perils of a democracy, it was argued one of the worst failures of such a system was to first agree to laws and edicts, and then to violate them at will.[31] Finally, in his account of the end of democracy in Athens by a group seeking to inaugurate an oligarchic system, Thucydides observed the Athenians were a group who had grown accustomed to their liberty, and we not about to let anyone deprive them of it—in short, a people robbed of their liberty.[32]

The Romans viewed liberty as an outgrowth of the civil law applicable only to citizens of Rome. Adopting the same ideology as the Greeks before them, the Romans believed government was the sole institution capable of protecting liberty and guarding against any encroachments. The historian Livy recognized that law was not an absolute, and its passage as well as repeal had dire consequences, thus every new law needed serious contemplation before being enacted. He quoted Cato's speech on the repeal of the *Lex Oppa*: "If every individual is to destroy or demolish any law which hinders him in his particular interests, what use will it be for the whole citizen body to pass measures which will soon be repealed by those whom they directed?"[33] The historian was also leery of crowds and their penchant for vigilantism, an argument he made when he recounted the oratory of So'pater on the assassination of King Hieronymous of Syracuse, who rued the bent of the crowd towards group violence.[34] Livy also noted the law inevitably changed due to circumstance, to which the Roman statesman Cicero added war drowned out the voice of the law.[35]

Cicero advocated a governmental system in which the essential law protected the rights of all citizens. He stated in *Die Legibus*, justice was entwined within the authority of law.[36] The law was not immune from the desires of ambitious men who held political office: It was often the actions of public officials through the laws they passed which often did the most damage:

> Injustice often arises through trickery, by an extremely cunning but ill-intentioned interpretation of the law. In consequences the saying "the more Justice, the more injustice" has now become a proverb.[37]

The statesman also echoed Roman attitudes towards the poor in one vital aspect: Life was in consort with the laws of nature.[38] In that context the law was the guarantor of the people to live their lives as they chose.[39] Citizens were to celebrate such liberty through the remembrance of times when they were deprived of it.[40]

For the historian Tacitus, liberty was best demonstrated in fairness, and when the people recanted on their belief in equality, they surrendered themselves to violence and selfishness.[41]

As for the British model, historian David Hume praised *Magna Carta* as having established civil liberties to all of the English people.[42] Historians Frederic Maitland and Frederick Pollard further explained its legal significance as the closest statement of essential rights the English people had ever declared up to that point. It demanded that all citizens, from the king down to the serf, were neither above nor below the law.[43]

Of specific importance to American constitutional history was Article #63 which guaranteed to male citizens "all the aforesaid liberties, rights and concessions".[44] Cited by both sides during the ratification debates, it was Anti-Federalist author "Brutus" who contended the 'Great Charter' had reaffirmed citizens were entitled to inalienable rights above and beyond any nation's constitution or codes of law.[45] In the spirit of *Magna Carta,* Section II of *The Petition of Right* specified neither the reigning monarch nor his privy council could act "against the laws and free custom of the realm", which was restated in Section XI.[46]

In the evolution of American constitutionalism and the idea of guaranteed civil liberties, the *English Bill of Rights* (1689) was among the most crucial. Though the bulk of the document castigated the legal abuses wrought by King James II, it also declared British subjects possessed irrefutable civil liberties. Among the stated freedoms were the right of free speech and debate, that subjects could petition the monarch with regards to grievances, the right to bear arms, and that "no declarations, judgments, doings or proceedings to the prejudice of the people in any of the said premises ought in any wise to be drawn" either by Parliament or the reigning monarch.[47]

Sir William Blackstone expounded upon the aspects of individual liberty found within British law. It was his assessment that citizens possessed civil liberties to the degree of the wellbeing of society, and possessed the responsibility to protect it against the usurpations of the monarchy, an essential philosophical tenet of the American colonists in their revolution against British rule.[48] Among the potent concepts was on the rights of citizens, as well as its 'wrongs'.[49] Properly defined, the law was the rule of civil conduct, and within those perimeters rights were the property of the citizenry; meanwhile, wrongs were infringements upon those rights. Thus, rights and wrongs coexisted and could not occur separately.[50]

Rights came in two delineations: 1) Those which are expected from citizens; and, 2) Those which are the possession of the citizens.[51] These were further demarcated in two different types: Natural, such as those found within nature itself, and artificial which were rights found within the construct of the law.[52] Finally, all rights also existed within an 'either/or' paradigm: absolute which pertained to all, and relative which concerned a specific group within the society.[53] The law was an accurate reflection of a society's morality or lack thereof. If the law unfairly benefitted one sector of the population while being prejudicial to another, it was an obvious indication of the dissipation of the society which had produced it.[54]

Within the purview of the law the concept of liberty had a specific Hobbesian definition: Freedom resided within the perimeters and silence of the law.[55] As Blackstone argued for equity under the law, he lamented those of wealth and political prestige had sought to compose the law as to provide for them unfair advantage, thus thwarting the essential notion of both the law and of rights.[56] This example was to demonstrate the difference between boundaries of these two, especially when entwined: Rights were meant to guarantee its citizens enduring refuge, while the law was staid and obdurate.[57] Yet, the acknowledgement of rights was dependent upon each citizen to possess the knowledge of right from wrong, good from evil, and the ability to choose between them which would reach the more desirable end.[58] Thus, in Blackstone's estimation, the legal restraint of freedom was necessary for the benefit of the general public.[59] Yet there were also legal protections of citizens' rights, among them was due process of law.[60]

There were specifically enumerated several rights which were guaranteed under British law, many of them stated within the *Statute of Westminster of 1275*.[61] Among them being: 1) protections from physical harm to their corporeal being; 2) protections from human actions which endanger human life and wellbeing; and, 3) protections against libel and slander.[62] Also stated was the defense of individual freedom which included that no one would be imprisoned except under the following circumstances: 1) by a fair verdict by a jury of one's peers; 2) Under an edict by the ruling monarch, with the exception being an indictment or subpoena; and, finally, 3) Afforded the right of habeas corpus within a court of law.[63] Furthermore, a citizen could not be forced to pay taxes gleaned without his consent.[64] Another among this list was the injustice of false imprisonment.[65] What Blackstone put forward as personal rights under the law were identical to that of the Framers' in their effort to 'establish justice'.

The Enlightenment political philosophers argued civil liberty was the outgrowth of the social contract, and without the latter to protect and nurture it, the former would not exist. In contrast, Niccolo Machiavelli stated there were only two denominations of states: Those who were adapted to monarchy, and those who were accustomed to freedom.[66] Most disturbing was his advice as to how to conquer a state living under the freedom of its own laws: 1) completely destroy their political institutions; 2) once conquered inhabit the state; and, 3) let the populace continue to live under their own laws while paying tribute to the conqueror.[67] In such a conquest the victor must pay heed to this warning: The ruler who conquers a city whose citizens are acculturated towards liberty, and does not crush such traditions, would fall victim to it regardless of how wise and benevolent be the ruler.[68] Thus, five centuries ago Machiavelli concluded once a populace had experienced liberty, the idea was embedded within its political conscience.

Thomas Hobbes proposed freedom existed solely within the silence and/or interpretation of the written law.[69] The philosopher's definition of a free man was one who had the strength and the will to do what he was able, and unhindered in doing so, though the terms 'liberty' and 'freedom' only applied to corporeal beings.[70] Consistent with Isaac Newton's Third Law of Motion, for every action there was an equal and opposite action, Hobbes argued liberty could not exist without fear.[71] Also, liberty and necessity were corresponding for the former was the result of the latter.[72] Furthermore, the idea of liberty set apart from the law to Hobbes was ridiculous for, in a practical sense, the law held no authority to protect without government; therefore, his conclusion was liberty was not the reward of any individual human being, but an award of the government and its laws.[73]

Hobbes reinforced his argument by pointing that when citizens entered into such an agreement with a sovereign authority, they accepted the amount of liberty provided for them by that sovereign in trade for their safety.[74] With rights, liberties and protections provided by the sovereign, the citizen held an obligation to act in accordance to the edicts of the head of state.[75] There was an exception: When a ruler demanded a subject to do bodily harm either to his own person, or to any other without legitimate cause. At that point the subject had the right to disobey.[76] As rights were a gift of the sovereign and under the legitimate purview of government authority, liberties were dependent upon the "Silence of the law."[77] Furthermore, the degree of rights were arbitrary, some societies having less while others possessed more.[78]

Hugo Grotius considered the philosophical concepts of liberty, equality, rights and justice. He defined liberty as the power a person has over themselves.[79] Nations were not constructed by the intelligence or will of the ruler, but by labors of the people and, therefore, it belonged to them, rather than the political authority which administered the government.[80] When it came to the allocation of rights there were specific contexts: One being the liberty of each individual to sovereignty over themselves which was unreserved; and, two, being a citizen within a society of other human beings which were dictated by a political authority.[81] This was a crucial point, all governments were not constructed for the benefit of the governed, but for the governor.[82] It was up to the political overseer for whom public policies would provide an advantage. Citing both Herodotus and Cicero, Grotius was clear in his assertion: "Kings were constituted to administer Justice to the People."[83]

As the government and the people were one entity, they were both bound by the laws passed under mutual agreement, as well as being liable for any punishments in violating them.[84] Grotius inferred the rights and liberties of the people guaranteed by the government retained the same force of law.[85] If the political authority infringed upon the rights of the citizens or the law, the people held the authority and the right to withdraw their allegiance.[86] In cases of political power gained by force at the cost of liberty, he concluded it was reasonable people would seek to recover their freedom.[87] As for equality Grotius contended justice was achieved among parties who were equivalent in political power.[88] He asserted there were levels of equality based upon a person's position within society.[89]

Grotius provided two separate definitions of rights. The first were private, for the benefit of both the individual and the community.[90] The second definition was personified within the law as obligations for the common good.[91] One citizen's rights did not provide the authority to traverse those of another person.[92] Civil Rights were provided by a political authority as the means by which citizens entered into the social contract for their mutual benefit, and which were subject to agreement between the people and their ruler.[93] It was the sovereign's duty to repeal any laws which interfered or impeded the rights of citizens.[94] Grotius defined justice was the positive consequence of right,[95] while injustice consisted of any political action which discounted any person within the polity from practicing rights guaranteed under the law.[96] Justice demanded punishment for transgression but only from one who lawfully possessed the right to do so.[97]

Algernon Sidney questioned Hobbes' contention the rights of citizens were derived from the sovereign, in the same manner as the divine authority to rule came from God.[98] In his assessment, liberty and monarchy could not co-exist[99] Though in principle he agreed with the foundations of the Hobbesian social contract, he did not concur one among them possessed an authority on the distribution and maintenance of rights and privileges.[100] Equality could only be maintained within a community by a populace who were equal to one another, and not at the discretion of those given an elevated status.[101] Sovereign power was a constraint upon the liberty of citizens, and allowed for the condemnation of those within the polity who claimed superiority over everyone else.[102]

Because all men were borne into liberty, any government which abrogated or impeded the essential liberty of its citizens was a revulsion which acted outside of the natural order of human existence.[103] Sidney qualified his assertion with the premise all honorable people were willing to abide by the law which in turn applied likewise to each citizen.[104] At the center of Sidney's views was the undercurrent of virtue, to which all human beings were born equally into.[105] In the best governed polities, those who were honored above all others had proven to their fellow citizens they were themselves worthy of such distinction, not automatically given due to social rank or position.[106] If a sovereign imposed upon either their liberty or rights under the law, the people had the right to rebel against those magistrates whom had authored such acts.[107] The law was not to be a tool of the sovereign to accomplish his personal aims, but was specifically wrought to protect the natural rights and liberties enjoyed by all citizens.[108]

John Locke echoed many of the ideas of Hobbes, Grotius and Sidney in his discussions on liberty and rights. Mankind in the state of nature was boorish and violent, and without the law and the sovereign power to enforce it, influenced men towards viciousness.[109] Because humans were born into a state of equality in nature, it was their right to share in all the rights afforded them.[110] When people entered into the social contract they agreed "*No man in Civil Society can be exempted from the Law*", as there was redress of grievances for any violation of it, even from the sovereign authorized to enforce it.[111] The rights of citizens within any community or commonwealth cannot exist without the creation of a government.[112] In turn, governments were instituted for preserving and defending the 'life, liberty and property', of those who had freely entered into the social contract.[113] Should the sovereign fail in this responsibility, citizens had not only the right, but the duty to withdraw their allegiance.[114]

John Trenchard and Thomas Gordon cautioned against the onset of tyranny which was, in their minds, an ever-present danger in a free society. The pair defined liberty as a government established for the good of all citizens, and which conducted itself as such.[115] In further outlining the specific tenets involved, they reasoned the foundation of the state was civil liberties, the protection of private property, and the equal justice under the law as being essential.[116] The pair indicated due to the nature of the social contract, no one was truly independent of society or religion, nor could they give up their essential rights to anyone else, nor possessed the authority to diminish those said rights to the following generations.[117] In practice, freedom also comprised of one's control over their individual actions, the right to enjoy the outcomes of their own efforts, and that it does not injure anyone else in the community.[118]

Corruption had been an intrinsic problem with all governments due to the instinctual greed of human beings, and it was the duty of every citizen to guard against it.[119] But in the struggle between liberty and power, if the citizen was not attentive in the protection of the former, the avarice of the one would eventually overtake the freedom of the many.[120] Though power was the natural enemy of liberty, the latter could exist without the former.[121] Tyranny was best confirmed by force, along with laws enforced through might, rather than right.[122] Under such conditions any talk of freedom or rights became a crime against the state.[123]

At the center of French philosopher Voltaire's view on rights and liberty was that only government could ensure both: "Freedom means being dependent only on the law."[124] It was a necessary tenet of human civilization, for the law protected the least important citizens from the whims of the most.[125] Liberty under the law and nature were consistent in that it can neither be regulated nor diminished by the law.[126] Yet strict adherence to the law was also shortsighted, as demonstrated by the character of the Englishman in his 1770 work *Dialogues Between A-B-C*, who touted his complete loyalty and obedience to the law, as it was the best bulwark in the protection of his civil liberties.[127] Rights and liberty are lost due to the citizens giving into their fears and not challenging those who sought to undermine them.[128]

Baron de Montesquieu claimed laws were inherent within nature itself, and refined with the evolution of human society.[129] The difference between the two was the former adhered to its laws faithfully and completely, while the latter deviated as the individual so desired.[130] It is in this context he contended law was the outgrowth of the fairness within civil liberties.[131] The state of war began when human beings realized they were masters of their own actions, and thus their fate.[132] It was to escape the state of war human beings banded together and entered into a social contract. Its terms involved rights of both the political authority and the citizen.[133] Montesquieu proposed liberty held as many meanings as there were human beings, each with their own context and perimeters in its comprehension.[134] True liberty was found only in judicious polities, those set up with a tradition of not abusing political power.[135]

Jean-Jacques Rousseau maintained the rights of citizens were entwined within the protections provided by government, and it was not prudent to challenge it unless it acted contrary to the public good.[136] People were born free, and thus they were the only ones who could give up their liberty; but, in renouncing their freedom they gave away their equality among others as well as their natural rights.[137] Doing so to adopt a social contract required the unanimous consent of those persons who entered into it.[138] In such a state all citizens were equal due to their individual commitment to their community, as well as their interdependence upon one another.[139] The conflict of government was best defined by the inconsistent need of its citizens to resolve political conflict in favor of their self-interest.[140] Thus the paradox between government and rights was that liberty could only be nurtured by one's servitude to it.[141] In the end, Rousseau came to a disturbing conclusion: "Freedom can be gained, but never recovered."[142]

Baron Samuel Von Pufendorf argued all law, rights and liberties originated in moral action, itself a reflection of natural law.[143] Law was at the center of human existence within the social contract, and civil liberties were the outgrowth of the laws which guaranteed them.[144] Rights were described as the freedom to use one's natural faculties within the realms of reason, and within the perimeters of the law.[145] Pufendorf asserted once a right was conferred by the sovereign, it was up to the citizens to make one another keep their oath to the social contract, by force of law if necessary.[146] The goal of laws, rights and liberty were to foster the best within the people for the common benefit.[147] He stressed all three elements together represented a commitment which bound society together and consisted of two essential rudiments: Equity and obligation.[148] To possess legitimacy, a right was obligated to provide a moral and ethical foundation for all the partners in the social contract.[149]

In the aftermath of the *Declaration of Independence* in 1776, the first mechanism of American government was wrought in committee under the leadership of John Dickinson: The *Articles of Confederation*. Though not ratified by the individual states until 1 March 1781, the final draft was accepted by the Second Continental Congress as a legitimate instrument of government in early 1777.[150] The system created from the *Articles* was state-centered, with a weak central authority which held the ability to negotiate treaties with other countries, but little else. Any other formal business had to obtain the unanimous approval of all the separate states.[151] Though during the actual war against Great Britain the *Articles* had been effective, when peace finally arrived on 3 September 1783 with the signing of the Treaty of Paris, these sovereign States proved themselves dysfunctional as one nation. Shays' Rebellion during the autumn and winter of 1786/7 had uncovered the inadequacies of the *Articles*, and inevitably led to the realization the creation of a new government was critical.[152]

During the Constitutional Convention the delegates focused their discussions upon practical mechanisms of government rather than the abstract concepts of rights, equality and justice. Their motivation was to rescue a country in freefall due to internal conflicts and popular uprisings. Thus, as Roger Sherman of Connecticut noted during a full session on the 28th of June 1787, in the thoughtful consideration of freedoms and privileges, the question before the delegates was which rights specifically belonged to the citizens as human beings, and those which were the grants of the government.[153] James Wilson of Pennsylvania posed that the delegates all should remember for whom they were constructing this new government, and in doing so, consider the people's reaction towards abstract ideas in times of crisis.[154] Nathaniel Gorham of Massachusetts asserted it had been Great Britain's needless violations of American liberties which had, in turn, influenced them to rebel, but did not elaborate upon which specific freedoms he was referring to.[155] Yet late into the convention proceedings on the 12th of September, George Mason of Virginia proposed a declaration of rights be added, but it was handily defeated.[156] Enumerating which rights were sacrosanct proved an impossible task, let along the determination as to how an instrument of government would effectively protect them.[157]

On the issue of equality Charles Coatesworth Pinckney of South Carolina spoke first, and defined a perfectionistic view of equality. He noted there were people of all classes who lived within its borders, and demanded the same protections as equivalent members of society, and to which they were entitled. It was the duty of the delegates gathered to ensure under a new governing charter that parity amongst all citizens was guaranteed and maintained, to reward industry and to minimalize poverty.[158] The rationale for Pinckney's assertions were based upon the Lockean notion that the accumulation of property was a guaranteed right.[159] He viewed the country as being the composite of three types of citizens: 1) A professional class who focused upon governmental affairs; 2) a commercial class; and, 3) the landed interests.[160] Alexander Hamilton of New York disagreed with Pinckney's assertion of equality, and reasoned inequality would exist so long as liberty did also.[161] Wealth and poverty were constant elements of differentiation in human society.[162] Though Roger Sherman agreed with Hamilton's assessment, he also added so far as equivalence was concerned, should some voluntarily gave more of their freedom than others in the cause of a just society, it would be an effort whose rewards would be reaped by all.[163] Sherman further noted the wealthy who contributed more in taxes to the community provided more of an investment than those of lesser means, but in the end the result was an equitable society.[164]

Issues of liberty, rights, equality, and justice played out more vigorously in the state ratification debates. The Framers were perceptive for to assure their Constitution would remain relevant in changing times, it was be necessary for the document to provide the means for its amending, along with the passage of additional necessary legislation. James Madison touted the flexibility of the Constitution by pointing out the provisions of Article V's amending power.[165] 'The Federal Farmer' critiqued this process as not being sufficiently democratic, for a few with means could use this authority to usurp the constitution altogether.[166] Alexander

Hamilton not only reinforced Madison's assessment, but also stated each amendment was a single proposition and would neither involve, nor evolve into a separate constitution.[167]

The foremost instruments of change within the Constitution were the amending powers of Article V and the Necessary-and-Proper Clause of Article I § 8. Under the procedures of Article V an amendment first needed the approval of two-thirds of both houses of Congress. After its passage, it was sent to the States, where their legislatures must either endorse, or defeat it.[168] When three-fourths of the State legislatures have approved the proposed amendment, it was then deemed ratified and added to the body of the Constitution where, under the authority of Article VI Paragraph 2, it became "the supreme law of the land".[169] James Madison disallowed the notion of the 'The Federal Farmer', if the Constitution was ratified, a constitutional convention must be called at every occasion the document needed to be amended.[170] Alexander Hamilton's reasoning was a direct attack upon the unanimity required of the *Articles of Confederation*, in that the ratification of the new federal constitution would resolve all the controversies surrounding it.[171]

The Necessary-and-Proper Clause of Article I § 8 was catalogued as one of the powers enumerated among many given specifically to the Congress. There was no further description or perimeters provided as to what constituted what was "necessary" or "proper"—the definition of which was left to the generations who followed to determine for themselves. Without such specificity it was not implausible a law wholly inconsistent with the Constitution could be passed by both houses of the Congress. This situation left it within the purview of either the president to thwart from becoming law through the veto power of Article II § 2; or, to mount a legal challenge to the Supreme Court and concluded with a decision rendered by that body as to its constitutionality. To the Federalists such checks upon power within these separate but equal branches of government was enough of a bulwark against political corruption.

But the greatest fear of the Anti-Federalists was the inherent power within this clause, in consort with the Supreme Law Clause of Article VI Paragraph 2, which would render the federal government in a position of dictatorship over the states. 'Brutus' claimed as the powers rendered under this clause were undefined, it provided the federal government with the authority to pass any law it saw fit, fair or not.[172] The author further contended with this authority listed within the document itself as a legitimate power given to the Congress, the Supreme Court would be powerless to nullify any law as inconsistent with the Constitution.[173]

Hamilton addressed this charge by stating such a power was consistent within all structures of government, whether state, national or otherwise.[174] Though he did not deny the clause held the authority the Anti-Federalist author claimed, Hamilton was noticeably careful not to definitively affirm it. He maintained arguments calling suspicion to this clause were those who sought to curtail as much governmental power as was in their legal authority to do so.[175] Such sovereignty was necessary to avoid the gridlock which had plagued the central government under the *Articles of Confederation*.[176] James Madison claimed any government lacking such authority would be powerless.[177] He then denigrated the clause's critics, claiming the Anti-Federalists had not offered any viable alternative.[178]

Within the context of American constitutional government personal liberties are the most intangible, as they are not clearly enumerated. They guarantee individuals will not only be secure in themselves, but also free to engage in the activities of their choice within the perimeters of the law. In short, they embody the citizens' right to be themselves, to hold whatever beliefs, morals and values they choose, and to pursue individual definitions of happiness without the intrusion of either the government, or other people. Thus, it is noteworthy the framers placed within the Preamble the goal of securing "the Blessings of Liberty" without concurrently inserting any specific clauses designed for that purpose. There are but two general clauses placed within the text itself which promote this adage: The Transportation Clause of Article IV § 2 and the No-Religious-Tests Clause of Article VI Paragraph 3.[179]

For the Anti-Federalists the inference that civil liberties were already innately protected was inadequate. They were quick to point out the Constitution did not contain a "bill of rights", in stark contrast to every State constitution at the time of ratification. 'The Federal Farmer' explained there were inalienable rights which were granted when citizens entered into the social contract, and they were of such a sacred nature the people would never disavow them at the whim of their sovereign.[180] 'Brutus' warned that by their unwillingness to include a declarations of rights, the Federalists were laboring to deceive the public while convincing them to ratify their own slavery.[181]

Alexander Hamilton maintained listing such protections was unnecessary. He first explained the purpose of a federal constitution was to govern, it was the responsibility of the individual states, through the instrument of their specific governing documents, to protect the rights of citizens.[182] Secondly, it was inappropriate to place the execution of such powers upon the federal government, as it depleted the individual States of their unique role within the Union.[183] The final protestation was the excessive cost to the federal government in the enforcement of any rights mandated to the people under the Constitution.[184]

In the interpretation of the Constitution, it is critical the document be read in its entirety, for as stated earlier, one clause is a part of a much larger picture when placed within the context of others. Due to the often ambiguous wording of the clauses, the construction of a consistent constitutional argument requires more than one clause to provide a level of specificity, especially when it pertains to civil liberties.

Such was the case with the doctrine of Church-and-State separation. Article VI paragraph 3 asserted: "[N]o religious test shall ever be required as a qualification to any office or public trust under the United States".[185] In this clause the Constitution guaranteed the right of people of all faiths, as well as those who do not hold such beliefs, whether they are citizens or residents, their inalienable right to serve the country as they see fit. In the assessment of James Madison such a clause was vital as a means of uniting the people under the Constitution, while thwarting religious-based bigotry:

> A zeal for different opinions concerning religion…have, in turn, divided mankind into parties, inflamed them with mutual animosity, and rendered them much more disposed to vex and oppress each other, than to co-operate for their common good.[186]

In addition, the First Amendment stated: "Congress shall make no law respecting an establishment of religion, or prohibiting the free exercise of".[187] In this clause the federal government was prohibited from passing any law granting ascent to any religious faith above any and all others. More succinct, though a sizeable majority of American citizens hold to the Christian faith, the federal government was specifically proscribed by the Constitution from passing a law which provided any religious faith an elevated status. It also barred the denigration of any religious faith into an inferior status and, when coupled with Article VI' No-Religious-Test Clause, allowed those of any and all faiths the opportunity to serve within the government of the United States.

The Fourth Amendment guaranteed "The right of the people to be secure in their persons, houses, papers and effects": Thus, one's corporeal being, personal attitudes, behaviors and conduct were protected from legal intercession so long as they did not infringe upon the same rights of others.[188] In this clause, within the context of church-and-state separation, every one possessed not only the right to hold whatever religious faith they so choose, but they were protected from persecution or legal denigration because of it, thus reinforcing the Establishment Clause of the First Amendment. Finally, the Fourteenth Amendment pledged "No state shall make or enforce any law which shall abridge the privileges or immunities of citizens of the United States; nor deny to any person within its jurisdiction the equal protection of the laws".[189] When placed within the context of the clauses cited above, the Fourteenth Amendment assured neither one religion, nor any of its adherents held any legal ascendency over any other. Believers and non-believers alike would not have their faith held against them in any American court on a religious basis alone.

Again, when taken together the Constitution clearly stated not only are church and state not to be entwined, but every belief or non-belief was acceptable within the United States. Every person, not just citizen under the authority of the U.S. federal government would not be persecuted for either holding a specific belief, practicing their faith, or injuring the rights and privileges of others with their religious inclinations. Finally, these specific clauses also guaranteed religion would hold neither exultance nor influence upon public policy, and neither would the government interfere with the conduct of churches so long as they act within the laws which governed the country as a whole.

Another potent example are the First Amendment protections of both free speech, protest and the press. With regard to the first, under the aegis of the First Amendment not only do citizens possess the right to free speech, but also the right to redress their grievances to the government, along with the right to peaceably assemble.[190] Thus, not only do we have the right to speak our minds, we have the right act in a peaceful manner in accordance with them. It was the Framers' fervent belief that the republic was best served when citizens expressed their views candidly, and when the press, no matter their ideological bent, reported the timbre of the debate, as well as printed its content. Benjamin Franklin asserted that free speech and expression was the foundation of a free government, and when this right was stifled, a government based upon liberty had ceased to exist.[191] They wanted spirited public debate and the last thing they intended was a populace too scared to speak up when they suspected questionable actions were being wrought by their government.

Concurrently, though all speech was protected, actions against fellow citizens wrought at the behest of such speech was not. This paradigm was reaffirmed by the U.S. Supreme Court, in *Chaplinsky v. New Hampshire* (1942), in which the Court speaking through Associate Justice Frank Murphy specified:

> Appellant assails the statute as a violation of all three freedoms, speech, press and worship, but only an attack on the basis of free speech is warranted. The spoken, not the written, word is involved. And we cannot conceive that cursing a public officer is the exercise of religion in any sense of the term. But even if the activities of the appellant which preceded the incident could be viewed as religious in character, and therefore entitled to the protection

> of the Fourteenth Amendment, they would not cloak him with immunity from the legal consequences for concomitant acts committed in violation of a valid criminal statute.[192]

Thus, no matter how objectionable or repugnant, free speech was protected, but the actions wrought from it were not, as they violate Fourth and Fourteenth Amendment protections of personal safety and equitable treatment under the law. Thus, the assurance of civil liberties also mandated the accessory of personal responsibility in their conduct. It was the bargain all citizens made when they entered into a social contract, which in the United States was embodied in the Constitution.

Finally, The Fourth Amendment guaranteed every citizen the fundamental right "to be secure in one's person".[193] In plain terms, this clause required both State and Federal governments hold the charge to keep citizens safe from people and objects which can and will do them harm. In *Poe v. Ullman* (1961), the Court, speaking through Justice John Marshall Harlan II, stated this definition of the Fourth Amendment's Security Clause was "a rational continuum which, broadly speaking, includes a freedom from all substantial arbitrary impositions and purposeless restraints."[194] Four years later, in *Griswold v. Connecticut* (1965) its meaning was expanded to include the right of citizens to their privacy. The Court speaking through Justice William O. Douglas explained:

> We deal with a right of privacy older than the Bill of Rights—older than our political parties, older than our school system. Marriage is a coming together for better or for worse, hopefully enduring, and intimate to the degree of being sacred. It is an association that promotes a way of life, not causes; a harmony in living, not political faiths; a bilateral loyalty, not commercial or social projects. Yet it is an association for as noble a purpose as any involved in our prior decisions.[195]

Thus, when somebody has fired a gun against another person causing them bodily harm, they have violated their essential constitutional right to be safe. It reiterates once again the paradigm put forward by the Framers: No right is absolute. One's rights end when they intrude upon those of another. To many this seems as a serious infringement upon the constitutional concept of "the blessings of liberty"; yet, in real sense, it is the sole manner by which a large cadre of people can live, flourish and thrive with some degree of freedom within the confines of civilization.

The question remains not which definition of freedom is the superlative, but how best to incorporate drive and ambition with civility and society to achieve a governing consensus. We can all agree freedom is foremost: The question is what form it takes to benefit the majority of American citizens. In our contemporary times we have witnessed the redefinition of liberty: The comprehensive invasion of our thoughts, lives and past to maintain our freedom. This theory was designed to root out potential national enemies as they covertly engage in clandestine activities against us. It is the embodiment of what author George Orwell termed as 'Doublethink': The paradigm of accepting two entirely conflicting ideas as a single truth.[196]

So what did the Framers mean by "the blessings of liberty"?

On the surface the phrase seems to be a literary generality reinforcing limitations on government power coupled with specific rights given to each American citizen. To the contrary, it was specific in both its meaning and its outcomes. James Wilson defined it as civil liberties: "[A] part of natural liberty [that] retains the free and generous exercise of all the human faculties, so far as it is compatible with the public welfare".[197] Alexander Hamilton demarcated them as social privileges which were denied revision and usurpation from the governments which guaranteed them.[198] As examples, Hamilton cited *Magna Carta*, the 1628 *Petition of Right*, and the 1689 *British Bill of Rights*.[199] 'The Federal Farmer' concurred with both Wilson's definition and Hamilton's examples.[200]

This constitutional conception of "the blessings of liberty" has its foundation the Lockean principle of active liberty: Once a group of people enter into the social contract they together possess the obligation to protect the liberty of all others in the society.[201] Within the construct of political society, each citizen is dependent upon all other members for their security and livelihood, as well as the abstract elements, features that could never be guaranteed within the state of nature. Stephen Breyer, associate justice of the United States Supreme Court, defined this concept as "an idea of freedom as old as antiquity, the freedom of the individual citizen to participate in the government and thereby share with others the right to make or to control the nation's public acts."[202] Liberty was neither the product of individual initiative, nor designed for the benefit of the individual: It was a group of people working together towards their common goal of freedom within the rules of their collective society.

John Adams stated in his 1776 work *Thoughts on Government* "the happiness of society is the end of government".[203] This is a bold assertion which begs a vital question: Of what intrinsic value is any government which favors one sector of the population over others; whose policies benefit one group, but not all; and, if the laws of society denigrate any group within the general public while coddling others? Under the Framers' definition, any such actions violate specific and essential constitutional protections. As citizen and representative alike were bound by the social contract, any violation nullifies the agreement between them, and thus causes the society itself to disintegrate.

Liberty has never been a 'safe' proposition, as demonstrated by the founding generation who engaged from a long, bloody war to gain this nation's independence. We dishonor them with every new piece of legislation which circumvents the rights for which they gave their lives, fortunes and sacred honor. If we, the people continue to accept the blatant subversion of our civil liberties to preserve our domiciles, we all shall wake up one day to find the door has been bolted and our every move under close scrutiny. And only then will we realize the value of the freedom we have so thoughtlessly given away.

Notes

1. Thomas Hobbes, *Leviathan*, ed. Richard Tuck (New York: Cambridge University Press, 1996), 89.
2. Aristotle, *The Constitution of the Athenians*, Section I, Part 2, trans. Sir Frederick G. Kenyon; at The Internet Classics Archive; http://classics.mit.edu/Aristotle/athenian_const.mb.txt. Accessed 14 June 2018.
3. *Ibid.*, Section I, Parts 8 and 16.
4. *Ibid.*, Section III, Part 63.
5. *Ibid.*, Section I, Part 22.
6. *Ibid.*, Section II, Part 39.
7. Plato, *The Republic*, trans. Francis MacDonald Cornford (New York: Oxford University Press, 1941), 267.
8. *Ibid.*, 282.
9. *Ibid.*, 283, 286.
10. *Ibid.*, 288.
11. Aristotle, *The Politics*, trans. Thomas Alan Sinclair, 1992 Edition (New York: Penguin Books, 1962), 168, 198.
12. *Ibid.*, 169.
13. *Ibid.*, 195.
14. *Ibid.*, 196.
15. *Ibid.*
16. *Ibid.*
17. *Ibid.*, 362.
18. *Ibid.*
19. *Ibid.*
20. *Ibid.*

21. Herodotus, *The Histories*, trans. Aubrey De Sélincourt. 1996 Reprint (New York: Penguin Books, 1954), 187–9.
22. *Ibid.*, 187.
23. *Ibid.*
24. *Ibid.*
25. *Ibid.*, 188.
26. *Ibid.*
27. *Ibid.*
28. *Ibid.*, 326.
29. Thucydides, *History of the Peloponnesian War*, trans. Rex Warner. 1972 Reprint (New York: Penguin Books, 1954), 74.
30. *Ibid.*, 147.
31. *Ibid.*, 213.
32. *Ibid.*, 577.
33. Livy, *Rome and the Mediterranean*, trans. Henry Bettenson. (New York: Penguin Books, 1976), 143.
34. Livy, *The War with Hannibal*, trans. Aubrey De Sélincourt. (New York: Penguin Books, 1965), 262.
35. Livy, *The Early History of Rome*, trans. Aubrey De Sélincourt. 1971 Reprint (New York: Penguin Books, 1960), 372. Cicero, "Pro Miloni"; in *The Speeches of M. Tullius Cicero*, ed. Herbert C. D. Blakiston. Reprint of 1894 edition (London: Forgotten Books, 2015), 150.
36. Cicero, "On the Law"; in *On the Commonwealth and On the Laws*, ed. James E. G. Zetzel (New York: Cambridge University Press, 1999), I20.
37. Cicero, *On Duties*, eds. M. T. Griffin and E. M. Atkings (Cambridge, England: Cambridge University Press, 1991), 14.
38. Cicero, "On the Law", in *On the Commonwealth and On the Laws*, 158.
39. Cicero, *On Duties*, 28.
40. Cicero, *On Duties*, 71.
41. Tacitus, *The Annals of Imperial Rome*, trans. Michael Grant. 1996 Reprint (New York: Penguin Books, 1956), 132.
42. David Hume, *The History of England From the Invasion of Julius Caesar to the Abdication of James II* (Boston: Phillips, Sampson, and Company, 1854), I: 429.
43. Frederick Pollard and Frederic William Maitland, *The History of English Law Before the Time of Edward I* (New York: Cambridge University Press, 1923), I: 173.
44. *Magna Carta* (1215); at http://www.constitution.org/eng/magnacar.htm. Accessed 15 June 2018.
45. Brutus, Letter #XVI, 30 January 1988, in *The Anti-Federalist: Writings by the Opponents of the Constitution*, ed. Herbert Storing (Chicago, IL: University of Chicago Press, 1981), 81.
46. 3 Car 1 c 1. This law is popularly known as the *Petition of Right* (1628).

47. 1 William & Mary Sess 2 c 2. This law is popularly known as *An Act Declaring the Rights and Liberties of the Subject and Settling the Succession of the Crown* (1689).
48. William Blackstone, *Commentaries on the Laws of England*, ed. William Draper Lewis, Reprint of 1922 edition (Clark, NJ: The Lawbook Exchange, 2004), IV: 1794.
49. *Ibid.*, I: 107–8.
50. *Ibid.*
51. *Ibid.*, I: 108.
52. *Ibid.*
53. *Ibid.*, I: 108–9.
54. *Ibid.*, I: 109.
55. *Ibid.*, I: 3.
56. *Ibid.*
57. *Ibid.*, I: 109–10.
58. *Ibid.*, I: 111.
59. *Ibid.*
60. *Ibid.*, I: 122.
61. *The Statute of Westminster of 1275*, 3. Edw. 1 c. 5 (1275).
62. Blackstone, I: 22.
63. Blackstone, I: 122–3.
64. *Ibid.*, I: 128–9.
65. *Ibid.*, III: 1124.
66. Niccolo Machiavelli, *The Prince*, eds. Quentin Skinner and Russell Price (New York: Cambridge University Press, 1988), 5.
67. *Ibid.*, 17–8.
68. *Ibid.*, 18.
69. Hobbes, 145, 194.
70. *Ibid.*, 146.
71. *Ibid.*
72. *Ibid.*, 146–7.
73. *Ibid.*, 147–9.
74. *Ibid.*, 150.
75. *Ibid.*
76. *Ibid.*, 151.
77. *Ibid.*, 152.
78. *Ibid.*
79. Hugo Grotius, *The Rights of War and Peace*, ed. Richard Tuck (Indianapolis, IN: The Liberty Fund, 2005), I: 138.
80. Grotius, I: 288.
81. *Ibid.*, I: 272.
82. *Ibid.*, I: 273.

83. *Ibid.*, I: 273–4.
84. *Ibid.*, I: 372–3; II: 604–5; II: 1142.
85. *Ibid.*
86. *Ibid.*, I: 376–7. Algernon Sidney, *Discourses Concerning Government*, ed. Thomas G. West (Indianapolis, IN: The Liberty Fund, 1996), 519. John Locke, *Two Treatises of Government*, ed. Peter Laslett (New York: Cambridge University Press, 1960), 412.
87. Grotius, II: 503. This point is reiterated in II: 1145.
88. *Ibid.*, I: 137.
89. *Ibid.*, II: 550–1.
90. *Ibid.*, I: 140.
91. *Ibid.*, I: 148. This point was reiterated in I: 156–7; II: 420.
92. *Ibid.*, I: 149.
93. *Ibid.*, I: 162; II: 505–6; II: 810.
94. *Ibid.*, II: 810–11.
95. *Ibid.*, II: 1132.
96. *Ibid.*, II: 451.
97. *Ibid.*, II: 953.
98. Sidney, 34.
99. *Ibid.*, 78.
100. *Ibid.*
101. *Ibid.*, 80.
102. *Ibid.*, 191.
103. *Ibid.*, 192.
104. *Ibid.*, 193.
105. *Ibid.*, 253.
106. *Ibid.*
107. *Ibid.*, 519. Grotius, I: 376–7. Locke, 412.
108. Sidney, 368.
109. Locke, 182.
110. *Ibid.*, 190.
111. *Ibid.*, 330. The italics are that of the original author.
112. *Ibid.*, 336.
113. *Ibid.*, 350.
114. *Ibid.*, 406–7.
115. John Trenchard and Thomas Gordon, "Essay #24", 8 April 1720; in *Cato's Letters; or, Essays on Liberty, Civil and Religious, and Other Important Subjects*, ed. Ronald Hamowy (Indianapolis, IN: The Liberty Fund, 1995), I: 176.
116. John Trenchard and Thomas Gordon, "Essay #63", 27 January 1721; in *Ibid.*, I: 436.
117. John Trenchard and Thomas Gordon, "Essay #59", 30 December 1721; in *Ibid.*, I: 406–7.
118. John Trenchard and Thomas Gordon, "Essay #62", 27 January 1721; in *Ibid.*, I: 427.

119. John Trenchard and Thomas Gordon, "Essay #60", 6 January 1721; in *Ibid.*, I: 416.
120. *Ibid.*
121. John Trenchard and Thomas Gordon, "Essay #33", 17 June 1721; in *Ibid.*, I: 239.
122. John Trenchard and Thomas Gordon, "Essay #63", 27 January 1721; in *Ibid.*, I: 437.
123. John Trenchard and Thomas Gordon, "Essay #129", 18 May 1723; in *Ibid.*, II: 895.
124. Voltaire, "Questions sur l'Encyclopédie" ("Questions on the Encyclopedia"), 1769; in *Political Writings*, ed. David Williams (New York: Cambridge University Press, 1994), 59. This is a point reiterated by Voltaire in his "Thoughts on Public Administration", 1752; in *Ibid.*, 216.
125. Voltaire, "L'A.B.C. Dialogue curieux" ("Dialogues Between A-B-C"), 1770; in *Ibid.*, 174.
126. *Ibid.*, 166.
127. *Ibid.*, 106.
128. *Ibid.*, 141.
129. Baron de Montesquieu, *Spirit of the Laws*, eds. Anne Cohler, Basia Miller, and Harold Stone (New York: Cambridge University Press, 1989), 3–4.
130. *Ibid.*, 4.
131. *Ibid.*
132. *Ibid.*, 7.
133. *Ibid.*
134. *Ibid.*, 154–5.
135. *Ibid.*, 155.
136. Jean-Jacques Rousseau, "Of the Social Contract", 1762; in, *The Social Contract and Other Later Political Writings*, ed. Victor Gourevitch (New York: Cambridge University Press, 1996), 119.
137. *Ibid.*, 45.
138. *Ibid.*, 123.
139. *Ibid.*, 61.
140. *Ibid.*, 105.
141. *Ibid.*, 115.
142. *Ibid.*, 73.
143. Samuel von Pufendorf, *Of the Law of Nature and Nations*, 8 vols., Reprint of 1712 edition, ed. Basil Kennet (Andover, Hampshire, England: Gale ECCO Print Editions; 2005), I: 58–9.
144. *Ibid.*, I: 59.
145. *Ibid.*, I: 59, 64.
146. *Ibid.*, I: 61. Sidney, 474. Locke, 406–7.
147. Pufendorf, III: 22–3.
148. *Ibid.*, III: 44–7.
149. *Ibid.*, III: 48.

150. Jack N. Rakove, *Original Meanings: Politics and Ideas in the Making of the Constitution* (New York: Alfred A. Knopf, 1977), 188–9.
151. *The Articles of Confederation*, Section II.
152. Rakove, 33–4.
153. Roger Sherman, quoted in James Madison, *Notes of Debates in the Federal Constitution of 1787* (Athens, OH: Ohio University Press, 1966, 1985), 208.
154. James Wilson, quoted in *Ibid.*, 221.
155. Nathan Gorham, quoted in *Ibid.*, 174.
156. *Ibid.*, 630.
157. *Ibid.*, 485–6, 630.
158. The views of Charles Coatesworth Pinckney summarized from *Ibid.*, 181.
159. *Ibid.*, 184–5.
160. *Ibid.*, 185–6.
161. *Ibid.*, 196.
162. *Ibid.*
163. *Ibid.*, 208.
164. *Ibid.*
165. James Madison, "Essay #40", in *The Federalist,* The Gideon Edition, eds. George W. Carey and James McClellan (Indianapolis, IN: The Liberty Fund, 2001), 201.
166. The Federal Farmer, Letter #IV, 12 October 1787; in *The Anti-Federalist*, 59.
167. Alexander Hamilton, Essay #85, in *The Federalist,* 456.
168. *United States Constitution*, Article V.
169. *United States Constitution*, Article V; Article VI.
170. The Federal Farmer, Letter #IV, 12 October 1787; in *The Anti-Federalist*, 59. James Madison, Essay #49, in *The Federalist,* 261.
171. Alexander Hamilton, Essay #85, in *The Federalist,* 456.
172. Brutus, Essay #I, 18 October 1787; in *The Anti-Federalist*, 112. The author reiterated this point in his Essay #5, dated 13 December 1787, in, *The Anti-Federalist*, 133–8.
173. Brutus, Essay #XI, 31 January 1788; in *The Anti-Federalist*, 166. This is a reference to the power of judicial review later asserted by Chief Justice John Marshall in *Marbury v. Madison* (1803). *Marbury v. Madison*, 5 U.S. 37 (1803).
174. Alexander Hamilton, Essay #33, in *The Federalist*, 158.
175. *Ibid.*, 159.
176. *Ibid.*, 161.
177. James Madison, Essay #44, in *The Federalist*, 233.
178. *Ibid.*
179. *U.S. Constitution*, Article IV § 2. *U.S. Constitution*, Article VI.
180. The Federal Farmer, Letter #II, 9 October 1787; in *The Anti-Federalist*, 40–1.
181. Brutus, Essay #II, 1 November 1787; in *The Anti-Federalist*, 122.
182. Alexander Hamilton, Essay #84, in *The Federalist*, 447.
183. *Ibid.*

184. *Ibid.*, 449.
185. *United States Constitution*, Article VI paragraph 3.
186. James Madison, Essay #10, in *The Federalist*, 44.
187. *United States Constitution*, First Amendment.
188. *United States Constitution*, Fourth Amendment.
189. *United States Constitution*, Fourteenth Amendment.
190. *U.S Constitution*, First Amendment.
191. Benjamin Franklin, "On Freedom of Speech and the Press", *Pennsylvania Gazette*, 20 November 1735; in Benjamin Franklin, *The Memoirs of Benjamin Franklin*, ed. William Temple Franklin (Philadelphia, PA: McCarty & Davis, 1840) II: 431.
192. *Chaplinsky v. New Hampshire*, 315 U.S. 568; 571 (1942).
193. *U.S. Constitution*, Fourth Amendment.
194. *Poe v. Ullman*, 367 U.S. 497; 543 (1961).
195. *Griswold v. Connecticut*, 381 U.S. 479; 486 (1965).
196. George Orwell, *1984* (New York: Penguin Group, 1983), 36.
197. James Wilson, Speech at the Pennsylvania Ratification Convention, 24 November 1787; in *Friends of the Constitution: Writings of the "Other" Federalists 1787–1788*, eds. Colleen A. Sheehan and Gary L. McDowell (Indianapolis, IN: The Liberty Fund; 1998), 82.
198. Alexander Hamilton, Essay #84, in *The Federalist,* 445.
199. *Ibid.*
200. The Federal Farmer, Letter #VI, 25 December 1787; in *The Anti*-Federalist, 71.
201. Locke, 353.
202. Stephen Breyer, *Active Liberty Interpreting Our Democratic Constitution* (New York: Alfred A. Knopf, 2005), 3.
203. John Adams, "Thoughts on Government: Applicable to the Present State of the American Colonies", 1776; in *The Revolutionary Writings of John Adams,* ed. C. Bradley Thompson (Indianapolis, IN: The Liberty Fund, 2000), 287.

Epilogue: "Do Ordain and Establish"

The Constitution and the Modern American Citizen

The United States has lost its way. Over the past several decades our elected representatives have scorned, and then deserted our nation's charter. And we are all to blame, each and every one of us: Conservatives and Liberals alike for championing destructive policies, and not fighting more effectively against their introduction. Foremost, we have fallen victims to our history, for we were content to be mere spectators while charlatans posing as servants of the people concocted and implemented legislative 'end-runs' which circumvented the Constitution, and with it undermined the very foundations of the American republic.

This country has abandoned its progressive Enlightenment legacy in the name of egotism and avarice. Our nation was borne from insurrection, a revolt against what we, the people had perceived as the tyrannical rule of a foreign power. It was to that end we established a government under laws, not inherited political power—a cause to which the Framers pledged their lives, their fortunes and their sacred honor to create. And we abandoned it all as we were self-centered, scared and greedy.

This country was once at the forefront of civil liberties. Our music echoed with a yearning for freedom, peace and justice. We used our popular media to inform and educate upon the social ills afflicting our nation, all while providing us with the moral conscience to do something about it. But we are now content to wallow in the insatiable excess of sex, gluttony and violence, craving ever more solely for our own curiosity and satisfaction. Is it any wonder why the nation is on the verge of self-destruction?

This country once truly believed in peace among our fellow nations of the world and intervened only when necessary, in the words of President Woodrow Wilson, "To make the world safe for democracy".[1] Through the work of former First Lady Eleanor Roosevelt, we championed human rights because it was the right thing to do. With the thrust of our finest minds, we sojourned into space and landed on the moon because a visionary president challenged us to. Yet, when some among us found they could make large profits for themselves by waging constant war, they convinced us that the rest of the world hated us for our freedom.[2] Afterward, a continuous slew of enemies arose, and collectively we abandoned human rights without any consideration of the cost in lives, both military and civilian, on all sides. And as the casualties mount, so do the profits of corporations, CEOs and shareholders.

When did we, the people ordain this? How was it ordained? And what does the future hold for a constitutional republic that has abandoned its constitution?

Since the close of the Second World War the military has been the driving force of the American national economy. Coupled with the death of domestic manufacturing through globalization and deregulation, defense spending is all that allows the United States to remain economically viable. As such, we have placed ourselves in the same situation as the European nations of a century ago, who found in concentrating their economic resources on a permanent arms industry, they either had to sell their weapons or use them to maintain their fiscal health. But it also brings to the fore several serious questions.

In our present economic state how long can the United States continue to assert itself as the world's police force? With our public education system in tatters, our infrastructure crumbling, our domestic economy outsourced to the point of an underemployment epidemic, can we honestly afford to plunge our country into further long-term military commitments? Or is it that we have no real choice, as American jobs are at stake? If we have, indeed, reached military overstretch, as predicted by historian Paul Kennedy a quarter-century ago, will the next military intervention be the final nail in the coffin of the American empire?[3]

In his *Second Treatise on Government* John Locke argued citizens not only possessed the right to protest acts of government, but they also held the duty to withdraw their allegiance.[4] Furthermore, this nation was founded upon the right of the citizens to protest and to rebel.[5] American citizens are now too paranoid of the world, as well as of themselves. They seek safety within the cloak of "law-and-order" and are willing to sacrifice their essential liberties to obtain it. Just as with the Communists over six-decades ago, they believe terrorists are lurking in every shadow, behind every corner looking for an opportunity to destroy "the American way of life".

Fear is the most influential of human emotions. Throughout human history it has been used by governments to hoist questionable policies upon their citizens. In that arena it requires a "great-Satan" as the target for manufactured hate, and when that foe has been toppled, it demands another enemy be created to keep the citizenry from discovering the true motives at work. After several generations of pointed national aggression, there have been a brave few who possessed the courage to speak truth to power. They have uncovered the unpleasant reality that within "a government of the people, by the people, and for the people", as President Abraham Lincoln so eloquently phrased it, essential rights have been undermined in the name of security.[6] Furthermore, the government has attempted not only to detain and incarcerate these brave citizens, but to destroy their personal reputation to maintain control over the masses and feed its collective hate. Such concentrated emotion has divided the populace against itself which, in turn, has rendered it powerless to force the government to change direction. This 'modus-operendi' has been woven within the fabric of American society in the incendiary debates over issues such as race, gender, religion, and sexual preference and identity—all of which divert attention away from policies which benefitted corporations over people, authorized wars in foreign countries to control their vital resources, and the established laws to render null and void the Constitution.

Not since the Civil War has American politics been so hopelessly divided, so adverse to political compromise. Citizens have become entrenched within an "either/or" political mentality which has inspired domestic disquiet and national divergence, wrought by popular media outlets who financially thrive on such dissonance. It is evocative of Orson Welles' masterpiece *Citizen Kane*, ranked among the greatest motion pictures ever made by the American Film Institute.[7] It is the story of newspaper magnate who acquired a fortune through the manipulation and distortion of the news.[8] At the turn of the last century, news magnates such as Joseph Pulitzer and William Randolph Hearst raked in millions of dollars every day with the practice of 'yellow journalism': The notion if reporters did not possess the facts, they simply made them up.[9] And everyday millions read these dailies and believed every word as gospel.

In our time six corporations own over 90% of news media outlets.[10] With the advent of digital media and the worldwide web, information is universal and there is no limit as to what can be posted, accurate or not. With this technology people possess the capability to access only the news which suits their specific ideology, and then to believe it with absolute certainty. The success of partisan politics is based upon perception: If people believe it to be true, in their minds it is true, and no evidence to the contrary will shift that perception.[11] Thus, if a person already holds distrust for the government specific news agencies nurture this proclivity until it festers into outright hatred, without the subject being aware this transformation has taken place. On the other hand, for those who support government policy, news feeds nurture their worldview in the same manner until the extreme is reached.

What is lost is *the truth*. Context and facts are nowhere to be found in the shuffle of propaganda which solely benefits those performing the manipulation. The evolution from hard news to propaganda began with the Reagan administration's rescinding of the Federal Communication Commission's Fairness Doctrine in 1987.[12] This cycle was made public when New World Communications of Tampa, Florida, a Fox News affiliate, was sued by an investigative reporter and former employee Jane Akre.[13] Defense counsel argued the First Amendment's Free Speech Clause provided the news outlet with its constitutional right to misinform their viewers.[14] What the public failed to comprehend in this instance was that nearly all media outlets engage in such practices, and under such circumstances the truth is obfuscated under the blare of ideologues on all sides shouting at the top of their lungs.[15]

When the federal constitution was ratified in 1788, it made a specific promise to all Americans to 'insure domestic tranquility'. As of late our government actively coddles brokerage, insurance and financial institutions who contribute to rising unemployment and homelessness. Our representatives give in to the will of lobbyists for the campaign cash they promise. Taxes are continuously lowered for the wealthiest 1% of the population, while our nation's public school systems produce functionally miseducated students, and its once formidable infrastructure crumbles into dust. All of these things and more have been wrought in the name of money. Thus, how have these policies met the constitutional obligation to 'insure domestic tranquility'?

Then there are those who advocate a violent overthrow of the government. In 2014 the popular media touted the results of a poll in which 25% of American citizens believed their state should secede from the Union.[16] More disturbing was 44% of self-described Republicans favored an armed insurrection to preserve their rights from federal government encroachment.[17] Do these people honestly believe if they launched a revolution armed with domestically sold firearms they would emerge victorious against the might of a government armed with drones and nuclear weapons?

In his essay #29 in *The Federalist*, Alexander Hamilton argued the government created by the Constitution had the inalienable right to exist and, thus, also possessed the authority to do whatever was necessary to preserve itself.[18] Article VI reinforces Hamilton's assertion by stating all laws made under the authority of the Constitution and the government created by it are the "supreme law of the land".[19] Also, the Preamble, the mission statement of the Constitution, specifically stated the government had the obligation to both 'insure domestic tranquility' [and] 'provide for the common defense'.[20] Any armed insurrection by definition would be a threat to that charge and, thus, would incur the full wrath of the federal government, and armed citizens would not stand a chance.

Historical precedent for such actions are numerous. During the Pullman Strike of 1894, thirteen strikers were killed and fifty-seven were wounded when President Grover Cleveland ordered U.S. marshals to break up a strike which had crippled the railroad industry for over three months.[21] In the Lattimer Massacre of 10 September 1897 nineteen unarmed striking mine workers were killed and thirty-six were wounded near Hazleton, Pennsylvania by a posse organized by the Luzerne County sheriff for refusing to disperse.[22] When a group of World War One veterans marched on the Capitol in 1932, President Herbert Hoover ordered the army under the command of General Douglas MacArthur to disperse the crowd by any necessary means.[23] Finally, in 1970, college students protesting the escalation of the Vietnam War at both Kent State University and Jackson State University were fired upon by members of the National Guard and law enforcement, in which six were killed and over twenty were wounded.[24] Thus, it would be foolhardy to think either of these incidences could not happen again.

But if armed insurrection is not an answer, how then can American citizens regain their rights from a government which has effectively marginalized them? The most successful and effective tactic used in the American past in such struggles has been non-violent non-cooperation: The prime example being Thurgood Marshall's efforts to reverse over a century of discriminatory federal government law by using the Constitution against itself. When dealing with a government which expects violence from 'insurgents', the best tactic is to use peaceful methods to promote change. Such efforts are not without martyrs, but it is the sole means at the citizen's disposal to implement change in a society which seeks safety in "law-and-order".

Over the past seven decades the United States of America has evolved into the very thing the founding generation had fought against during the American

Revolution: An empire. With the successful conclusion of the Spanish-American War in 1898, and with it the defeat of the Spanish Empire, the United States assumed the stewardship of its own colonies: Puerto Rico, Guam and the Philippine Islands.[25] In the afterglow of this victory on 6 December 1904, President Theodore Roosevelt announced to the world the U.S. was, by virtue of its new imperial status, the police force of the world.[26] Subsequently the U.S. abandoned a national economy based upon commercial trade and domestic manufacturing, and embraced instead a state of permanent war in which nearly three-quarters of its national economy was tied to armed conflict. In turn, this country sacrificed its public education, social responsibilities, national infrastructure and, most disturbingly civil liberties to this Hobbesian 'leviathan'. To maintain its national economic solvency, the federal government is obligated to: 1) wage war on at least one front, preferably two;[27] 2) create national enemies abroad with which to involve itself in as a justification for outrageous military spending allocations;[28] 3) encourage armed conflict between other nations or terrorist groups to procure further customers;[29] and, 4) maintain a large deployment of troops abroad as the means to exclude them from a domestic economy that can neither absorb nor sustain them.[30] It is a disturbing way for a national government to operate.

The U.S. accounts for nearly 50% of worldwide military expenditures.[31] On-budget federal allocations for the fiscal year 2015 were set at over $620 billion, which is significantly larger than the Defense Department's request of $496 billion.[32] When taking into account off-budget military provisions, total U.S. spending on its military came to $716 billion.[33] More disturbing is since 1996 the Pentagon has either lost track of, or has outright wasted over $8.5 trillion in federally allocated taxpayer funds.[34]

The initial step in this evolution was the Roosevelt Corollary to the Monroe Doctrine, a statement of American imperialistic intentions. It presumed the United States to be both the preeminent military and moral power of the world, as well as a pronounced threat of U.S. invasion and occupation to any foreign government who disagreed with our authority. Beginning in 1905, the Corollary was used as justification for an American invasion of the Dominican Republic in 1916, afterwards placing the island nation under U.S. jurisdiction until the situation had stabilized.[35] Afterward U.S. troops invaded Latin American countries nearly three-dozen times. Add to the Corollary the policy of "Dollar Diplomacy", implemented by Roosevelt's hand-picked successor, William Howard Taft, and the true beneficiary becomes apparent: The American business community.[36] Among the most disquieting instances of its use was as justification by the Nixon Administration in the violent overthrow of Chile's popularly elected President

Salvador Allende on 11 September 1973, and the rise to power of military dictator General Augusto Pinochet.[37]

Another potent step in this evolution was the development and employment of the atomic bomb. In the aftermath of its use against the Japanese at the close of the Second World War, the U.S. actively concerned itself with the nuclear threat posed from "rogue" nations. Yet this delineation is curious, as the United States remains the sole power to have actually used this weapon of mass-destruction on a civilian population not once, but twice. Also, no other nation at that time was on an equal par with the U.S. in the development of atomic weapons, and we knew its destructive power for President Truman acknowledged it.[38] Using the atomic bomb to bring about the conclusion of the Pacific front in World War Two was unnecessary, as by the opening of 1945 the Japanese had been pushed back to their mainland by U.S. naval and air forces.[39] In the years afterwards, the United States aggressively deterred other nations from possessing their own nuclear programs though we had them, made more of them, and threatened to use them at the slightest provocation. Such actions are blatant hypocrisy.

The next step was the abandonment of a national economy based upon domestic manufacturing in favor of a permanent military industry, a transition which began as the U.S. was engulfed in World War Two. The Second World War made billions of dollars for those manufacturing and distributing war materials. War profiteering led to the creation of a permanent war economy via the Cold War, as well as a union between defense manufacturers, the military itself and the government known to the world as the Military-Industrial Complex.[40]

The process involved is both interlocking and circular in that each of the parties involved depend upon one another for a successful transaction; but, it is not clear when the cycle actually begins. Business is conducted in the following manner: 1) military contractors and manufacturers present products for manufacture, or projects which require further massive funding for development; 2) the Department of Defense specifically requests these items either for peacetime defense or wartime advantage; 3) either through the executive, or the legislative branches of government, or both working with one another, adopt the Defense Department recommendations and place them into the annual federal budget; and, 4) media outlets are utilized to purvey the desired message to the general public of pending military conflict due to either peacetime security or military deployment.[41] The sole guarantee for federal revenue allocations is a permanent state of war, either with a nation, or in contemporary times a terrorist group. It was these specific circumstances which led to U.S. entry into the Cold War with the Soviet Union;[42] into Southeast Asia following the exit of French forces;[43]

into the Persian Gulf with the invasion of Kuwait by Iraqi dictator Saddam Hussein;[44] and, the "War on Terror" initiated against Islamic jihadist groups such as Al Qaeda and the Taliban after the 9/11 attack.[45] More disturbingly, it in his farewell address to the nation on 17 January 1961, President Dwight Eisenhower, the former supreme commander of allied forces during World War Two and five-star general, warned:

> In the councils of government, we must guard against the acquisition of unwarranted influence, whether sought or unsought, by the military-industrial complex. The potential for the disastrous rise of misplaced power exists and will persist. We must never let the weight of this combination endanger our liberties or democratic processes.[46]

The last American president who took significant actions to dismantle the permanent arms industry was John Kennedy. Following the Cuban Missile Crisis of October 1962, rather than marveling at how close the world had come to nuclear war, President Kennedy personally reached out to Soviet Premier Nikita Khrushchev and successfully negotiated the first nuclear test ban treaty in history.[47] Afterwards, the president shut down "Operation Mongoose", the second CIA-led invasion of Cuba;[48] put into place an ordered withdrawal of all American troops from Vietnam by Christmas 1965;[49] and, at his commencement speech at American University, announced his intent to end the Cold War with the Soviet Union.[50] Within the text of that speech President Kennedy made the case for peace between the then-prominent superpowers:

> So, let us not be blind to our differences—but let us also direct attention to our common interests and to means by which those differences can be resolved. And if we cannot end now our differences, at least we can help make the world safe for diversity. For, in the final analysis, our most basic common link is that we all inhabit this small planet. We all breathe the same air. We all cherish our children's future. And we are all mortal.[51]

Unfortunately for the country and the world, President Kennedy was assassinated during a political visit to Dallas, Texas on Friday, 22 November 1963. His successors saw fit to incrementally escalate the country's proclivity towards its military, as well as its economic dependency on war manufacturing.

Finally, in providing a degree of safety, the price American citizens paid for it has been their civil liberties. The Patriot Act of 2001, passed in the jingoistic fervor which followed the 9/11 attacks, and signed into law by President George W. Bush, was among the most significant.[52] In the name of public safety, it authorized the National Security Administration to monitor all forms of private communication from cellular telephone calls to books checked out of the public library. Upon this was added the National Defense Authorization Act of 2011 signed by President Barack Obama which codified a policy of indefinite detention.[53] Under these acts combined, the federal government possesses the necessary authorization to arrest a citizen on the grounds they *may* commit a crime, and detain them indefinitely without charge, without examination of the witnesses and/or evidence against them; or, without the benefit of a trial by a jury of their peers. Furthermore, the U.S. Supreme Court in its majority opinion in *Hamdan v. Rumsfeld* (2006) ruled such practices exceeded executive authority, especially when wrought by military tribunals established under the authority of the president of the United States, under his constitutional role as commander-in-chief.[54] Yet, these laws remain stringently enforced.

Upon a careful examination of the intent of the Framers, and the specific clauses of the U.S. Constitution which govern the military, an imperative question should immediately come to mind: Has this sacrifice of our civil liberties been worth the price for our personal safety? It was obvious in their words the Framers did not see this trade-off as equitable. They had fought a bloody and destructive war against a mighty empire to secure those rights. Perhaps, this is why they held civil liberties to be of ultimate value, the very things which made Americans special among other nations.

When compared to the attitudes of contemporary Americans, the founding generation were more aware of the social benefits of "promoting the general welfare". Consistent with their understanding of "the public good", the Framers were convinced a nation's greatness was gauged by its level of benevolence to the less fortunate, not by its military strength or financial accumulation. As the country became better educated the abuses of society would be lessened. The first U.S. president George Washington, in his 1790 letter to American citizens of the Roman Catholic faith, articulately stated:

> As mankind becomes more liberal, they will be more apt to allow that all those who conduct themselves as worthy members of the community are equally entitled to the protections of civil government. I hope ever to see America among the foremost nations of justice and liberality.[55]

The Framing generation concurred an educated citizenry was the best guard against the corruption of the country. James Madison voiced so eloquently the value of public education: "Learned institutions ought to be favorite objects with every free people."[56] Similar to what John Adams had written in 1765, the Fourth President of the United States was convinced the greatest leveling element in American society to be public education, as it was the manner by which the poorest citizen could rise to among the most innovative and productive members of their community.[57] Furthermore, others of the revolutionary generation such as George Washington, John Adams, Benjamin Franklin, Thomas Jefferson and Alexander Hamilton viewed education as a right due every citizen. In a letter to Dr. Benjamin Rush, future Chief Justice John Jay wrote he considered public education to be the 'soul' of the nation, a guard against the rise of ambitious politicians who sought glory and power for themselves at the public's peril.[58] The Land Ordinance of 1785, enacted on 20 May 1785 was a compromise agreement between the states on the issue of land usage and city planning. This law set the standards by which towns settled in the western territories must adhere, one of the sections being devoted to the establishment of a public school.[59] The Northwest Ordinance of 1787 was a law passed by the Confederation Congress which put into place standard procedures as to how public lands would be sold to private citizens.[60] Among the specifications in this legislation was a clause which encouraged all of the governmental entities within the territories to promote public education.[61]

The Framing generation were also mindful of the consequences upon both individual communities, as well as the nation as a whole of rampant disease among those who could not afford treatment. It was this realization which influenced Benjamin Franklin to create the first hospital in Philadelphia which treated the illness of the poor.[62] In his appeal to the city's citizens, Franklin gave voice to the need to address issues of public health: "The good particular men may do separately, in relieving the sick, is small, compared with what they may do collectively."[63] During his single term as governor of the Commonwealth of Virginia, Thomas Jefferson voiced his support for a public health initiative,[64] but as president of the United States he retained the idea the interests of public health were best served if left for state governments to attend.[65] Thus, it has been demonstrated the Framing generation had given serious consideration of issues of public health, but were unready to take the next step: the use the power of the federal government to rectify the problem.

Yet there was an area of the 'general welfare' in which the majority of the Framers lacked empathy: the relief of poverty itself. Perhaps as they were all men of wealth the ravages of poverty were alien to them. This lack of understanding of the plight of the poor was voiced in much of their personal correspondence. Consistent with the above interpretation, as governor of the Commonwealth of Virginia, Thomas Jefferson looked toward private charities to assist the destitute.[66] With regards to poverty relief, contrary to modern interpretations of the Preamble's General Welfare Clause, James Madison himself lamented if the government used the public money for the relief of the poor, it would no longer be a limited government, but an all-powerful entity.[67] Yet, any assessment of the Constitutional provisions for promoting the "general welfare", for Thomas Paine the task would not be complete until the elderly and the poor were relieved, the prisons were empty, beggars were non-existent, and tax rates were reasonably set.[68] Unfortunately, the push for national public education, as well as public health and poverty relief initiatives ended with the presidency of Andrew Jackson. In his view, all such programs were not within the purview of federal authority. According to the president it was for the states to determine for themselves, and if the states did not view such issues as a priority, so be it.[69]

As there were no explicit instructions either from the Framers or within the document itself as to what promoted 'the general welfare', the lack of specificity made Article I § 8 elastic in its application.[70] Yet those who constructed the Constitution were ardent it be flexible as to provide the means by which contemporary issues could be effectively addressed. Therefore, it only stands to reason if contemporary Americans, many generations separated from the Framers, found the Constitution useful in resolving a modern crisis, it is essential to do so. If it were otherwise, the Constitution could never be a living entity: It would have been fundamental law trapped within the last decade of the eighteenth century.

Until the dawn of the twentieth century both members of the Congress and presidents were reticent to use the power of the Constitution's General Welfare Clause to address the social ills of their time. This was specifically due to a 'strict constructionist' understanding of the document in which action was constrained as to exactly what the language of any given clause specifically stated. It was a pattern demonstrated by President Franklin Pierce in his 1854 Veto Message for a land grant bill of benefit to "indigent insane persons":

> I cannot find any authority in the Constitution for making the Federal Government the great almoner of public charity throughout the United States. To do so would, in my judgment, be contrary to the letter and spirit of the Constitution and subversive of the whole theory upon which the Union of these States is founded.[71]

Yet, as new generations of Americans were born, and the nation moved further away from the time of the Framers, as well as their attitudes towards poverty relief, it brought with it modern interpretations of the nation's social contract. Members of all three branches of the federal government began to view the Constitution as the means to address issues of dire poverty within society. Progressive Era presidents such as Theodore Roosevelt and Woodrow Wilson took a different approach towards interpreting the document: A 'loose constructionist' methodology in which if the Constitution did not specifically forbid such action, it was constitutional. This method is supported by a statement from President John F. Kennedy's Inaugural Address: "If a free society cannot help the many who are poor, it cannot save the few who are rich."[72] This change demonstrates the flexibility of the Constitution—a condition which allowed it to remain relevant after over two centuries.

How can a nation which proclaims itself to the world the "land of the free" and simultaneously allow such inequity to continue, especially when it holds the constitutional means to address these problems? How does such cowardice promote "the General Welfare"? Perhaps, the answer is though Americans sincerely revere their Constitution, they possess not a clue as what is in it. In his 1987 book, *The Machine That Would Go of Itself: The Constitution in American Culture*, historian Michael Kammen made that very argument.[73]

In example, the federal income tax was instituted by the Sixteenth Amendment to the Constitution, which under the aegis of Article V, was approved by a two-thirds vote in both houses of Congress, and ratified by more than two-thirds of the existing states.[74] Upon ratification it became a part of the Constitution itself and, thus, under Article VI was the "supreme law of the land".[75] Furthermore, upon reading Alexander Hamilton's essays #30-through-35 in *The Federalist* it is clear the Framers had no problem with the government possessing the specific power to tax anything, anywhere, and under whatever circumstances it so chose.[76] One of the specific reasons for the Supreme Law Clause of Article VI, along with the Necessary-and-Proper Clause of Article I § 8 as previously discussed, was to give such authority in case it was necessary, a power first used by President Abraham Lincoln to finance the Union army during the Civil War, as there was no federal bank at the time.[77]

Finally, it was proposed to effectively wrestle control of the American economy from the influence of the 'Robber Barons'. Prior to the income tax the government was financed by import/export tariffs and, as a result, often ran short of operating funds. In both 1872 and in 1907, financier J. P. Morgan personally provided loans to the federal government at exorbitant interest rates which, in turn, allowed him to dictate what bills the Congress could consider, or actions the government could take (i.e. the 1892 Pullman Strike).[78] President William Howard Taft reasoned this was neither a power a good man should want, nor a bad man should have. *That* is why he proposed the federal income tax.[79] History has proven Taft's reasoning to be sound. Ponder for a moment all the services tax revenues pay for: public education; interstate infrastructure; social responsibility programs; national defense. As Associate Justice Oliver Wendell Holmes, Jr. argued: "Taxes are the price we pay for a civilized society".[80] This is how the Constitution can be used as a progressive instrument to rectify situations in the promotion of the "general welfare".

In a 1755 memorandum to the Pennsylvania State Assembly Benjamin Franklin maintained that citizens who were willing to forfeit any portion of their freedom in the hope of safety merited neither.[81] Yet, throughout our relatively short history, Americans have viewed this trade-off as acceptable. There are many instances where either laws or socially mandated sanctions have hindered the civil liberties of specific ethnic or political groups, as evidenced by President Woodrow Wilson's forced exile of socialists and communists during World War One,[82] and President Franklin Roosevelt's detainment of Japanese-Americans at the onset of World War Two.[83] More disturbing was in a country who extolled "the blessings of liberty", human chattel slavery was not only an accepted practice, but was also an indispensable element of the United States' pre-Civil War national economy.[84]

Within recent American history, there are two eras disturbingly demonstrative of the popular acceptance of safety over liberty: The Red Scare and 9/11.

"The Red Scare" was a crisis invented by President Harry Truman as the means to pass his post-war reconstruction legislation, known as The Marshall Plan, through a hostile Congress. In instituting a national panic against Communism, the president effectively turned our ally during World War Two into our nemesis.[85] Because the menace was purported to be all-encompassing, the federal government passed laws designed to "protect" the public at the cost of their civil liberties. It also encouraged the public to channel their First Amendment rights and demonstrate in support of such government action, as well as for citizens to act as informants against their neighbors who conducted themselves in a "suspicious manner".

Claiming authority under the Constitution's Article II, the *Pendleton Act of 1883*, and the *Hatch Act of 1939*, President Harry Truman instituted mandatory loyalty oaths and extensive background checks on employees in the federal government on 22 March 1947.[86] In his executive order the president authorized the investigation into both personal and professional records of all federal employees to gauge their loyalty to the United States.[87] The order also specified the manner by which a "disloyal" government employee was to be discharged through the establishment of a Loyalty Review Board under the authority of the Civil Service Commission.[88] Once a government employee was found to be "disloyal" their names and records were to be transferred to both the Federal Bureau of Investigation for further inquiry and to the Department of Justice for federal prosecution.[89]

The Immigration and Nationality Act—popularly known as the *McCarran-Walter Internal Security Act*—provided to the federal government the authority to deport both immigrants and naturalized citizens who were engaged in seditious activities.[90] The statute also empowered the government to deny entry in the United States of suspected foreign-born subversives. Furthermore, it also affected naturalized citizens who had ceased to have an affiliation with subversive groups for several years. This bill was considered offensive by President Truman and he vetoed the legislation because it was "un-American". It was nonetheless re-passed by the Congress, overriding the president's veto.[91]

The elements of this law were a defilement of the "personal rights" the Framers had sought to protect within the Constitution, with its requirement all "Communists" register with the federal government and, as such, their activities were subject to monitoring. Not only was this a violation of the freedom of association in the First Amendment's Assembly Clause, but the desecration of the Equal Protection Clause of the Fourteenth Amendment which applied to people gathered into specific groups for political purposes. Once this list was completed, and all Communists were known due to such a requirement, how easy would it have been to pass legislation to proscribe the Communist Party in the United States altogether, and then incarcerate and try them as criminals? With the passage of the *Communist Control Act* on 24 August 1954 that is exactly what happened. The Communist Party was made illegal and its participants were made criminals of the state.[92]

Two controversial decisions of the U.S. Supreme Court undermined the civil liberties of citizens during this era. In their *per curiam* decision in *Morford v. United States* (1950), the Court refused to review contempt of Congress convictions against two screenwriters under Executive Order #9835.[93] By doing so the Court upheld the authority of Congressional committees to force witnesses to reveal their political affiliations, thereby exempting witnesses from Fifth Amendment protections against self-incrimination. A year later, in *Rogers v. United States* (1951), the Court upheld the constitutionality of the *Alien Registration Act of 1940*, also known as The Smith Act, which made any act or speech which advocated the violent overthrow of the government illegal.[94] The Court speaking through Chief Justice Fred Vinson stated "where criminating facts have been voluntarily revealed, the [Fifth Amendment] privilege cannot be invoked to avoid disclosure of the details".[95]

Though the 'threat' of international communism remained at the fore of American foreign policy, the domestic threat lessened to a large degree in the public eye. Only in specific circles did the label of "communist" stimulate disfavor. However, during the Red Scare, one essential paradigm had been proven: Given the choice between civil liberties and safety, the public will choose the latter over the former. This realization provided the impetus for a "war on terror" called for by President George W. Bush and authorized by Congress in the wake of an unspeakable national tragedy.

Over five decades following the Red Scare, in the wake of the 9/11 tragedy, the Congress passed and President George W. Bush signed into law the *USA Patriot Act*: Legislation to tighten security in our nation under the premise it would make Americans safe.[96] It not only created the Department of Homeland Security,[97] but it also authorized the U.S. Government with the authority to monitor telephone calls, emails, ground mail, and all other forms of personal communication, as well as to monitor everything from a citizen's credit score to the books they had checked out of their local library *without the need of a warrant.*[98] As such, the necessity for a nationwide organization to centralize all government digital surveillance—a program first proposed by Deputy National Security Advisor John Poindexter to President Ronald Reagan in 1983—was incorporated into the National Security Agency.[99]

In both cases, the threat of terrorism was used by the federal government to infringe upon constitutionally guaranteed civil liberties, the most blatant being those inherent within the right to privacy. We were led to believe communists in the post-World War II era, and Islamic terrorists in our time were lurking in the shadows awaiting every opportunity to destroy the American way of life. Sadly, such fear-mongering accomplished the creation of a populace paranoid of one another and willing to give up their essential freedoms for the fleeting comfort of feeling safe.

Yet, the greatest assaults against civil liberties were neither wrought through the passage of a bill by the Congress, nor the result of an executive order issued by the president: It was rendered by two recent decisions of the United States Supreme Court.

The first was *Citizens United v. Federal Communications Commission* (2010), in which the U.S. Supreme Court contended the First Amendment prohibited spending limits in political campaigns.[100] This decision removed campaign contribution limits which had been set through federal legislation in the wake of the Watergate scandal of the mid-1970s.[101] It was not the Court's exemplar which elevated the voice of the wealthy over working- and middle-class citizens that violated the civil liberties of the American people, but the reaffirmation corporations exercised the same rights as individuals, a doctrine first declared by the Court in *Santa Clara County v. Southern Pacific Railroad* (1886).[102] Speaking through Associate Justice Anthony Kennedy, the Court argued in the area of free speech, the law did not recognize "that political speech of corporations or other associations should be treated differently under the First Amendment simply because such associations are not 'natural persons'".[103] Furthermore, the Court contended: "This rule that political speech cannot be limited based on a speaker's wealth is a necessary consequence of the premise that the First Amendment generally prohibits the suppression of political speech based upon the speaker's identity."[104] In the end, the body concluded corporate entities possessed the same First Amendment rights as flesh-and-blood citizens, for to distinguish between them would be to commit a constitutional error which would favor one above the other.[105]

The primary flaw of the Court's majority opinion in *Citizen's United* was that it failed to recognize that there is indeed a difference between corporate and human entities. In potential earning power alone the difference between the average American worker and the corporations becomes apparent. The average annual salary of the former, according to the Bureau of Labor Statistics, is $44,200 per year, while the latter earns in the billions of dollars.[106] In federal income taxes, according to a 2013 Government Accountability Office (GAO) report, large corporations pay an average rate of 12% in taxes, in comparison to the average worker earning $44,200 who pays a rate of 25%.[107] The variances are large and obvious, yet the most disturbing aspect of this financial differential is the manner by which it proved to be prejudicial. In a lawsuit filed by a human citizen against a corporate entity, which side possesses the necessary funds to maintain credible counsel? And in a political campaign, what is the potential audience an individual voter or candidate when relying upon their personal financial resources, as opposed to that of a corporate entity?

The second was *Burwell v. Hobby Lobby Stores, Inc.* (2014), in which the Court further defined corporate personhood to include religious beliefs.[108] The Court speaking through Associate Justice Samuel Alito rejected the premise put forward by the Department of Health and Human Services, "the owners of the companies forfeited all RFRA (*Religious Freedom Restoration Act*) protections when they decided to organize their businesses as corporations".[109] Furthermore, the Court pointed out that the DHHS had allowed for exceptions based upon religious grounds to non-profit corporations, which was an unlawful discrimination against for-profit corporate entities.[110] Furthermore the Department had "failed to demonstrate a compelling interest in enforcing the mandate" against the businesses in question which, in the estimation of the Court, was improper.[111] Therefore, their conclusion was in the same manner as an individual can exercise a religious preference, a corporation operated by a collection of individuals possesses the same rights under the Constitution.[112] It was also stated that the decision in this case could not be used as precedent for similar cases, nor as the foundation for new cases to be filed under its authority.[113]

Congruent with legal traditions dating back to ancient Rome, all decisions of the U.S. Supreme Court are based upon specific clauses within the Constitution, coupled with past decisions made by the Court itself. As such, *all* Court decisions become precedent for later cases. In the future, if a business concludes to specifically discriminate on the basis of religion, they can and will inevitably cite *Burwell v. Hobby Lobby* (2014) as precedent, which will provide legal sanction for its actions. Thus, this decision blatantly violated the Constitution in five essential ways:

First, as previously stated, the U.S. Constitution has provided for the separation of church and state in the clauses found in Article VI and the First, Fourth, and Fourteenth Amendments. Burwell violates the doctrine of church-and-state separation for it has legally taken sides in what is essentially a religious debate. In previous cases where religion was at its vital center, with the plaintiff arguing for special and complete dispensation of the law, the Court had consistently ruled against it. This was seen in such cases as *Reynolds v. United States* (1878), where the Mormon Church argued for the right of polygamy as a religious practice; and, *Employment Division v. Smith* (1990), in which a Native nation argued for the legal use of peyote as a religious rite.[114]

Second, the U.S. Constitution requires all people to be secure in their persons, which is a foundational clause for privacy rights. This right was guaranteed under the Court's decision in *Griswold v. Connecticut* (1965), which established the right of privacy based upon the Fourth Amendment's Security Clause. But instead of a woman's reproductive rights being an issue between herself and her physician, due to the interposition of her employer's right to deny coverage for specific forms of birth control on religious grounds, her employer becomes a partner in those health care decisions.[115]

Third, under the aegis of the Fourteenth Amendment, the U.S. Constitution provides all people under its authority "equal protection under the law".[116] Though Hobby Lobby, Inc. can refuse to cover specific forms of birth control for women, the company ironically provided coverage for vasectomies and Viagra for men.[117] This means that under the *Burwell* decision, the reproductive rights of men are of greater legal concern and value than those of women, an obvious unequal application of the law. For this to be an equal application, either all birth control options are covered, or none.

Four, this decision violated the doctrine of religious freedom as put forward in the Establishment Clause of the First Amendment, as it places the owner's religious faith above the 'general welfare' of their female employees.[118] Moreover, it provides more cadence towards the religious belief of one over the physical needs of another; or, in a more disturbing scenario, the religious beliefs of a corporate entity over that of a human individual. As one of the primary charges of the Constitution, as stated in the Preamble, is to "promote the general welfare", this application of the law violates that opening clause under the guise of "religious freedom".[119]

Yet the foremost danger this decision poses is as a precedent for business owners to discriminate against citizens in the rendering of services on the grounds of religious faith. The precedent has now been set to allow businesses to refuse service to people of color, or to members of the LGBTQ community, or people of different faiths based solely upon their religious beliefs. Thus, what legislation could not accomplish in states such as Arizona and Mississippi, the Court via the *Burwell* decision has provided the necessary legal framework to occur without federal government reprisal. Thus it will ultimately divide us further as a nation, and as Abraham Lincoln said so eloquently: "A nation divided against itself cannot stand."[120]

What has been taken from us through deceit and fear can only be reclaimed through candor and vigilance. Drawing upon the Constitution itself and the words of the Framers, the following constitutional amendments should be taken under consideration:

1. Only flesh-and-blood human beings can be considered "persons" within the clauses of the Constitution—not corporations, or similar artificial entities.
2. All legislation should be authorized not by a numerical majority, but by a concurrent majority consisting of two/thirds of the members of both houses.
3. Monetary funds and/or *quid pro quo* services are forbidden as an undue influence upon any role in either the construction or implementation of public policy, nor in our choice of the candidates, nominees, elected officials or public servants who represent in any manner the people and/or government of the United States.
4. All direct theological influence upon the construction or implementation of either legislation or public policy is strictly forbidden under penalty of law.
5. As wars are a necessary evil, they should be entered into only under specific criterion based upon a verifiable threat, with an enemy easily identifiable.

All proposals for such military action must contain a precise strategy; reasonable armistice terms; and a proposal for peace to be mutually enforced.
6. There are areas within the public sector which are to remain out of the realm of privately managed for-profit business models, which include, but are not limited to the following: military operations and procurement of necessary arms and materiel; public education; utilities, health care, and institutions involving the corrections system (prisons, probation, and parole). All such private business interests engaged in any of the aforementioned endeavors must immediately cease and desist.
7. The Electoral College must be reestablished and remain an independent entity, free from the influence of any political party, candidate, elected representative, or any person engaged in the profession of politics.

The aforementioned concepts are meant to promote a peaceful transition from our current state, and towards the reconstruction of the constitutional republic we once were.

As the keepers of America's constitutional legacy, our generation has failed. Rather than being the protector of our collective liberty, we have acceded our rights to the wealthy few who have bastardized the Constitution to suit themselves. Rather than a system which guaranteed a free and competitive society, we have tacitly allowed the document to be warped into a justification for a feudal system in which it is acceptable for our fellow citizens to go without food or shelter, while being denied the essential means to procure it through gainful employment. Yes, it is we who have betrayed the trust given us by the framing generation, not only in creating a permanent military of imperial proportions, but also having embraced the notion of empire they themselves pledged their lives, fortunes and sacred honor to free both themselves and their posterity from.

As children we learn from our parents what 'acceptable' behavior is, and we were rewarded when we acted accordingly, as well as punished when we did not. Bearing in mind our current fear and complacency, what sort of constitutional example are we now implementing for our children? A country where rights once sacred have been easily discarded in favor of fleeting safety, and where fear of reprisal has undermined the practice of a free people, and where might has made right rather, than reason and morality.

During these trying times in our nation's history, this historian remains optimistic towards the future. Young people are abandoning the conventional wisdom of their parents and embracing what they believe to be in their best long-term interests. They are questioning established traditions and values, as well as actively challenging authority. They are rebelling against economic pedophilia, defined as the wholesale rape and pillage of fiscal, environmental and political resources for the sole benefit of the elder generation.

Like locusts to a harvest we, the baby-boom generation, viewed it as our right to own and consume everything we could lay our hands on while, in the wake, we left our children with nothing upon which to build their own futures. In our belief it was our right to be rich, we decided self-gratification was worth leaving our children in poverty. To secure more wealth for ourselves we shipped vital jobs overseas, taking advantage of cheap labor and called it "globalization". We encouraged our children to procure a college education knowing their degrees would be obsolete by the time they were obtained, all the while leaving the next generation with a morass of debt they cannot hope to pay off, and which ultimately benefitted us. While we polluted the air, poisoned the aquifers, and cut down trees in masse which made it more difficult for the planet to provide the necessary elements of life itself, we called anyone who protested environmental annihilation "tree-huggers". More despicably, we incarcerated people in record numbers not just because they violated our ill-constructed laws, but to increase profit for both shareholders and ourselves. We touted our right to weapons, which gave us cover to do nothing as our children were being brutally slaughtered in their schools by the guns we so treasure.

And we have the utter gall to call them "lazy" and "narcissistic" when they asked "why?"

Is it not obvious why they are in rebellion against the status quo their Baby-Boom parents constructed for them? Is it any wonder why they eagerly embrace alternative lifestyles, abandon religion, and laugh at our values? They refuse to accept the future their parents presented them with; they decline to adhere to the norms and values we taught them; and, they reject notions of "conformity". They will be the ones who will return a nation lost in self-centeredness and avarice to its progressive Enlightenment legacy inherent within its constitution.

As stated at the beginning of this essay, the United States has lost its way because its citizens have abandoned the Constitution. Furthermore, we, the people of the United States lack the sufficient impetus and courage to stand up to those who have robbed us of that legacy. They deceived us into believing the easy road to wealth was meant for us, appealing to our own avarice and greed. And it did. Now, here we are, at the brink of national abyss.

Yet, if our country is in a dire condition due to the desertion of constitutional principles, it stands to reason we can regain our lost glory by returning to them. Let us not forget this nation was born out of a revolution. Also the founding generation were children of the Enlightenment who voraciously read books banned by the mother country. It is this legacy we must reclaim.

We, the people must utilize our constitutional right to protest—freedom of speech; freedom to petition; freedom to peaceably assemble—to demand a restoration of the document at the heart of our national identity. Once again, it must be a precondition of holding elected office to "preserve, protect and defend the Constitution of the United States", as well as we, the people must hold them strictly accountable for doing so.[121] The ideas within the Preamble must be at the vital center of all public policy. No other course will allow us the crucial rebirth of our forlorn country.

Yes, this is a burning cry for an insurgency against those who view this country as source of their own profit, against those who view themselves as being above the laws of this land, and who have disinherited our constitutional republic and denigrated our national legacy. They are the lawbreakers, not we. Americans must stand together against this injustice, or live out the rest of our days as serfs in a modern feudal system. And if it must be the latter, then the America we once knew has, indeed, vanished forever.

Notes

1. Woodrow Wilson, *Address to a Joint Session of Congress*, 2 April 1917; at National Archives and Records Administration, Washington, DC. https://www.ourdocuments.gov/doc_large_image.php?flash=false&doc=61. Accessed 16 June 2018.
2. George W. Bush, *Address to the Nation*, 20 September 2001; at http://www.washingtonpost.com/wp-srv/nation/specials/attacked/transcripts/bushaddress_092001.html. Accessed 16 June 2018.
3. Paul Kennedy, *The Rise and Fall of the Great Powers* (New York: Random House, Inc., 1987), 530–1.
4. John Locke, *Two Treatises of Government*, ed. Peter Laslett (New York: Cambridge University Press, 1960), 415–17.
5. *U.S. Constitution*, First Amendment.
6. Abraham Lincoln, "Address at Gettysburg, Pennsylvania", 19 November 1863; in *Lincoln: Speeches and Writings 1859–1865*, ed. Don E. Fahrenbacher (New York: Literary Classics of the United States, Inc., 1989), 536.
7. "AFI's 100 Greatest Films of All Time", *American Film Institute*, Hollywood, CA, 2013; at http://www.afi.com/100Years/movies.aspx. Accessed 16 June 2018. Orson Welles, Joseph Cotton, and Agnes Moorhead, *Citizen Kane*, Directed by Orson Welles; Hollywood, CA: R.K.O Pictures, 1941.

8. *Citizen Kane*.
9. Shirley Biagi, *Media Impact: An Introduction to Mass Media*, Tenth Edition (Boston, MA: Wadsworth Publishing Company, Inc., 2011), 56.
10. James B. Stewart, "When Media Mergers Limit More Than Competition", *New York Times*, 25 July 2014; at, http://www.nytimes.com/2014/07/26/business/a-21st-century-fox-time-warner-merger-would-narrow-already-dwindling-competition.html?_r=0. Accessed 23 May 2018. Michael Sproule, "Propaganda and Public Discourse", in *Propaganda and American Democracy*, ed. Nancy Snow (Baton Rouge, LA: Louisiana State University Press, 2014), 86–7.
11. Beverly Kelley, "In Politics, Perception is the Reality", *Los Angeles Times*, Los Angeles, CA, 17 January 1999; at http://articles.latimes.com/1999/jan/17/local/me-64527. Simon Kellner, "Perception is Reality: The Facts Won't Matter in Next Year's General Election", *The Independent, London*, England, 30 October 2014; at http://www.independent.co.uk/voices/comment/perception-is-reality-the-facts-wont-matter-in-next-years-general-election-9829132.html. "Public Perception is Just Wrong About Key Obama Issues", *Bloomberg Political Report*, New York, 9 December 2014; at http://www.bloomberg.com/politics/articles/2014-12-09/perceptions-blur-reality-when-it-comes-to-obamas-key-issues. All accessed 16 June 2018.
12. Kathleen Anne Ruane, *Fairness Doctrine: History and Constitutional Issues* (Washington, DC: Congressional Research Service, 2011), 5. "Editorial: 'Fairness' is censorship", *The Washington Times*, Washington, DC, 17 June 2008; at https://www.washingtontimes.com/news/2008/jun/17/fairness-is-censorship/. Accessed 17 June 2018.
13. *New World Communications of Tampa, Inc. v. Jane Akre* (2D01-529–2003); at http://caselaw.findlaw.com/fl-district-court-of-appeal/1310807.html. Accessed 16 June 2018.
14. *Ibid.*
15. Andrew O'Hagan, "The Joys of Propaganda", *New York Times Style Magazine*, New York, 22 February 2017; at https://www.nytimes.com/2017/02/22/t-magazine/joys-of-propaganda.html?rref=collection%2Ftimestopic%2FPropaganda&action=click&contentCollection=timestopics&region=stream&module=stream_unit&version=latest&contentPlacement=9&pgtype=collection. Accessed 16 June 2018.
16. Jim Gaines, "One-in-four Americans want their state to secede from the U.S., but why?", *Reuters News Service*, New York, 19 September 2014; at http://blogs.reuters.com/jamesrgaines/2014/09/19/one-in-four-americans-want-their-state-to-secede-from-the-u-s-but-why/. Accessed 16 June 2018.
17. "New Poll: Armed Revolution Could Be Necessary, 29 Percent of Voters Believe", *Huffington Post*, Washington, DC, 2 May 2013; at http://www.huffingtonpost.com/2013/05/02/poll-armed-revolution_n_3203315.html. Accessed 16 June 2018.
18. Alexander Hamilton, Essay #29; in *The Federalist,* The Gideon Edition, eds. George W. Carey and James McClellan (Indianapolis, IN: The Liberty Fund, 2001), 141–2.
19. *U.S. Constitution*, Article VI clause 3.

20. *U.S. Constitution*, Preamble.
21. Allan Nevins, *Grover Cleveland: A Study in Courage* (New York: Dodd, Mead & Company, 1934), 609–24.
22. *The Lattimer Massacre Trial: Revealing Newspaper Article Reports and Artist Sketches As And When It Happened*, ed. Pasco L. Schiavo (Pittsburg, PA: Dorrance Publishing Company, 1920), 54.
23. Paul Dickson and Thomas B. Allen, *The Bonus Army: An American Epic* (New York: Walker & Company, 2004), 182–3.
24. John Kifner, "4 Kent State Students Killed by Troops: 8 Hurt as Shooting Follows Reported Sniping at Rally", *New York Times*, New York, 5 May 1970; at http://www.nytimes.com/learning/general/onthisday/big/0504.html?mcubz=0#article. William W. Scranton, *The Report on the President's Commission on Campus Unrest* (Washington, DC: U.S. Government Printing Office, 1970), 422–4. Accessed 16 June 2018.
25. *Treaty of Peace between the United States and Spain*, (30 Stat. 1754; TS 343; 11 Bevans 615) 10 December 1898; at http://avalon.law.yale.edu/19th_century/sp1898.asp. Accessed 16 June 2018.
26. Theodore Roosevelt, "Fourth Annual Message to Congress", 6 December 1904; in *A Compilation of the Messages and Papers of the Presidents*, 1789–1908, ed. James D. Richardson (Washington, DC: Bureau of National Literature and Art, 1909) 10: 831–2.
27. James Petras, "The Soaring Profits of the Military Industrial Complex, the Soaring Costs of Military Casualties", *Global Research*, Montreal, Quebec, Canada; 24 June 2014; at http://www.globalresearch.ca/the-soaring-profits-of-the-military-industrial-complex-the-soaring-costs-of-military-casualties/5388393. Accessed 16 June 2018.
28. Doug Bandow, "How Many Enemies, How Much Military Spending", *Huffington Post*, Washington, DC, 25 May 2011; at http://www.huffingtonpost.com/doug-bandow/how-many-enemies-how-much_b_262509.html. Accessed 16 June 2018.
29. Jonathan Turley, "Big Money Behind War: the Military-Industrial Complex", *Al Jezeera*, Doha, Quatar, 11 January 2014; at http://www.aljazeera.com/indepth/opinion/2014/01/big-money-behind-war-military-industrial-complex-20141473026736533.html. Accessed 16 June 2018.
30. *Total Military Personnel and Dependent End Strength by Service Region Area, and Country*, Defense Manpower Data Center, Washington, DC, 30 September 2014.
31. Thomas C. Frohlich and Alexander Kent, "Countries Spending the Most on Military", *USA Today*, McLean, Virginia, 12 July 2014: at http://www.usatoday.com/story/money/business/2014/07/12/countries-spending-most-on-military/12491639/. Accessed 16 June 2018.
32. *United States Department of Defense Fiscal Year 2015 Budget Request* (Washington, DC: Department of Defense, 2014) 1–1; at http://comptroller.defense.gov/

Portals/45/Documents/defbudget/fy2015/fy2015_Budget_Request_Overview_Book.pdf. Accessed 16 June 2018.

33. Brad Plumer, "America's Staggering Defense Budget, in Charts", *Washington Post*, Washington, DC, 7 January 2013; at http://www.washingtonpost.com/blogs/wonkblog/wp/2013/01/07/everything-chuck-hagel-needs-to-know-about-the-defense-budget-in-charts/. Accessed 16 June 2018.
34. Scot J. Paltrow, "Special Report: The Pentagon's Doctored Ledgers Conceal Epic Waste", *Reuters New Service*, New York, 18 November 2013; at http://www.reuters.com/article/2013/11/18/us-usa-pentagon-waste-specialreport-idUSBRE9AH0LQ20131118. Accessed 16 June 2018.
35. P. C. Emmer, Bridget Brereton, and B. W. Higman, *General History of the Caribbean: The Caribbean in the Twentieth Century* (New York: Macmillan Educational Publishers, 2004), 609.
36. Scott Nearing and Joseph Freeman, *Dollar Diplomacy: A Study in American Imperialism* (New York: B. W. Heubsch and The Viking Press, 1925), 1–312.
37. "Remembering Chile's 9/11: democracy's final triumph over General Pinochet", *The Guardian*, 9 September 2003, at http://www.theguardian.com/commentisfree/2013/sep/09/chile-911-pinochet-baltasar-garzon. Uri Friedman, "The Other 9/11: A CIA Agent Remembers the Chile Coup", *The Atlantic Monthly*, 11 September 2014; at http://www.theatlantic.com/international/archive/2014/09/chile-coup-salvador-allende-cia/380082/. Both accessed 16 June 2018.
38. Hugh Thomas, *Armed Truce: The Beginnings of the Cold War 1945–1946* (New York: Atheneum Books, 1987), 436–7.
39. Gar Alperovitz, "The War Was Won Before Hiroshima—And the Generals Who Dropped the Bomb Knew It: Seventy Years After the Bombing, will Americans Face the Brutal Truth?" *The Nation*, New York, 8 August 2015; at https://www.thenation.com/article/why-the-us-really-bombed-hiroshima/. Accessed 16 June 2018.
40. Alex Roland, "The Military-Industrial Complex: Lobby and Trope"; in *The Long War: A New History of U.S. National Security Policy Since World War II* , ed. Andrew J. Bacevitch (New York: Columbia University Press, 2009), 335–70.
41. Walter Adams and William James Adams, "The Military-Industrial Complex: A Market Structure Analysis", *The American Economic Review*, Nashville, TN, 1 March 1972. Lewis Uchitelle, "The U.S. Still Leans on the Military-Industrial Complex", *New York Times*, New York, 22 September 2017; at https://www.nytimes.com/2017/09/22/business/economy/military-industrial-complex.html?mcubz=0. Accessed 16 June 2018.
42. Andrew H. Kydd, *Trust and Mistrust in International Relations* (Princeton, NJ: Princeton University Press, 2005), 107.
43. Frank Cain, *America's Vietnam War and Its French Connection* (Abingdon, UK: Routledge Books, 2016), 23.

44. John E. Peters and Howard Deshong, *Out of Area or Out of Reach?: European Military Support for Operations in Southeast Asia* (Santa Monica, CA: RAND Corporation, 1995), 28–32.
45. Michel Chossudrovsky, "9/11 and America's 'War on Terrorism'", *The Center for Research on Globalization*, Montreal, Quebec, Canada, 13 September 2017; at https://www.globalresearch.ca/9-11-and-america-s-war-on-terrorism/24975. Accessed 16 June 2018.
46. Dwight Eisenhower, *Address to the Nation*, 17 January 1961; at https://eisenhower.archives.gov/research/online_documents/farewell_address.html. Accessed 27 May 2018.
47. Richard Reeves, *President Kennedy: Profile of Power* (New York: Simon & Schuster, 1993), 346–7; 439–40; 476–7; 540–1. Ralph G. Martin, *A Hero for Our Time: An Intimate Story of the Kennedy Years* (New York: Macmillan Publishing Company, 1983), 443–7.
48. Evan Thomas, *Robert Kennedy: His Life* (New York: Simon & Schuster, 2000), 149–52; 234–5.
49. John F. Kennedy, "National Security Action Memorandum 263", 11 October 1963; at http://www.jfklibrary.org/Asset-Viewer/w6LJoSnW4UehkaH9Ip5IAA.aspx. Reeves, 613–4. Martin, 441–2. Accessed 16 June 2018.
50. Reeves, 513–4.
51. John F. Kennedy, "Commencement Speech at American University", 10 June 1963; at *The John F. Kennedy Presidential Library*, Boston, MA. https://www.jfklibrary.org/Asset-Viewer/BWC7I4C9QUmLG9J6I8oy8w.aspx. Accessed 16 June 2018.
52. *The USA Patriot Act* (115 Stat. 272 Public Law 107–56).
53. *National Defense Authorization Act of 2011* (Pub.L 112–81. 1021(d)). Peter Finn and Anne E. Kornblut, "Obama Creates Indefinite Detention System for Prisoners at Guantanamo Bay", *The Washington Post*, Washington, DC, 8 March 2011; at http://www.washingtonpost.com/wp-dyn/content/article/2011/03/07/AR2011030704871.html?noredirect=on. Accessed 17 June 2018.
54. *Hamdan v. Rumsfeld*, 548 U.S. 557 (2006).
55. George Washington, Letter to the Roman Catholics in the United States, 15 March 1790; in *George Washington: A Collection*, ed. W. B. Allen (Indianapolis, IN: The Liberty Fund, 1988), 189.
56. James Madison, Letter to W. T. Barry, 4 August 1822; in *The Founder's Constitution*, eds. Philip B. Kurland and Ralph Lerner. 2004 Reprint (Indianapolis, IN: The Liberty Fund, 1987), I: 690.
57. *Ibid.*
58. John Jay, Letter to Benjamin Rush, 24 March 1785; in *The Correspondence and Public Papers of John Jay, Vol. III, 1782–1793*, ed. Henry P. Johnston (New York: G. P. Putnam's Sons, 1891), III: 139.
59. The Land Ordinance of 1785, *Congress of the Confederation*, at http://memory.loc.gov/cgi-bin/ampage?collId=lljc&fileName=028/lljc028.db&recNum=386&itemLink=r?ammem/hlaw:@field(DATE+17850520)::%230280388&linkText=1.

Edmund C. Burnett, *The Continental Congress* (New York: W.W. Norton and Company, 1941), 613–32. Accessed 16 June 2018.

60. The Northwest Ordinance of 1787, *Congress of the Confederation*, 13 July 1787; at http://usa.usembassy.de/etexts/democrac/5.htm. Bill Hubbard, Jr., *American Boundaries: The Nation, the States, the Rectangular Survey* (Chicago, IL: University of Chicago Press, 2009), 46–7; 114. Accessed 16 June 2018.
61. *Ibid.*
62. Benjamin Franklin, "Appeal for the Hospital", 8 August 1751; in *The Papers of Benjamin Franklin*, ed. Leonard B. Labaree (New Haven, CT: Yale University Press, 1961), IV: 147.
63. *Ibid.*
64. Thomas Jefferson, Letter to Patrick Henry, 27 March 1779; in *Writings*, 770.
65. Thomas Jefferson, "Fifth Annual Message to Congress", 3 December 1805; at http://avalon.law.yale.edu/19th_century/jeffmes5.asp. Accessed 16 June 2018.
66. Thomas Jefferson, "Notes on the State of Virginia" (1785); in *Writings*, 259.
67. James Madison, Letter to Edmund Pendleton, 12 January 1792; original source in *The Writings of James Madison*, 9 vols., ed. Gaillard Hunt (New York: G. P. Putnam's Sons, 1900), available online through The Liberty Fund at https:// http://oll.libertyfund.org/titles/madison-the-writings-of-james-madison-9-vols, accessed 11 May 2018.
68. Thomas Paine, *The Rights of Man* (New York: Oxford University Press, 1995), 326.
69. Robert V. Remini, *The Life of Andrew Jackson* (New York: HarperCollins Publishing Company, 2011), 307.
70. *U.S. Constitution*, Article I § 8.
71. Franklin Pierce, "Veto Message", 3 May 1854; in *The Papers of Franklin Pierce* (Microfiche Collection), The National Archives and Records Administration, Washington, DC.
72. John F. Kennedy, "Inaugural Address", 20 January 1961; at *The John F. Kennedy Presidential Library*, Boston, MA. https://www.jfklibrary.org/Asset-Viewer/BqXIEM9F4024ntFl7SVAjA.aspx. Accessed 16 June 2018.
73. Michael Kammen, *The Machine That Would Go of Itself: The Constitution in American Culture* (New York: Alfred A. Knopf, Inc., 1987), 4–5.
74. *U.S. Constitution*, Sixteenth Amendment. William Howard Taft, *Presidential Addresses and State Papers of William Howard Taft: From March 4, 1909 to March 4, 1910* (New York: Doubleday, Page and Company, 1910), I: 166–9.
75. *U.S. Constitution*, Article VI Clause 2.
76. Alexander Hamilton, Essay #33; in *The Federalist*, 159.
77. Phillip Shaw Paludan, *The Presidency of Abraham Lincoln* (Lawrence, KS: University Press of Kansas, 1994), 83.
78. Allen Nevins, *Grover Cleveland: A Study in Courage* (New York: Dodd, Mead & Company, 1934), 626–7.

79. *Presidential Addresses and State Papers of William Howard Taft,* I: 167–8.
80. Oliver Wendell Holmes, Jr., dissenting opinion in *Compania General de Tabacos De Filipinas v. Collector of Internal Revenue*, 275 U.S. 87, 100 (1927).
81. Benjamin Franklin, "Pennsylvania Assembly: Reply to the Governor", 11 November 1755; in http://franklinpapers.org/franklin/framedVolumes.jsp?vol=6&page=238a. Accessed 16 June 2018.
82. August Heckshur, *Woodrow Wilson: A Biography* (New York: Charles Scribner's Sons, 1991), 619–20.
83. Franklin D. Roosevelt, *Executive Order #9066*, 19 February 1942. *An Act to Provide a Penalty for Restriction of Orders With Respect to Persons Entering, Remaining In, or Committing Any Act in Military Areas or Zones* (Pub.L. 77–503 56 Stat. 173) 21 March 1942.
84. Robert William Fogel and Stanley Engerman, *Time on the Cross: The Economics of American Negro Slavery* (Boston: Little, Brown and Company, 1974), 74, 76, 82, 90, 154, 193.
85. Harry S Truman, *Inaugural Address*, 20 January 1949; at http://www.presidency.ucsb.edu/ws/index.php?pid=13282. Accessed 16 June 2018.
86. *The Pendleton Civil Service Reform Act* (ch. 27, 22 Stat. 403) (1883); *An Act to Prevent Pernicious Political Activities* (a.k.a. The Hatch Act) 5 U.S.C. §§ 1501–1508, 7321–7326 (1939).
87. Harry S Truman, *Executive Order #9835*, 22 March 1947.
88. *Ibid.*
89. *Ibid.*
90. *The Immigration and Nationality Act of 1952* (a.k.a. The McCarran-Walter Act) (Pub. L. 82–414, 66 Stat. 163, 27 June 1952), 33–55.
91. Harry S. Truman, *Veto Message of the Internal Security Bill*, 22 September 1950; at https://trumanlibrary.org/publicpapers/index.php?pid=883. Accessed 16 June 2018.
92. *The Communist Control Act* (68 Stat. 775, 50 U.S.C. 841–844).
93. *Morford v. United States*, 339 U.S. 258 (1950).
94. *Rogers v. United States*, 340 U.S. 367 (1951); *The Alien Registration Act of 1940* (a.k.a The Smith Act) ch. 439, 54 Stat. 670, 18 U.S.C. § 2385.
95. *Rogers v. United States*, 373.
96. *The USA Patriot Act* (115 Stat. 272 Public Law 107–56).
97. *The Homeland Security Act* (Pub.L. 107–296, 116 Stat. 2135).
98. *The USA Patriot Act*, Title II; *The Computer Fraud and Abuse Act* (18 U.S.C. § 1030(e)(2)), Ch. 19.
99. Shane Harris, *The Watchers: The Rise of America's Surveillance State* (New York: Penguin Books, 2011), 24.
100. *Citizens United v. Federal Communications Commission*, 556 U.S. 310 (2010).
101. *Ibid.*, 576.

102. *Santa Clara County v. Southern Pacific Railroad*, 118 U.S. 394 (1886); *Citizens United*, 590.
103. *Citizens United*, 591.
104. *Ibid.*, 622.
105. *Ibid.*, 624.
106. Occupational Outlook Handbook, *Bureau of Labor Statistics*, Washington, DC, 17 December 2015; at http://www.bls.gov/ooh/community-and-social-service/social-workers.htm. Accessed 16 June 2018.
107. http://money.cnn.com/2013/07/01/news/economy/corporate-tax-rate/; http://taxfoundation.org/article/comparison-tax-burden-labor-oecd. Accessed 16 June 2018.
108. *Burwell v. Hobby Lobby Stores, Inc.*, 573 U.S. ___ (2014).
109. *Ibid.*, 2.
110. *Ibid.*, 3.
111. *Ibid.*, 15.
112. *Ibid.*, 19.
113. *Ibid.*, 45.
114. *Reynolds v. United States*, 98 U.S. 145 (1878); *Employment Division v. Smith*, 494 U.S. 872 (1990).
115. *Griswold v. Connecticut*, 381 U.S. 479 (1965).
116. *U.S. Constitution*, Fourteenth Amendment.
117. Alexander C. Kaufman, "Hobby Lobby Still Covers Vasectomies and Viagra", *Huffington Post*, Washington, DC, 2 July 2014; at http://www.huffingtonpost.com/2014/06/30/hobby-lobby-viagra_n_5543916.html. Accessed 16 June 2018.
118. *U.S. Constitution*, First Amendment.
119. *U.S. Constitution*, Preamble.
120. Abraham Lincoln, "Speech at Springfield, Illinois", 16 June 1858; in *Abraham Lincoln: Speeches and Writings 1832–1858*, ed. Roy P. Basler (New York: Literary Classics of America, 1989), 426.
121. *U.S. Constitution*, Article II § 1.

Appendix A: Thoughts on Government

Applicable to the Present State of the American Colonies; In a letter from a Gentleman to his Friend A Pamphlet by John Adams April 1776

My dear Sir,

If I was equal to the task of forming a plan for the government of a colony, I should be flattered with your request, and very happy to comply with it; because as the divine science of politicks is the science of social happiness, and the blessings of society depend entirely on the constitutions of government, which are generally institutions that last for many generations, there can be no employment more agreeable to a benevolent mind, than a research after the best.

Pope flattered tyrants too much when he said,

"For forms of government let fools contest,
That which is best administered is best."

Nothing can be more fallacious than this: But poets read history to collect flowers not fruits—they attend to fanciful images, not the effects of social institutions. Nothing is more certain from the history of nations, and the nature of man, than that some forms of government are better fitted for being well administered than others.

We ought to consider, what is the end of government, before we determine which is the best form. Upon this point all speculative politicians will agree, that the happiness of society is the end of government, as all Divines and moral Philosophers will agree that the happiness of the individual is the end of man. From this principle it will follow, that the form of government, which communicates ease, comfort, security, or in one word happiness to the greatest number of persons, and in the greatest degree, is the best.

All sober enquiries after truth, ancient and modern, Pagan and Christian, have declared that the happiness of man, as well as his dignity consists in virtue. Confucius, Zoroaster, Socrates, Mahomet, not to mention authorities really sacred, have agreed in this.

If there is a form of government then, whose principle and foundation is virtue, will not every sober man acknowledge it better calculated to promote the general happiness than any other form?

Fear is the foundation of most governments; but is so sordid and brutal a passion, and renders men, in whose breasts it predominates, so stupid, and miserable, that Americans will not be likely to approve of any political institution which is founded on it.

Honor is truly sacred, but holds a lower rank in the scale of moral excellence than virtue. Indeed the former is but a part of the latter, and consequently has not equal pretensions to support a frame of government productive of human happiness.

The foundation of every government is some principle or passion in the minds of the people. The noblest principles and most generous affections in our nature then, have the fairest chance to support the noblest and most generous models of government.

A man must be indifferent to the sneers of modern Englishmen to mention in their company the names of Sidney, Harrington, Locke, Milton, Nedham, Neville, Burnet, and Hoadley. No small fortitude is necessary to confess that one has read them. The wretched condition of this country, however, for ten or fifteen years past, has frequently reminded me of their principles and reasonings. They will convince any candid mind, that there is no good government but what is Republican. That the only valuable part of the British constitution is so; because the very definition of a Republic, is "an Empire of Laws, and not of men." That, as a Republic is the best of governments, so that particular arrangement of the powers of society, or in other words that form of government, which is best contrived to secure an impartial and exact execution of the laws, is the best of Republics.

Of Republics, there is an inexhaustable variety, because the possible combinations of the powers of society, are capable of innumerable variations.

As good government, is an empire of laws, how shall your laws be made? In a large society, inhabiting an extensive country, it is impossible that the whole should assemble, to make laws: The first necessary step then, is, to depute power from the many, to a few of the most wise and good. But by what rules shall you chuse your Representatives? Agree upon the number and qualifications of persons, who shall have the benefit of choosing, or annex this priviledge to the inhabitants of a certain extent of ground.

The principal difficulty lies, and the greatest care should be employed in constituting this Representative Assembly. It should be in miniature, an exact portrait of the people at large. It should think, feel, reason, and act like them. That it may be the interest of this Assembly to do strict justice at all times, it should be an equal representation, or in other words equal interest among the people should have equal interest in it. Great care should be taken to effect this, and to prevent unfair, partial, and corrupt elections. Such regulations, however, may be better made in times of greater tranquility than the present, and they will spring up of themselves naturally, when all the powers of government come to be in the hands of the people's friends. At present it will be safest to proceed in all established modes to which the people have been familiarised by habit.

A representation of the people in one assembly being obtained, a question arises whether all the powers of government, legislative, executive, and judicial, shall be left in this body? I think a people cannot be long free, nor ever happy, whose government is in one Assembly. My reasons for this opinion are as follow.

1. A single Assembly is liable to all the vices, follies and frailties of an individual. Subject to fits of humour, starts of passion, flights of enthusiasm, partialities of prejudice, and consequently productive of hasty results and absurd judgments: And all these errors ought to be corrected and defects supplied by some controuling power.
2. A single Assembly is apt to be avaricious, and in time will not scruple to exempt itself from burthens which it will lay, without compunction, on its constituents.
3. A single Assembly is apt to grow ambitious, and after a time will not hesitate to vote itself perpetual. This was one fault of the long parliament, but more remarkably of Holland, whose Assembly first voted themselves from annual to septennial, then for life, and after a course of years, that all vacancies happening by death, or otherwise, should be filled by themselves, without any application to constituents at all.
4. A Representative Assembly, altho' extremely well qualified, and absolutely necessary as a branch of the legislature, is unfit to exercise the executive power, for want of two essential properties, secrecy and dispatch.

5. A Representative Assembly is still less qualified for the judicial power; because it is too numerous, too slow, and too little skilled in the laws.
6. Because a single Assembly, possessed of all the powers of government, would make arbitrary laws for their own interest, execute all laws arbitrarily for their own interest, and adjudge all controversies in their own favour.

But shall the whole power of legislation rest in one Assembly? Most of the foregoing reasons apply equally to prove that the legislative power ought to be more complex—to which we may add, that if the legislative power is wholly in one Assembly, and the executive in another, or in a single person, these two powers will oppose and enervate upon each other, until the contest shall end in war, and the whole power, legislative and executive, be usurped by the strongest.

The judicial power, in such case, could not mediate, or hold the balance between the two contending powers, because the legislative would undermine it. And this shews the necessity too, of giving the executive power a negative upon the legislative, otherwise this will be continually encroaching upon that.

To avoid these dangers let a [distinct] Assembly be constituted, as a mediator between the two extreme branches of the legislature, that which represents the people and that which is vested with the executive power.

Let the Representative Assembly then elect by ballot, from among themselves or their constituents, or both, a distinct Assembly, which for the sake of perspicuity we will call a Council. It may consist of any number you please, say twenty or thirty, and should have a free and independent exercise of its judgment, and consequently a negative voice in the legislature.

These two bodies thus constituted, and made integral parts of the legislature, let them unite, and by joint ballot choose a Governor, who, after being stripped of most of those badges of domination called prerogatives, should have a free and independent exercise of his judgment, and be made also an integral part of the legislature. This I know is liable to objections, and if you please you may make him only President of the Council, as in Connecticut: But as the Governor is to be invested with the executive power, with consent of Council, I think he ought to have a negative upon the legislative. If he is annually elective, as he ought to be, he will always have so much reverence and affection for the People, their Representatives and Councillors, that although you give him an independent exercise of his judgment, he will seldom use it in opposition to the two Houses, except in cases the public utility of which would be conspicuous, and some such cases would happen.

In the present exigency of American affairs, when by an act of Parliament we are put out of the royal protection, and consequently discharged from our allegiance; and it has become necessary to assume government for our immediate security, the Governor, Lieutenant-Governor, Secretary, Treasurer, Commissary, Attorney-General, should be chosen by joint Ballot, of both Houses. And these and all other elections, especially of Representatives, and Councillors, should be annual, there not being in the whole circle of the sciences, a maxim more infallible than this, "Where annual elections end, there slavery begins."

These great men, in this respect, should be, once

a year

"Like bubbles on the sea of matter borne,

They rise, they break, and to that sea return."

This will teach them the great political virtues of humility, patience, and moderation, without which every man in power becomes a ravenous beast of prey.

This mode of constituting the great offices of state will answer very well for the present, but if, by experiment, it should be found inconvenient, the legislature may at its leisure devise other methods of creating them, by elections of the people at large, as in Connecticut, or it may enlarge the term for which they shall be chosen to seven years, or three years, or for life, or make any other alterations which the society shall find productive of its ease, its safety, its freedom, or in one word, its happiness.

A rotation of all offices, as well as of Representatives and Councillors, has many advocates, and is contended for with many plausible arguments. It would be attended no doubt with many advantages, and if the society has a sufficient number of suitable characters to supply the great number of vacancies which would be made by such a rotation, I can see no objection to it. These persons may be allowed to serve for three years, and then excluded three years, or for any longer or shorter term.

Any seven or nine of the legislative Council may be made a Quorum, for doing business as a Privy Council, to advise the Governor in the exercise of the executive branch of power, and in all acts of state.

The Governor should have the command of the militia, and of all your armies. The power of pardons should be with the Governor and Council.

Judges, Justices and all other officers, civil and military, should be nominated and appointed by the Governor, with the advice and consent of Council, unless you choose to have a government more popular; if you do, all officers, civil and military, may be chosen by joint ballot of both Houses, or in order to preserve the independence and importance of each House, by ballot of one House, concurred by the other. Sheriffs should be chosen by the freeholders of counties—so should Registers of Deeds and Clerks of Counties.

All officers should have commissions, under the hand of the Governor and seal of the Colony.

The dignity and stability of government in all its branches, the morals of the people and every blessing of society, depends so much upon an upright and skillful administration of justice, that the judicial power ought to be distinct from both the legislative and executive, and independent upon both, that so it may be a check upon both, as both should be checks upon that. The Judges therefore should always be men of learning and experience in the laws, of exemplary morals, great patience, calmness, coolness and attention. Their minds should not be distracted with jarring interests; they should not be dependant upon any man or body of men. To these ends they should hold estates for life in their offices, or in other words their commissions should be during good behaviour, and their salaries ascertained and established by law. For misbehaviour the grand inquest of the Colony, the House of Representatives, should impeach them before the Governor and Council, where they should have time and opportunity to make their defence, but if convicted should be removed from their offices, and subjected to such other punishment as shall be thought proper.

A Militia Law requiring all men, or with very few exceptions, besides cases of conscience, to be provided with arms and ammunition, to be trained at certain seasons, and requiring counties, towns, or other small districts to be provided with public stocks of ammunition and entrenching utensils, and with some settled plans for transporting provisions after the militia, when marched to defend their country against sudden invasions, and requiring certain districts to be provided with field-pieces, companies of matrosses and perhaps some regiments of light horse, is always a wise institution, and in the present circumstances of our country indispensible.

Laws for the liberal education of youth, especially of the lower class of people, are so extremely wise and useful, that to a humane and generous mind, no expence for this purpose would be thought extravagant.

The very mention of sumptuary laws will excite a smile. Whether our countrymen have wisdom and virtue enough to submit to them I know not. But the happiness of the people might be greatly promoted by them, and a revenue saved sufficient to carry on this war forever. Frugality is a great revenue, besides curing us of vanities, levities and fopperies which are real antidotes to all great, manly and warlike virtues.

But must not all commissions run in the name of
a king? No. Why may they not as well run thus,
"The Colony of ___________ to A. B. greeting," and be
tested by the Governor?

Why may not writs, instead of running in the name of a King, run thus, "The Colony of ___________ to
the Sheriff, &c." and be tested by the Chief Justice.

Why may not indictments conclude, "against the peace of the Colony of ___________ and the dignity
of the same?"

A Constitution, founded on these principles, introduces knowledge among the People, and inspires them with a conscious dignity, becoming Freemen. A general emulation takes place, which causes good humour, sociability, good manners, and good morals to be general. That elevation of sentiment, inspired by such a government, makes the common people brave and enterprizing. That ambition which is inspired by it makes them sober, industrious and frugal. You will find among them some elegance, perhaps, but more solidity; a little pleasure, but a great deal of business—some politeness, but more civility. If you compare such a country with the regions of domination, whether Monarchial or Aristocratical, you will fancy yourself in Arcadia or Elisium.

If the Colonies should assume governments separately, they should be left entirely to their own choice of the forms, and if a Continental Constitution should be formed, it should be a Congress, containing a fair and adequate Representation of the Colonies, and its authority should sacredly be confined to these cases, viz. war, trade, disputes between Colony and Colony, the Post-Office, and the unappropriated lands of the Crown, as they used to be called.

These Colonies, under such forms of government, and in such a union, would be unconquerable by all the Monarchies of Europe.

You and I, my dear Friend, have been sent into life, at a time when the greatest law-givers of antiquity would have wished to have lived. How few of the human race have ever enjoyed an opportunity of making an election of government more than of air, soil, or climate, for themselves or their children. When! Before the present epocha, had three millions of people full power and a fair opportunity to form and establish the wisest and happiest government that human wisdom can contrive? I hope you will avail yourself and your country of that extensive learning and indefatigable industry which you possess, to assist her in the formations of the happiest governments, and the best character of a great People. For myself, I must beg you to keep my name out of sight, for this feeble attempt, if it should be known to be mine, would oblige me to apply to myself those lines of the immortal John Milton, in one of his sonnets,

"I did but teach the age to quit their cloggs
By the plain rules of ancient Liberty,
When lo! a barbarous noise surrounded me,
Of owls and cuckoos, asses, apes and dogs."

Text used through the courtesy of the Massachusetts Historical Society.

Appendix B: Articles of Confederation and Perpetual Union

15 November 1777
Adopted 1 March 1781

To all to whom these Presents shall come, we the undersigned Delegates of the States affixed to our Names send greeting.

Articles of Confederation and perpetual Union between the states of New Hampshire, Massachusetts-bay Rhode Island and Providence Plantations, Connecticut, New York, New Jersey, Pennsylvania, Delaware, Maryland, Virginia, North Carolina, South Carolina and Georgia.

I.

The Stile of this Confederacy shall be
"The United States of America".

II.

Each state retains its sovereignty, freedom, and independence, and every power, jurisdiction, and right, which is not by this Confederation expressly delegated to the United States, in Congress assembled.

III.

The said States hereby severally enter into a firm league of friendship with each other, for their common defense, the security of their liberties, and their mutual and general welfare, binding themselves to assist each other, against all force offered to, or attacks made upon them, or any of them, on account of religion, sovereignty, trade, or any other pretense whatever.

IV.

The better to secure and perpetuate mutual friendship and intercourse among the people of the different States in this Union, the free inhabitants of each of these States, paupers, vagabonds, and fugitives from justice excepted, shall be entitled to all privileges and immunities of free citizens in the several States; and the people of each State shall free ingress and regress to and from any other State, and shall enjoy therein all the privileges of trade and commerce, subject to the same duties, impositions, and restrictions as the inhabitants thereof respectively, provided that such restrictions shall not extend so far as to prevent the removal of property imported into any State, to any other State, of which the owner is an inhabitant; provided also that no imposition, duties or restriction shall be laid by any State, on the property of the United States, or either of them.

If any person guilty of, or charged with, treason, felony, or other high misdemeanor in any State, shall flee from justice, and be found in any of the United States, he shall, upon demand of the Governor or executive power of the State from which he fled, be delivered up and removed to the State having jurisdiction of his offense.

Full faith and credit shall be given in each of these States to the records, acts, and judicial proceedings of the courts and magistrates of every other State.

V.

For the most convenient management of the general interests of the United States, delegates shall be annually appointed in such manner as the legislatures of each State shall direct, to meet in Congress on the first Monday in November, in every year, with a power reserved to each State to recall its delegates, or any of them, at any time within the year, and to send others in their stead for the remainder of the year.

No State shall be represented in Congress by less than two, nor more than seven members; and no person shall be capable of being a delegate for more than three years in any term of six years; nor shall any person, being a delegate, be capable of holding any office under the United States, for which he, or another for his benefit, receives any salary, fees or emolument of any kind.

Each State shall maintain its own delegates in a meeting of the States, and while they act as members of the committee of the States.

In determining questions in the United States in Congress assembled, each State shall have one vote.

Freedom of speech and debate in Congress shall not be impeached or questioned in any court or place out of Congress, and the members of Congress shall be protected in their persons from arrests or imprisonments, during the time of their going to and from, and attendance on Congress, except for treason, felony, or breach of the peace.

VI.

No State, without the consent of the United States in Congress assembled, shall send any embassy to, or receive any embassy from, or enter into any conference, agreement, alliance or treaty with any King, Prince or State; nor shall any person holding any office of profit or trust under the United States, or any of them, accept any present, emolument, office or title of any kind whatever from any King, Prince or foreign State; nor shall the United States in Congress assembled, or any of them, grant any title of nobility.

No two or more States shall enter into any treaty, confederation or alliance whatever between them, without the consent of the United States in Congress assembled, specifying accurately the purposes for which the same is to be entered into, and how long it shall continue.

No State shall lay any imposts or duties, which may interfere with any stipulations in treaties, entered into by the United States in Congress assembled, with any King, Prince or State, in pursuance of any treaties already proposed by Congress, to the courts of France and Spain.

No vessel of war shall be kept up in time of peace by any State, except such number only, as shall be deemed necessary by the United States in Congress assembled, for the defense of such State, or its trade; nor shall any body of forces be kept up by any State in time of peace, except such number only, as in the judgement of the United States in Congress assembled, shall be deemed requisite to garrison the forts necessary for the defense of such State; but every State shall always keep up a well-regulated and disciplined militia, sufficiently armed and accoutered, and shall provide and constantly have ready for use, in public stores, a due number of filed pieces and tents, and a proper quantity of arms, ammunition and camp equipage.

No State shall engage in any war without the consent of the United States in Congress assembled, unless such State be actually invaded by enemies, or shall have received certain advice of a resolution being formed by some nation of Indians to invade such State, and the danger is so imminent as not to admit of a delay till the United States in Congress assembled can be consulted; nor shall any State grant commissions to any ships or vessels of war, nor letters of marque or reprisal, except it be after a declaration of war by the United States in Congress assembled, and then only against the Kingdom or State and the subjects thereof, against which war has been so declared, and under such regulations as shall be established by the United States in Congress assembled, unless such State be infested by pirates, in which case vessels of war may be fitted out for that occasion, and kept so long as the danger shall continue, or until the United States in Congress assembled shall determine otherwise.

VII.

When land forces are raised by any State for the common defense, all officers of or under the rank of colonel, shall be appointed by the legislature of each State respectively, by whom such forces shall be raised, or in such manner as such State shall direct, and all vacancies shall be filled up by the State which first made the appointment.

VIII.

All charges of war, and all other expenses that shall be incurred for the common defense or general welfare, and allowed by the United States in Congress assembled, shall be defrayed out of a common treasury, which shall be supplied by the several States in proportion to the value of all land within each State, granted or surveyed for any person, as such land and the buildings and improvements thereon shall be estimated according to such mode as the United States in Congress assembled, shall from time to time direct and appoint.

The taxes for paying that proportion shall be laid and levied by the authority and direction of the legislatures of the several States within the time agreed upon by the United States in Congress assembled.

IX.

The United States in Congress assembled, shall have the sole and exclusive right and power of determining on peace and war, except in the cases mentioned in the sixth article—of sending and receiving ambassadors—entering into treaties and alliances, provided that no treaty of commerce shall be made whereby the legislative power of the respective States shall be restrained from imposing such imposts and duties on foreigners, as their own people are subjected to, or from prohibiting the exportation or importation of any species of goods or commodities whatsoever—of establishing rules for deciding in all cases, what captures on land or water shall be legal, and in what manner prizes taken by land or naval forces in the service of the United States shall be divided or appropriated—of granting letters of marque and reprisal in times of peace—appointing courts for the trial of piracies and felonies commited on the high seas and establishing courts for receiving and determining finally appeals in all cases of captures, provided that no member of Congress shall be appointed a judge of any of the said courts.

The United States in Congress assembled shall also be the last resort on appeal in all disputes and differences now subsisting or that hereafter may arise between two or more States concerning boundary, jurisdiction or any other causes whatever; which authority shall always be exercised in the manner following. Whenever the legislative or executive authority or lawful agent of any State in controversy with another shall present a petition to Congress stating the matter in question and praying for a hearing, notice thereof shall be given by order of Congress to the legislative or executive authority of the other State in controversy, and a day assigned for the appearance of the parties by their lawful agents, who shall then be directed to appoint by joint consent, commissioners or judges to constitute a court for hearing and determining the matter in question: but if they cannot agree, Congress shall name three persons out of each of the United States, and from the list of such persons each party shall alternately strike out one, the petitioners beginning, until the number shall be reduced to thirteen; and from that number not less than seven, nor more than nine names as Congress shall direct, shall in the presence of Congress be drawn out by lot, and the persons whose names shall be so drawn or any five of them, shall be commissioners or judges, to hear and finally determine the controversy, so always as a major part of the judges who shall hear the cause shall agree in the determination: and if either party shall neglect to attend at the day appointed, without showing reasons, which Congress shall judge sufficient, or being present shall refuse to strike, the Congress shall proceed to nominate three persons out of each State, and the secretary of Congress shall strike in behalf of such party absent or refusing; and the judgement and sentence of the court to be appointed, in the manner before prescribed, shall be final and conclusive; and if any of the parties shall refuse to submit to the authority of such court, or to appear or defend their claim or cause, the court shall nevertheless proceed to pronounce sentence, or judgement, which shall in like manner be final and decisive, the judgement or sentence and other proceedings being in either case transmitted to Congress, and lodged among the acts of Congress for the security of the parties concerned: provided that every commissioner, before he sits in judgement, shall take an oath to be administered by one of the judges of the supreme or superior court of the State, where the cause shall be tried, 'well and truly to hear and determine the matter in question, according to the best of his judgement, without favor, affection or hope of reward': provided also, that no State shall be deprived of territory for the benefit of the United States.

All controversies concerning the private right of soil claimed under different grants of two or more States, whose jurisdictions as they may respect such lands, and the States which passed such grants are adjusted, the said grants or either of them being at the same time claimed to have originated antecedent to such settlement of jurisdiction, shall on the petition of either party to the Congress of the United States, be finally determined as near as may be in the same manner as is before presecribed for deciding disputes respecting territorial jurisdiction between different States.

The United States in Congress assembled shall also have the sole and exclusive right and power of regulating the alloy and value of coin struck by their own authority, or by that of the respective States—fixing the standards of weights and measures throughout the United States—regulating the trade and managing all affairs with the Indians, not members of any of the States, provided that the legislative right of any State within its own limits be not infringed or violated—establishing or regulating post offices from one State to another, throughout all the United States, and exacting such postage on the papers passing through the same as may be requisite to defray the expenses of the said office—appointing all officers of the land forces, in the service of the United States, excepting regimental officers—appointing all the officers of the naval forces, and commissioning all officers whatever in the service of the United States—making rules for the government and regulation of the said land and naval forces, and directing their operations.

The United States in Congress assembled shall have authority to appoint a committee, to sit in the recess of Congress, to be denominated 'A Committee of the States', and to consist of one delegate from each State; and to appoint such other committees and civil officers as may be necessary for managing the general affairs of the United States under their direction—to appoint one of their members to preside, provided that no person be allowed to serve in the office of president more than one year in any term of three years; to ascertain the necessary sums of money to be raised for the service of the United States, and to appropriate and apply the same for defraying the public expenses—to borrow money, or emit bills on the credit of the United States, transmitting every half-year to the respective States an account of the sums of money so borrowed or emitted—to build and equip a navy—to agree upon the number of land forces, and to make requisitions from each State for its quota, in proportion to the number of white inhabitants in such State; which requisition shall be binding, and thereupon the legislature of each State shall appoint the regimental officers, raise the men and cloath, arm and equip them in a solid-like manner, at the expense of the United States; and the officers and men so cloathed, armed and equipped shall march to the place appointed, and within the time agreed on by the United States in Congress assembled. But if the United States in Congress assembled shall, on consideration of circumstances judge proper that any State should not raise men, or should raise a smaller number of men than the quota thereof, such extra number shall be raised, officered, cloathed, armed and equipped in the same manner as the quota of each State, unless the legislature of such State shall judge that such extra number cannot be safely spread out in the same, in which case they shall raise, officer, cloath, arm and equip as many of such extra number as they judeg can be safely spared. And the officers and men so cloathed, armed, and equipped, shall march to the place appointed, and within the time agreed on by the United States in Congress assembled.

The United States in Congress assembled shall never engage in a war, nor grant letters of marque or reprisal in time of peace, nor enter into any treaties or alliances, nor coin money, nor regulate the value thereof, nor ascertain the sums and expenses necessary for the defense and welfare of the United States, or any of them, nor emit bills, nor borrow money on the credit of the United States, nor appropriate money, nor agree upon the number of vessels of war, to be built or purchased, or the number of land or sea forces to be raised, nor appoint a commander in chief of the army or navy, unless nine States assent to the same: nor shall a question on any other point, except for adjourning from day to day be determined, unless by the votes of the majority of the United States in Congress assembled.

The Congress of the United States shall have power to adjourn to any time within the year, and to any place within the United States, so that no period of adjournment be for a longer duration than the space of six months, and shall publish the journal of their proceedings monthly, except such parts thereof relating to treaties, alliances or military operations, as in their judgement require secrecy; and the yeas and nays of the delegates of each State on any question shall be entered on the journal, when it is desired by any delegates of a State, or any of them, at his or their request shall be furnished with a transcript of the said journal, except such parts as are above excepted, to lay before the legislatures of the several States.

X.

The Committee of the States, or any nine of them, shall be authorized to execute, in the recess of Congress, such of the powers of Congress as the United States in Congress assembled, by the consent of the nine States, shall from time to time think expedient to vest them with; provided that no power be delegated to the said Committee, for the exercise of which, by the Articles of Confederation, the voice of nine States in the Congress of the United States assembled be requisite.

XI.

Canada acceding to this confederation, and adjoining in the measures of the United States, shall be admitted into, and entitled to all the advantages of this Union; but no other colony shall be admitted into the same, unless such admission be agreed to by nine States.

XII.

All bills of credit emitted, monies borrowed, and debts contracted by, or under the authority of Congress, before the assembling of the United States, in pursuance of the present confederation, shall be deemed and considered as a charge against the United States, for payment and satisfaction whereof the said United States, and the public faith are hereby solemnly pleged.

XIII.

Every State shall abide by the determination of the United States in Congress assembled, on all questions which by this confederation are submitted to them. And the Articles of this Confederation shall be inviolably observed by every State, and the Union shall be perpetual; nor shall any alteration at any time hereafter be made in any of them; unless such alteration be agreed to in a Congress of the United States, and be afterwards confirmed by the legislatures of every State.

And Whereas it hath pleased the Great Governor of the World to incline the hearts of the legislatures we respectively represent in Congress, to approve of, and to authorize us to ratify the said Articles of Confederation and perpetual Union. Know Ye that we the undersigned delegates, by virtue of the power and authority to us given for that purpose, do by these presents, in the name and in behalf of our respective constituents, fully and entirely ratify and confirm each and every of the said Articles of Confederation and perpetual Union, and all and singular the matters and things therein contained: And we do further solemnly plight and engage the faith of our respective constituents, that they shall abide by the determinations of the United States in Congress assembled, on all questions, which by the said Confederation are submitted to them. And that the Articles thereof shall be inviolably observed by the States we respectively represent, and that the Union shall be perpetual.

In Witness whereof we have hereunto set our hands in Congress. Done at Philadelphia in the State of Pennsylvania the ninth day of July in the Year of our Lord One Thousand Seven Hundred and Seventy-Eight, and in the Third Year of the independence of America.

Agreed to by Congress 15 November 1777 In force after ratification by Maryland, 1 March 1781.

Appendix C: The Constitution of the United States

17 September 1787
Adopted 21 June 1788

We the People of the United States, in Order to form a more perfect Union, establish Justice, insure domestic Tranquility, provide for the common defence, promote the general Welfare, and secure the Blessings of Liberty to ourselves and our Posterity, do ordain and establish this Constitution for the United States of America.

Article. I.

Section. 1.

All legislative Powers herein granted shall be vested in a Congress of the United States, which shall consist of a Senate and House of Representatives.

Section. 2.

The House of Representatives shall be composed of Members chosen every second Year by the People of the several States, and the Electors in each State shall have the Qualifications requisite for Electors of the most numerous Branch of the State Legislature.

No Person shall be a Representative who shall not have attained to the Age of twenty five Years, and been seven Years a Citizen of the United States, and who shall not, when elected, be an Inhabitant of that State in which he shall be chosen.

Representatives and direct Taxes shall be apportioned among the several States which may be included within this Union, according to their respective Numbers, which shall be determined by adding to the whole Number of free Persons, including those bound to Service for a Term of Years, and excluding Indians not taxed, three fifths of all other Persons. The actual Enumeration shall be made within three Years after the first Meeting of the Congress of the United States, and within every subsequent Term of ten Years, in such Manner as they shall by Law direct. The Number of Representatives shall not exceed one for every thirty Thousand, but each State shall have at Least one Representative; and until such enumeration shall be made, the State of New Hampshire shall be entitled to chuse three, Massachusetts eight, Rhode-Island and Providence Plantations one, Connecticut five, New-York six, New Jersey four, Pennsylvania eight, Delaware one, Maryland six, Virginia ten, North Carolina five, South Carolina five, and Georgia three.

When vacancies happen in the Representation from any State, the Executive Authority thereof shall issue Writs of Election to fill such Vacancies.

The House of Representatives shall chuse their Speaker and other Officers; and shall have the sole Power of Impeachment.

Section. 3.

The Senate of the United States shall be composed of two Senators from each State, chosen by the Legislature thereof for six Years; and each Senator shall have one Vote.

Immediately after they shall be assembled in Consequence of the first Election, they shall be divided as equally as may be into three Classes. The Seats of the Senators of the first Class shall be vacated at the Expiration of the second Year, of the second Class at the Expiration of the fourth Year, and of the third Class at the Expiration of the sixth Year, so that one third may be chosen every second Year; and if Vacancies happen by Resignation, or otherwise, during the Recess of the Legislature of any State, the Executive thereof may make temporary Appointments until the next Meeting of the Legislature, which shall then fill such Vacancies.

No Person shall be a Senator who shall not have attained to the Age of thirty Years, and been nine Years a Citizen of the United States, and who shall not, when elected, be an Inhabitant of that State for which he shall be chosen.

The Vice President of the United States shall be President of the Senate, but shall have no Vote, unless they be equally divided.

The Senate shall chuse their other Officers, and also a President pro tempore, in the Absence of the Vice President, or when he shall exercise the Office of President of the United States.

The Senate shall have the sole Power to try all Impeachments. When sitting for that Purpose, they shall be on Oath or Affirmation. When the President of the United States is tried, the Chief Justice shall preside: And no Person shall be convicted without the Concurrence of two thirds of the Members present.

Judgment in Cases of Impeachment shall not extend further than to removal from Office, and disqualification to hold and enjoy any Office of honor, Trust or Profit under the United States: but the Party convicted shall nevertheless be liable and subject to Indictment, Trial, Judgment and Punishment, according to Law.

Section. 4.

The Times, Places and Manner of holding Elections for Senators and Representatives, shall be prescribed in each State by the Legislature thereof; but the Congress may at any time by Law make or alter such Regulations, except as to the Places of chusing Senators.

The Congress shall assemble at least once in every Year, and such Meeting shall be on the first Monday in December, unless they shall by Law appoint a different Day.

Section. 5.

Each House shall be the Judge of the Elections, Returns and Qualifications of its own Members, and a Majority of each shall constitute a Quorum to do Business; but a smaller Number may adjourn from day to day, and may be authorized to compel the Attendance of absent Members, in such Manner, and under such Penalties as each House may provide.

Each House may determine the Rules of its Proceedings, punish its Members for disorderly Behaviour, and, with the Concurrence of two thirds, expel a Member.

Each House shall keep a Journal of its Proceedings, and from time to time publish the same, excepting such Parts as may in their Judgment require Secrecy; and the Yeas and Nays of the Members of either House on any question shall, at the Desire of one fifth of those Present, be entered on the Journal.

Neither House, during the Session of Congress, shall, without the Consent of the other, adjourn for more than three days, nor to any other Place than that in which the two Houses shall be sitting.

Section. 6.

The Senators and Representatives shall receive a Compensation for their Services, to be ascertained by Law, and paid out of the Treasury of the United States. They shall in all Cases, except Treason, Felony and Breach of the Peace, be privileged from Arrest during their Attendance at the Session of their respective Houses, and in going to and returning from the same; and for any Speech or Debate in either House, they shall not be questioned in any other Place.

No Senator or Representative shall, during the Time for which he was elected, be appointed to any civil Office under the Authority of the United States, which shall have been created, or the Emoluments whereof shall have been encreased during such time; and no Person holding any Office under the United States, shall be a Member of either House during his Continuance in Office.

Section. 7.

All Bills for raising Revenue shall originate in the House of Representatives; but the Senate may propose or concur with Amendments as on other Bills.

Every Bill which shall have passed the House of Representatives and the Senate, shall, before it become a Law, be presented to the President of the United States: If he approve he shall sign it, but if not he shall return it, with his Objections to that House in which it shall have originated, who shall enter the Objections at large on their Journal, and proceed to reconsider it. If after such Reconsideration two thirds of that House shall agree to pass the Bill, it shall be sent, together with the Objections, to the other House, by which it shall likewise be reconsidered, and if approved by two thirds of that House, it shall become a Law. But in all such Cases the Votes of both Houses shall be determined by yeas and Nays, and the Names of the Persons voting for and against the Bill shall be entered on the Journal of each House respectively. If any Bill shall not be returned by the President within ten Days (Sundays excepted) after it shall have been presented to him, the Same shall be a Law, in like Manner as if he had signed it, unless the Congress by their Adjournment prevent its Return, in which Case it shall not be a Law.

Every Order, Resolution, or Vote to which the Concurrence of the Senate and House of Representatives may be necessary (except on a question of Adjournment) shall be presented to the President of the United States; and before the Same shall take Effect, shall be approved by him, or being disapproved by him, shall be repassed by two thirds of the Senate and House of Representatives, according to the Rules and Limitations prescribed in the Case of a Bill.

Section. 8.

The Congress shall have Power To lay and collect Taxes, Duties, Imposts and Excises, to pay the Debts and provide for the common Defence and general Welfare of the United States; but all Duties, Imposts and Excises shall be uniform throughout the United States;

To borrow Money on the credit of the United States;

To regulate Commerce with foreign Nations, and among the several States, and with the Indian Tribes;

To establish an uniform Rule of Naturalization, and uniform Laws on the subject of Bankruptcies throughout the United States;

To coin Money, regulate the Value thereof, and of foreign Coin, and fix the Standard of Weights and Measures;

To provide for the Punishment of counterfeiting the Securities and current Coin of the United States;

To establish Post Offices and post Roads;

To promote the Progress of Science and useful Arts, by securing for limited Times to Authors and Inventors the exclusive Right to their respective Writings and Discoveries;

To constitute Tribunals inferior to the supreme Court;

To define and punish Piracies and Felonies committed on the high Seas, and Offences against the Law of Nations;

To declare War, grant Letters of Marque and Reprisal, and make Rules concerning Captures on Land and Water;

To raise and support Armies, but no Appropriation of Money to that Use shall be for a longer Term than two Years;

To provide and maintain a Navy;

To make Rules for the Government and Regulation of the land and naval Forces;

To provide for calling forth the Militia to execute the Laws of the Union, suppress Insurrections and repel Invasions;

To provide for organizing, arming, and disciplining, the Militia, and for governing such Part of them as may be employed in the Service of the United States, reserving to the States respectively, the Appointment of the Officers, and the Authority of training the Militia according to the discipline prescribed by Congress;

To exercise exclusive Legislation in all Cases whatsoever, over such District (not exceeding ten Miles square) as may, by Cession of particular States, and the Acceptance of Congress, become the Seat of the Government of the United States, and to exercise like Authority over all Places purchased by the Consent of the Legislature of the State in which the Same shall be, for the Erection of Forts, Magazines, Arsenals, dock-Yards, and other needful Buildings;—And

To make all Laws which shall be necessary and proper for carrying into Execution the foregoing Powers, and all other Powers vested by this Constitution in the Government of the United States, or in any Department or Officer thereof.

Section. 9.

The Migration or Importation of such Persons as any of the States now existing shall think proper to admit, shall not be prohibited by the Congress prior to the Year one thousand eight hundred and eight, but a Tax or duty may be imposed on such Importation, not exceeding ten dollars for each Person.

The Privilege of the Writ of Habeas Corpus shall not be suspended, unless when in Cases of Rebellion or Invasion the public Safety may require it.

No Bill of Attainder or ex post facto Law shall be passed.

No Capitation, or other direct, Tax shall be laid, unless in Proportion to the Census or enumeration herein before directed to be taken.

No Tax or Duty shall be laid on Articles exported from any State.

No Preference shall be given by any Regulation of Commerce or Revenue to the Ports of one State over those of another; nor shall Vessels bound to, or from, one State, be obliged to enter, clear, or pay Duties in another.

No Money shall be drawn from the Treasury, but in Consequence of Appropriations made by Law; and a regular Statement and Account of the Receipts and Expenditures of all public Money shall be published from time to time.

No Title of Nobility shall be granted by the United States: And no Person holding any Office of Profit or Trust under them, shall, without the Consent of the Congress, accept of any present, Emolument, Office, or Title, of any kind whatever, from any King, Prince, or foreign State.

Section. 10.

No State shall enter into any Treaty, Alliance, or Confederation; grant Letters of Marque and Reprisal; coin Money; emit Bills of Credit; make any Thing but gold and silver Coin a Tender in Payment of Debts; pass any Bill of Attainder, ex post facto Law, or Law impairing the Obligation of Contracts, or grant any Title of Nobility.

No State shall, without the Consent of the Congress, lay any Imposts or Duties on Imports or Exports, except what may be absolutely necessary for executing it's inspection Laws: and the net Produce of all Duties and Imposts, laid by any State on Imports or Exports, shall be for the Use of the Treasury of the United States; and all such Laws shall be subject to the Revision and Controul of the Congress.

No State shall, without the Consent of Congress, lay any Duty of Tonnage, keep Troops, or Ships of War in time of Peace, enter into any Agreement or Compact with another State, or with a foreign Power, or engage in War, unless actually invaded, or in such imminent Danger as will not admit of delay.

Article. II.

Section. 1.

The executive Power shall be vested in a President of the United States of America. He shall hold his Office during the Term of four Years, and, together with the Vice President, chosen for the same Term, be elected, as follows:

Each State shall appoint, in such Manner as the Legislature thereof may direct, a Number of Electors, equal to the whole Number of Senators and Representatives to which the State may be entitled in the Congress: but no Senator or Representative, or Person holding an Office of Trust or Profit under the United States, shall be appointed an Elector.

The Electors shall meet in their respective States, and vote by Ballot for two Persons, of whom one at least shall not be an Inhabitant of the same State with themselves. And they shall make a List of all the Persons voted for, and of the

Number of Votes for each; which List they shall sign and certify, and transmit sealed to the Seat of the Government of the United States, directed to the President of the Senate. The President of the Senate shall, in the Presence of the Senate and House of Representatives, open all the Certificates, and the Votes shall then be counted. The Person having the greatest Number of Votes shall be the President, if such Number be a Majority of the whole Number of Electors appointed; and if there be more than one who have such Majority, and have an equal Number of Votes, then the House of Representatives shall immediately chuse by Ballot one of them for President; and if no Person have a Majority, then from the five highest on the List the said House shall in like Manner chuse the President. But in chusing the President, the Votes shall be taken by States, the Representation from each State having one Vote; A quorum for this purpose shall consist of a Member or Members from two thirds of the States, and a Majority of all the States shall be necessary to a Choice. In every Case, after the Choice of the President, the Person having the greatest Number of Votes of the Electors shall be the Vice President. But if there should remain two or more who have equal Votes, the Senate shall chuse from them by Ballot the Vice President.

The Congress may determine the Time of chusing the Electors, and the Day on which they shall give their Votes; which Day shall be the same throughout the United States.

No Person except a natural born Citizen, or a Citizen of the United States, at the time of the Adoption of this Constitution, shall be eligible to the Office of President; neither shall any Person be eligible to that Office who shall not have attained to the Age of thirty five Years, and been fourteen Years a Resident within the United States.

In Case of the Removal of the President from Office, or of his Death, Resignation, or Inability to discharge the Powers and Duties of the said Office, the Same shall devolve on the Vice President, and the Congress may by Law provide for the Case of Removal, Death, Resignation or Inability, both of the President and Vice President, declaring what Officer shall then act as President, and such Officer shall act accordingly, until the Disability be removed, or a President shall be elected.

The President shall, at stated Times, receive for his Services, a Compensation, which shall neither be increased nor diminished during the Period for which he shall have been elected, and he shall not receive within that Period any other Emolument from the United States, or any of them.

Before he enter on the Execution of his Office, he shall take the following Oath or Affirmation:—"I do solemnly swear (or affirm) that I will faithfully execute the Office of President of the United States, and will to the best of my Ability, preserve, protect and defend the Constitution of the United States."

Section. 2.

The President shall be Commander in Chief of the Army and Navy of the United States, and of the Militia of the several States, when called into the actual Service of the United States; he may require the Opinion, in writing, of the principal Officer in each of the executive Departments, upon any Subject relating to the Duties of their respective Offices, and he shall have Power to grant Reprieves and Pardons for Offences against the United States, except in Cases of Impeachment.

He shall have Power, by and with the Advice and Consent of the Senate, to make Treaties, provided two thirds of the Senators present concur; and he shall nominate, and by and with the Advice and Consent of the Senate, shall appoint Ambassadors, other public Ministers and Consuls, Judges of the supreme Court, and all other Officers of the United States, whose Appointments are not herein otherwise provided for, and which shall be established by Law: but the Congress may by Law vest the Appointment of such inferior Officers, as they think proper, in the President alone, in the Courts of Law, or in the Heads of Departments.

The President shall have Power to fill up all Vacancies that may happen during the Recess of the Senate, by granting Commissions which shall expire at the End of their next Session.

Section. 3.

He shall from time to time give to the Congress Information of the State of the Union, and recommend to their Consideration such Measures as he shall judge necessary and expedient; he may, on extraordinary Occasions, convene both Houses, or either of them, and in Case of Disagreement between them, with Respect to the Time of Adjournment, he may adjourn them to such Time as he shall think proper; he shall receive Ambassadors and other public Ministers; he shall take Care that the Laws be faithfully executed, and shall Commission all the Officers of the United States.

Section. 4.

The President, Vice President and all civil Officers of the United States, shall be removed from Office on Impeachment for, and Conviction of, Treason, Bribery, or other high Crimes and Misdemeanors.

Article III.

Section. 1.

The judicial Power of the United States shall be vested in one supreme Court, and in such inferior Courts as the Congress may from time to time ordain and establish. The Judges, both of the supreme and inferior Courts, shall hold their Offices during good Behaviour, and shall, at stated Times, receive for their Services a Compensation, which shall not be diminished during their Continuance in Office.

Section. 2.

The judicial Power shall extend to all Cases, in Law and Equity, arising under this Constitution, the Laws of the United States, and Treaties made, or which shall be made, under their Authority;—to all Cases affecting Ambassadors, other public Ministers and Consuls;—to all Cases of admiralty and maritime Jurisdiction;—to Controversies to which the United States shall be a Party;—to Controversies between two or more States;—between a State and Citizens of another State,—between Citizens of different States,—between Citizens of the same State claiming Lands under Grants of different States, and between a State, or the Citizens thereof, and foreign States, Citizens or Subjects.

In all Cases affecting Ambassadors, other public Ministers and Consuls, and those in which a State shall be Party, the supreme Court shall have original Jurisdiction. In all the other Cases before mentioned, the supreme Court shall have appellate Jurisdiction, both as to Law and Fact, with such Exceptions, and under such Regulations as the Congress shall make.

The Trial of all Crimes, except in Cases of Impeachment, shall be by Jury; and such Trial shall be held in the State where the said Crimes shall have been committed; but when not committed within any State, the Trial shall be at such Place or Places as the Congress may by Law have directed.

Section. 3.

Treason against the United States, shall consist only in levying War against them, or in adhering to their Enemies, giving them Aid and Comfort. No Person shall be convicted of Treason unless on the Testimony of two Witnesses to the same overt Act, or on Confession in open Court.

The Congress shall have Power to declare the Punishment of Treason, but no Attainder of Treason shall work Corruption of Blood, or Forfeiture except during the Life of the Person attainted.

Article. IV.

Section. 1.

Full Faith and Credit shall be given in each State to the public Acts, Records, and judicial Proceedings of every other State. And the Congress may by general Laws prescribe the Manner in which such Acts, Records and Proceedings shall be proved, and the Effect thereof.

Section. 2.

The Citizens of each State shall be entitled to all Privileges and Immunities of Citizens in the several States.

A Person charged in any State with Treason, Felony, or other Crime, who shall flee from Justice, and be found in another State, shall on Demand of the executive Authority of the State from which he fled, be delivered up, to be removed to the State having Jurisdiction of the Crime.

No Person held to Service or Labour in one State, under the Laws thereof, escaping into another, shall, in Consequence of any Law or Regulation therein, be discharged from such Service or Labour, but shall be delivered up on Claim of the Party to whom such Service or Labour may be due.

Section. 3.

New States may be admitted by the Congress into this Union; but no new State shall be formed or erected within the Jurisdiction of any other State; nor any State be formed by the Junction of two or more States, or Parts of States, without the Consent of the Legislatures of the States concerned as well as of the Congress.

The Congress shall have Power to dispose of and make all needful Rules and Regulations respecting the Territory or other Property belonging to the United States; and nothing in this Constitution shall be so construed as to Prejudice any Claims of the United States, or of any particular State.

Section. 4.

The United States shall guarantee to every State in this Union a Republican Form of Government, and shall protect each of them against Invasion; and on Application of the Legislature, or of the Executive (when the Legislature cannot be convened), against domestic Violence.

Article. V.

The Congress, whenever two thirds of both Houses shall deem it necessary, shall propose Amendments to this Constitution, or, on the Application of the Legislatures of two thirds of the several States, shall call a Convention for proposing Amendments, which, in either Case, shall be valid to all Intents and Purposes, as Part of this Constitution, when ratified by the Legislatures of three fourths of the several States, or by Conventions in three fourths thereof, as the one or the other Mode of Ratification may be proposed by the Congress; Provided that no Amendment which may be made prior to the Year One thousand eight hundred and eight shall in any Manner affect the first and fourth Clauses in the Ninth Section of the first Article; and that no State, without its Consent, shall be deprived of its equal Suffrage in the Senate.

Article. VI.

All Debts contracted and Engagements entered into, before the Adoption of this Constitution, shall be as valid against the United States under this Constitution, as under the Confederation.

This Constitution, and the Laws of the United States which shall be made in Pursuance thereof; and all Treaties made, or which shall be made, under the Authority of the United States, shall be the supreme Law of the Land; and the Judges in every State shall be bound thereby, any Thing in the Constitution or Laws of any State to the Contrary notwithstanding.

The Senators and Representatives before mentioned, and the Members of the several State Legislatures, and all executive and judicial Officers, both of the United States and of the several States, shall be bound by Oath or Affirmation, to support this Constitution; but no religious Test shall ever be required as a Qualification to any Office or public Trust under the United States.

Article. VII.

The Ratification of the Conventions of nine States, shall be sufficient for the Establishment of this Constitution between the States so ratifying the Same.

The Word, "the," being interlined between the seventh and eighth Lines of the first Page, the Word "Thirty" being partly written on an Erazure in the fifteenth Line of the first Page, The Words "is tried" being interlined between the thirty second and thirty third Lines of the first Page and the Word "the" being interlined between the forty third and forty fourth Lines of the second Page.

Attest William Jackson Secretary

done in Convention by the Unanimous Consent of the States present the Seventeenth Day of September in the Year of our Lord one thousand seven hundred and Eighty seven and of the Independance of the United States of America the Twelfth In witness whereof We have hereunto subscribed our Names.

Bibliography

A List of Sources Cited and Consulted

Primary Sources

Adams, John. *Thoughts on Government.* The Adams Papers Digital Edition. Boston: Massachusetts Historical Society, 2018. http://www.masshist.org/publications/adams-papers/. Original source: Papers of John Adams, Volume 4 (February–August 1776).

Appian, *The Civil Wars.* John Carter, trans. New York: Penguin Books, 1996.

Aquinas, St. Thomas. *The Pocket Aquinas.* Vernon J. Bourke, ed. New York: Simon & Schuster, 1960.

Aristotle. *The Constitution of the Athenians.* Sir Frederick G. Kenyon, trans. New York: Hafner Publishing Co., Inc., 1950.

———. *The Politics.* T. A. Sinclair, ed. 1992 reprint. New York: Penguin Books, 1962.

———. *The Politics.* William Ellis, ed. Buffalo, NY: Prometheus Books, 1986.

Beccaria, Cesare. *On Crimes and Punishments and Other Writings.* Richard Bellamy, ed. New York: Cambridge University Press, 1995.

Bede. *Ecclesiastical History of the English People.* Leo Shirley-Price, trans. 1990 reprint. New York: Penguin Group, Inc., 1955.

Blackstone, William. *Commentaries on the Laws of England.* 4 volumes. William Draper Lewis, ed. Reprint of 1922 edition. Clark, NJ: The Lawbook Exchange, 2004.

Bodin, Jean. *Six Books of the Commonwealth.* M. J. Tooley, ed. Oxford, England: Basil Blackwell, 1955.

Burke, Edmund. *Reflections on the Revolution in France.* J. G. A. Pocock, ed. Indianapolis, IN: Hackett Publishing Company, 1987.

Bush, George W. *Address to the Nation.* Washington, DC, 20 September 2001.

Cato's Letters, or Essays on Liberty, Civil and Religious, and Other Important Subjects. 2 volumes. Ronald Hamowy, ed. Indianapolis, IN: The Liberty Fund, 1995.

Chaucer, Geoffrey. *The Canterbury Tales.* R. M. Lumiansky, ed. New York: Washington Square Press, 1971.

Cicero. *On the Commonwealth* and *On the Laws.* James E. G. Zetzel, ed. New York: Cambridge University Press, 1999.

———. *On Duties.* M. T. Griffin and E. M. Atkings, eds. New York: Cambridge University Press, 1991.

———. *On the Good Life.* Michael Grant, ed. New York: Penguin Books, 1971.

Eisenhower, Dwight. *Address to the Nation.* Abilene, KS: The Dwight D. Eisenhower Presidential Library, 17 January 1961.

Franklin, Benjamin. *The Memoirs of Benjamin Franklin.* William Temple Franklin, ed. Philadelphia, PA: McCarty & Davis, 1840.

Friends of the Constitution: Writings of the "Other" Federalists. Colleen A. Sheehan and Gary L. MacDowell, eds. Indianapolis, IN: The Liberty Fund, 1998.

Geoffrey of Monmouth. *The History of the Kings of Britain.* Lewis Thorpe, ed. New York: Penguin Books, 1966.

George Washington: A Collection. W. B. Allen, ed. Indianapolis, IN: The Liberty Fund, 1988.

Grotius, Hugo. *The Rights of War and Peace.* 3 volumes. Richard Tuck, ed. Indianapolis, IN: The Liberty Fund, 2005.

Herodotus, *The Histories.* John M. Marincola, ed. New York: Penguin Books, 1996.

Hobbes, Thomas. *Leviathan.* Richard Tuck, ed. New York: Cambridge University Press, 1996.

Hume, David. *The History of England from the Invasion of Julius Caesar to the Abdication of James the Second, 1688.* 6 volumes. Boston, MA: Phillips, Sampson, and Company, 1850.

James Madison: Writings. Jack Rakove, ed. New York: Literary Classics of the United States, Inc., 1995.

Jefferson, Thomas. *Fifth Annual Message to Congress.* New Haven, CT: The Avalon Project at Yale University, 3 December 1805.

———. *Sixth Annual Message to Congress.* New Haven, CT: The Avalon Project at Yale University, 2 December 1806.

Kennedy, John F. *Commencement Speech at American University.* Boston, MA: John F. Kennedy Presidential Library, 10 June 1963.

———. *Inaugural Address.* Boston, MA: John F. Kennedy Presidential Library, 20 January 1961.

Languet, Hubert. *Vindiciae, contra tyrannos; Or, Concerning the Legitimate Power of a Prince over the People, and of the People over a Prince.* George Garnett, ed. New York: Cambridge University Press, 2003.

Lincoln, Abraham. *Lincoln: Speeches and Writings 1859–1865.* Don E. Fahrenbacher, ed. New York: Literary Classics of the United States, Inc., 1989.

———. *Speeches and Writings 1832–1858.* Roy P. Basler, ed. New York: Literary Classics of the United States, Inc., 1989.

Livy, *Early History of Rome*. Aubrey De Sélincourt, trans. New York: Penguin Books, 1960.

———. *Rome and Italy: Books VI–X of The History of Rome From Its Foundations*. Betty Radice, ed. New York: Penguin Books, 1982.

———. *Rome and the Mediterranean*. Henry Bettenson, trans. New York: Penguin Books, 1976.

———. *The War With Hannibal*. Aubrey DeSélincourt, trans. 1972 reprint. New York: Penguin Books, 1965.

Locke, John. *Two Treatises on Government*. Peter Laslett, ed. New York: Cambridge University Press, 1960.

Lucretius. *The Nature of the Universe*. Ronald Latham, ed. Baltimore, MD: Penguin Books, 1951.

Macaulay, Thomas Lord. *The History of England*. Trevor Roper, ed. New York: Penguin Books, 1979.

———. *The History of England from the Accession to James II*. 2 volumes. New York: Harper and Brothers, 1849.

Machiavelli, Niccolo. *The Prince*. Quentin Skinner and Russell Price, eds. New York: Cambridge University Press, 1988.

Madison, James. *Notes of Debates in the Federal Constitution of 1787*. 1985 reprint. Athens, OH: Ohio University Press, 1966.

Mariana, Juan de. *De Rege et Regis Institutione; Or, The King and the Education of a King*. London: Forgotten Books, 2017.

Montesquieu, Baron de. *The Spirit of the Laws*. Anne Cohler, Basia Miller, and Harold Stone, eds. New York: Cambridge University Press, 1989.

Occupational Outlook Handbook. Bureau of Labor Statistics. Washington, DC, 17 December 2015.

Paine, Thomas. *Common Sense*. Issac Kramnick, ed. New York: Penguin Books, 1986.

———. *The Rights of Man*. New York: Oxford University Press, 1995.

Pierce, Franklin. *Veto Message*. Washington, DC: The National Archives and Records Administration, 3 May 1854.

Plato. *The Republic*. Francis Cornford, trans. New York: Oxford University Press, 1941.

Plutarch. *The Complete Collection of Plutarch's Parallel Lives*. John Dryden, trans. CreateSpace Independent Publishing Platform from Outskirts Press, 2014.

———. *Fall of the Roman Republic*. Rex Warner, trans. 1972 reprint. New York: Penguin Books, 1958.

Polybius. *The Rise of the Roman Empire*. Ian Scott-Kilvert, trans. New York: Penguin Books, 1979.

Pufendorf, Samuel von. *Of the Law of Nature and Nations*. 8 volumes. Basil Kennet, ed. Andover, Hampshire, England: Gale ECCO Print Editions, 2005.

Roosevelt, Theodore. *Fourth Annual Message. A Compilation of the Messages and Papers of the Presidents*, 1789–1908. James D. Richardson, ed. Washington, DC: Bureau of National Literature and Art, 1909.

Rousseau, Jean-Jacques. *The Social Contract and Other Later Political Writings*. C. D. H. Cole, ed. Rutland, VT: Charles E. Tuttle Co., Inc., 1973.

———. *The Social Contract and Other Later Political Writings*. Victor Gourevitch, ed. New York: Cambridge University Press, 1996.

Ruane, Kathleen Anne. *Fairness Doctrine: History and Constitutional Issues*. Washington, DC: Congressional Research Service, 2011.

Scranton, William W. *The Report on the President's Commission on Campus Unrest.* Washington, DC: U.S. Government Printing Office, 1970.

Select Orations and Letters of Cicero. J. B. Greenough and G. L. Kittredge, eds. Boston, MA: Ginn and Company, 1902.

Sidney, Algernon. *Discourses Concerning Government.* Thomas G. West, ed. Indianapolis, IN: The Liberty Fund, 1996.

Smith, Adam. *An Inquiry Into the Wealth of Nations.* Abridged. Edwin Cannan, ed. 1976 reprint. Chicago, IL: The University of Chicago Press, 1904.

St. Augustine of Hippo. *The City of God.* Vernon J. Bourke, ed. New York: Image Books, 1958.

Suarez, Francisco. *On Efficient Causality: Metaphysical Disputations 17, 18, and 19.* Alfred J. Freddoso, ed. New Haven, CT: Yale University Press, 1994.

Suetonius. *The Twelve Caesars.* Robert Graves, trans. 1989 reprint. New York: Penguin Books, 1957.

Tacitus. *The Agricola* and *The Germania.* Harold Mattingly, ed. New York: Penguin Books, 1970.

———. *The Annals of Imperial Rome.* Michael Grant, trans. 1971 reprint. New York: Penguin Books, 1956.

———. *The Histories.* Kenneth Wellesley, ed. New York: Penguin Books, 1964.

Taft, William Howard. *Presidential Addresses and State Papers of William Howard Taft: From March 4, 1909 to March 4, 1910.* New York: Doubleday, Page and Company, 1910.

The Anti-Federalists: Selected Writings and Speeches. Bruce Frohnen, ed. Washington, DC: Regnery Publishing, Inc., 1999.

The Anti-Federalist: Writings by the Opponents of the Constitution. Herbert Storing, ed. Chicago, IL: University of Chicago Press, 1981.

The Correspondence and Public Papers of John Jay. 4 volumes. Henry P. Johnston, ed. New York: G. P. Putnam's Sons, 1891.

The Federalist. The Gideon Edition. George W. Carey and James McClellan, eds. Indianapolis, IN: The Liberty Fund, 2001.

The Founders' Constitution. 5 volumes. Philip B. Kurland and Ralph Lerner, eds. 2000 reprint. Indianapolis, IN: The Liberty Fund, 1987.

The Holy Bible. New International Version. New York: Zodervan/HarperCollins Christian Publishing, 1973.

The Papers of Alexander Hamilton. 26 volumes. Harold C. Syrett, ed. New York: Columbia University Press, 1975.

The Papers of Benjamin Franklin. Volume IV. Leonard B. Larabee, ed. New Haven, CT: Yale University Press, 1961.

The Papers of George Mason. 3 volumes. Robert A. Rutland, ed. Chapel Hill, NC: University of North Carolina Press, 1970.

The Political Writings of John Adams. George A. Peek, ed. New York: Liberal Arts Press, 1954.

The Revolutionary Writings of John Adams. C. Bradley Thompson, ed. Indianapolis, IN: The Liberty Fund, 2000.

The Struggle For Sovereignty: Seventeenth-Century English Political Tracts. Joyce Lee Malcolm, ed. Indianapolis, IN: The Liberty Fund, 1999.

Thomas Jefferson: Writings. Merrill D. Peterson, ed. New York: The Library of America, 1984.

Thucydides. *History of the Peloponnesian War.* Rex Warner, trans. New York: Penguin Books, 1972.

Tocqueville, Alexis de. *Democracy in America*. Phillips Bradley, ed., 2 volumes. New York: Vintage Books, 1990.

Total Military Personnel and Dependent End Strength by Service Region Area, and Country. Defense Manpower Data Center. Washington, DC, 30 September 2014.

Truman, Harry S. *Inaugural Address*. Independence, MO: The Harry S Truman Presidential Library, 20 January 1949.

———. *Veto Message of the Internal Security Bill.* Independence, MO: The Harry S Truman Presidential Library, 22 September 1950.

Tucker, St. George. *View of the Constitution of the United States, with Selected Writings*. Clyde N. Wilson, ed. Indianapolis, IN: The Liberty Fund, 1999.

United States Department of Defense Fiscal Year 2015 Budget Request. Department of Defense, Washington, DC, 2014.

Voltaire. *Political Writings*. David Williams, ed. New York: Cambridge University Press, 1994.

Wilson, Woodrow. *Address to a Joint Session of Congress*. Washington, DC: The National Archives and Records Administration, 2 April 1917.

———. *An Address to a Joint Session of Congress*. New Haven, CT: The Avalon Project at Yale University, 8 January 1918.

Primary Sources, Court Cases, Laws, and Statutes

Ableman v. Booth, 62 U.S. 506 (1859).

An Act Declaring the Rights and Liberties of the Subject and Settling the Succession of the Crown. 1 William & Mary Sess 2 c 2. (1689).

An Act for the Union of the Two Kingdoms of England and Scotland, 1706 c. 11. *An Act Ratifying the Treaty of Union of the Two Kingdoms of Scotland and England*, 1707 c. 7.

An Act to Prevent Pernicious Political Activities (a.k.a. The Hatch Act) 5 U.S.C. §§ 1501–1508, 7321–7326 (1939).

An Act to Provide a Penalty for Restriction of Orders With Respect to Persons Entering, Remaining In, or Committing Any Act in Military Areas or Zones. Pub.L. 77–503 56 Stat. 173 (1942).

Articles of Confederation and Perpetual Union (1777).

Bas v. Tingy, 4 U.S. 37 (1800).

Burwell v. Hobby Lobby Stores, Inc., 573 U.S. ___ (2014).

Calder v. Bull, 3 U.S. 386 (1798).

Chaplinsky v. New Hampshire, 315 U.S. 568 (1942).

Charles River Bridge v. Warren Bridge, 36 U.S. 420 (1837).

Citizens United v. Federal Communications Commission, 556 U.S. 310 (2010).

Compania General de Tabacos De Filipinas v. Collector of Internal Revenue, 275 U.S. 87 (1927).

Corpus Juris Civilis (*The Institutes of Justinian*). J. B. Moyle, ed. New York: Oxford University Press, 1913.

Declaration of What Offences Shall Be Adjudged Treason, A. 25 Edw 3 St. 5 c 2. (1351).

Employment Division v. Smith, 494 U.S. 872 (1990).

Executive Order #9066 (1942).
Executive Order #9835 (1947).
Ex Parte Bollman; *Ex Parte Swartwart*, 8 U.S. 75 (1807).
Ex Parte Milligan, 71 U.S. 2 (1866).
Fairfax's Devisee v. Hunter's Lessee, 11 U.S. 603 (1813).
Fletcher v. Peck, 10 U.S. 87 (1810).
Gibbons v. Ogden, 22 U.S. 1 (1824).
Griswold v. Connecticut, 381 U.S. 479 (1965).
Hamdan v. Rumsfeld, 548 U.S. 557 (2006).
Houston v. Moore, 18 U.S. 1 (1820).
Justices Commitment Act, 17 Geo. II c. 5 (1743).
Little v. Barreme, 6 U.S. 170 (1804).
Magna Carta (1215).
Marbury v. Madison, 5. U.S. 137 (1803).
Martin v. Hunter's Lessee, 14 U.S. 304 (1816).
Martin v. Mott, 25 U.S. 19 (1827).
McCulloch v. Maryland, 17 U.S. 316 (1819).
Morford v. United States, 339 U.S. 258 (1950).
National Defense Authorization Act, Pub.L 112–81 (2011).
National Security Action Memorandum No. 263 (1963).
New World Communications of Tampa, Inc. v. Jane Akre (2D01-529–2003).
Poe v. Ullman, 367 U.S. 497 (1961).
Reynolds v. United States, 98 U.S. 145 (1878).
Rogers v. United States, 340 U.S. 367 (1951).
R v Richardson (1758) 97 ER 426.
Santa Clara County v. Southern Pacific Railroad, 118 U.S. 394 (1886).
Scott v. Sandford, 60 U.S. 393 (1857).
The Act of Settlement of 1701, 12 and 13 Will. 3 c. 2. (1701).
The Alien Registration Act of 1940 (a.k.a The Smith Act) ch. 439, 54 Stat. 670, 18 U.S.C. § 2385 (1940).
The Bounty Act of 1714. 1 Geo, 1. St. 2. (1714).
The Code of Hammurabi. Santa Cruz, CA. Evinity Publishing, Inc., 2011.
The Communist Control Act. 68 Stat. 775, 50 U.S.C. 841–844 (1954).
The Constitution of the Iroquois Nations. Lawrence, KS: The University of Kansas Press, 1985.
The Habeas Corpus Act of 1679. 31 Cha. 2 c. 2 (1679).
The Homeland Security Act. Pub.L. 107–296, 116 Stat. 2135 (2001).
The Immigration and Nationality Act of 1952 (a.k.a. The McCarran-Walter Act) Pub. L. 82–414, 66 Stat. 163 (1952).
The Judiciary Act of 1789, 1 Stat. 73.
The Land Ordinance of 1785 (1785).
The Limitation Acts. 21 Jac. 1 c. 24 (1623).
The Northwest Ordinance of 1787 (1787).
The Pendleton Civil Service Reform Act. ch. 27, 22 Stat. 403 (1883).

The Petition of Right. 3 Car. 1 c 1. (1628).
The Poor Act, 5 and 6 Edw. VI c. 2 (1551).
The Poor Act, 39 Eliz. I c. 3 (1597).
The Process of Exigent Act, 25 Edw. 3 c. 17 (1351).
The Religious Freedom Restoration Act, Pub. L. No. 103–141, 107 Stat. 1488 (1993).
The Statute of Westminster of 1275, 3. Edw. 1 c. 5 (1275).
The Treaty of Amity, Commerce and Navigation between His Brittanic Majesty and the United States of America (1796).
The Treaty of Paris (1763).
The Treaty of Paris (1783).
Treaty of Peace between the United States and Spain. 30 Stat. 1754; TS 343; 11 Bevans 615 (1898).
Trustees of Dartmouth College v. Woodward, 17 U.S. 518 (1819).
The USA Patriot Act. 115 Stat. 272 Public Law 107–56 (2001).
United States Constitution (1787).
Vagabonds and Beggars Act, 11 Hen. VII c. 2 (1495).

Secondary Sources Cited

Ackerman, Bruce. *We the People: Foundations*. Cambridge, MA: The Belknap Press of Harvard University Press, 1991.
Alden, John Richard. *The American Revolution: 1775–1783*. New York: Harper and Brothers Publishers, 1954.
Ashe, Geoffrey. *The Discovery of King Arthur*. London: Guild Books, Ltd., 1985.
Bailyn, Bernard. *The Ideological Origins of the American Revolution*. Cambridge, MA: The Belknap Press of Harvard University Press, 1967.
Barber, Richard. *Henry Plantagenet 1133–1189: A Biography*. 1993 reprint. New York: Barnes and Noble, Inc., 1964.
Belz, Herman. *A Living Constitution or Fundamental Law? American Constitutionalism in Historical Perspective*. Lanham, MD: Rowan & Littlefield Publishers, Inc., 1998.
Beveridge, Albert. *The Life of John Marshall*. 4 volumes. Boston and New York: Houghton Mifflin Company, 1916.
Biagi, Shirley. *Media Impact: An Introduction to Mass Media*. 10th edition. Boston, MA: Wadsworth Publishing Company, Inc., 2011.
Bloch, Marc. *Feudal Society*. 2 volumes. L. A. Manyon, ed. Chicago, IL: Phoenix Books, University of Chicago Press, 1961.
Borkowski's Textbook on Roman Law. Paul du Plessis, ed. 4th edition. New York: Oxford University Press, 2010.
Bradford, M. E. *Founding Fathers: Brief Lives of the Framers of the United States Constitution*. 1994 reprint. Lawrence, KS: University of Kansas Press, 1981.
Breyer, Stephen. *Active Liberty Interpreting Our Democratic Constitution*. New York: Alfred A. Knopf, 2005.

Burnett, Edmund C. *The Continental Congress.* New York: W.W. Norton and Company, 1941.

Cain, Frank. *America's Vietnam War and Its French Connection.* Abingdon, England: Routledge Books, 2016.

Cantor, Norman F. *The Civilization of the Middle Ages.* New York: HarperCollins Publishers, 1993.

Cardozo, Benjamin Nathan. *The Growth of the Law.* New Haven, CT: Yale University Press, 1924.

City and Country in the Ancient World. John Rich and Andrew Wallace-Hadrill, eds. London: Routledge Books, 1992.

Davis, Sue. *American Political Thought: Four Hundred Years of Ideas and Ideologies.* Englewood Cliffs, NJ: Prentice Hall, Inc., 1996.

Dickson, Paul, and Thomas B. Allen. *The Bonus Army: An American Epic.* New York: Walker & Company, 2004.

Douglas, William O. *A Living Bill or Rights.* Garden City, NJ: Doubleday & Company, Inc., 1961.

Edward the Confessor: The Man and the Legend. Richard Mortimer, ed. Woodbridge, Suffolk, England: The Boydell Press, 2009.

Ehrenberg, Victor. *From Solon to Socrates: Greek History and Civilization during the 6th and 5th Centuries B.C.* 3rd edition. Abington, England: Routledge Books, 2011.

Emmer, P. C., Bridget Brereton, and B. W. Higman. *General History of the Caribbean: The Caribbean in the Twentieth Century.* New York: Macmillan Educational Publishers, 2004.

Fogel, Robert William, and Stanley Engerman. *Time on the Cross: The Economics of American Negro Slavery.* Boston, MA: Little, Brown and Company, 1974.

Frazier, James Gregory. *The Golden Bough.* New York: Collier Books, 1922.

Gellner, Ernest. *Nations and Nationalism.* Ithaca, NY: Cornell University Press, 1983.

Gibbon, Edward. *The Decline and Fall of the Roman Empire.* 3 volumes. J. B. Bury, ed. New York: The George Macy Companies, Inc., 1946.

Grant, Michael. *Constantine the Great: The Man and His Times.* New York: Charles Scribner's Sons, 1993.

———. *The Founders of the Western World: A History of Greece and Rome.* New York: Charles Scribner's Sons, 1991.

———. *History of Rome.* New York: Charles Scribner's Sons, 1978.

Greene, Jack P. *Negotiated Authorities: Essays in Colonial Political and Constitutional History.* Charlottesville, VA: University Press of Virginia, 1994.

Hale, John. *The Civilization of Europe in the Renaissance.* New York: Athenaeum Books, 1994.

Hamilton, Edith. *Mythology.* Boston, MA: Little, Brown and Company, 1942.

Harris, Shane. *The Watchers: The Rise of America's Surveillance State.* New York: Penguin Books, 2011.

Harris, William C. *Lincoln's Rise to the Presidency.* Lawrence, KS: The University Press of Kansas, 2007.

Heckscher, August. *Woodrow Wilson: A Biography.* New York: Charles Scribner's Sons, 1991.

Hubbard, Bill, Jr. *American Boundaries: The Nation, the States, the Rectangular Survey.* Chicago, IL: University of Chicago Press, 2009.

Hutchison, Harold F. *Edward II: 1284–1327.* New York: David Bolt Associates, 1971.

Jenks, Edward. *The Government of the British Empire.* Boston: Little, Brown, and Company, 1918.

Jolowicz, H. F. *Historical Introduction to the Study of Roman Law*. New York: Cambridge University Press, 1932.

Kammen, Michael. *A Machine That Would Go of Itself: the Constitution in American Culture*. New York: St. Martin's Press, 1986.

Keen, Maurice. *The Outlaws of Medieval Legend*. London: Routledge Books/Taylor & Francis Group, 2013.

Kennedy, Paul. *The Rise and Fall of the Great Powers: Economic Change and Military Conflict from 1500 to 2000*. New York: Random House, Inc., 1986.

Ketcham, Ralph. *James Madison: A Biography*. Charlottesville, VA: University Press of Virginia, 1971.

Kramer, Samuel Noah. *History begins at Sumer: Thirty-Nine Firsts in Recorded History*. Philadelphia, PA: University of Pennsylvania Press, 1988.

Kydd, Andrew H. *Trust and Mistrust in International Relations*. Princeton, NJ: Princeton University Press, 2005.

Maguire, Daniel C. and A. Nicholas Fargnoli. *On Moral Grounds: The Art/Science of Ethics*. New York: The Crossroad Publishing Company, 1991.

Maier, Pauline. *American Scripture: Making the Declaration of Independence*. New York: Alfred A. Knopf, Inc., 1997.

Maitland, Frederic William. *The Constitutional History of England*. H. A. L. Fisher, ed. 1965 reprint. Cambridge, England: Cambridge University Press, 1908.

Maritan, Jacques. *Man and the State*. Washington, DC: The Catholic University of America Press, 1951.

Martin, Ralph G. *A Hero for Our Time: An Intimate Story of the Kennedy Years*. New York: Macmillan Publishing Company, 1983.

McDonald, Forrest. *E Pluribus Unum: The Formation of the American Republic 1776–1790*. 1979 reprint. Indianapolis, IN: The Liberty Fund, 1965.

McFeely, William S. *Frederick Douglass*. New York: W. W. Norton & Company, Inc., 1991.

Miller, John C. *Origins of the American Revolution*. Boston, MA: Little, Brown, and Company, 1943.

———. *Triumph of Freedom 1775–1783*. Boston, MA: Little, Brown & Company, 1948.

Miller, Nathan. *F.D.R.: An Intimate History*. Garden City, NY: Doubleday and Company, Inc., 1983.

Morris, Richard B. *Witness at the Creation: Hamilton, Madison, Jay, and the Constitution*. New York: Henry Holt and Company, Inc., 1985.

Nearing, Scott, and Joseph Freeman. *Dollar Diplomacy: A Study in American Imperialism*. New York: B. W. Heubsch and The Viking Press, 1925.

Nevins, Allan. *Grover Cleveland: A Study in Courage*. New York: Dodd, Mead & Company, 1934.

Nietzsche, Friedrich. *Beyond Good and Evil*. R. J. Hollingdale, trans. 1990 reprint. New York: Penguin Books, 1973.

Orwell, George. *1984*. New York: Penguin Books, 1983.

Paludan, Phillip Shaw. *The Presidency of Abraham Lincoln*. Lawrence, KS: The University Press of Kansas, 1994.

Pollard, Frederick, and Frederic William Maitland. *The History of English Law Before the Time of Edward I.* 2 volumes. Cambridge, England: Cambridge University Press, 1923.

Poverty in the Roman World. Margaret Atkins and Robin Osborne, eds. Cambridge, England: Cambridge University Press, 2006.

Propaganda and American Democracy. Nancy Snow, ed. Baton Rouge, LA: Louisiana State University Press, 2014.

Rakove, Jack N. *Original Meanings: Politics and Ideas in the Making of the Constitution.* New York: Vintage Books, 1997.

Reeves, Richard. *President Kennedy: Profile of Power.* New York: Simon & Schuster, 1993.

Remini, Robert V. *The Life of Andrew Jackson.* New York: HarperCollins Publishing Company, 2011.

Sharp, James Roger. *American Politics in the Early Republic: The New Nation in Crisis.* New Haven, CT: Yale University Press, 1993.

Smith, Jean Edward. *John Marshall: Definer of a Nation.* New York: Henry Holt & Company, Inc., 1996.

Smith, Page. *John Adams.* 2 volumes. Garden City, NY: Doubleday & Company, Inc., 1962.

Social Contract. Ernest Barker, ed. New York: Oxford University Press, 1960.

Storing, Herbert J. *What the Anti-Federalists Were For: The Political Thought of the Opponents of the Constitution.* Chicago, IL: University of Chicago Press, 1981.

The American Founding: Essays on the Formation of the Constitution. J. Jackson Barlow, Leonard W. Levy, and Ken Masugi, eds. Santa Barbara, CA: Praeger Books, 1988.

The American Heritage History of the Presidency. Marcus Cunliffe, ed. New York: American Heritage Publishing Co., Inc., 1968.

The Lattimer Massacre Trial: Revealing Newspaper Article Reports and Artist Sketches As And When It Happened. Pasco L. Schiavo, ed. Pittsburg, PA: Dorrance Publishing Company, 1920.

The Long War: A New History of U.S. National Security Policy Since World War II. Andrew J. Bacevitch, ed. New York: Columbia University Press, 2009.

Thomas, Evan. *Robert Kennedy: His Life.* New York: Simon & Schuster, 2000.

Thomas, Hugh. *Armed Truce: The Beginnings of the Cold War 1945–1946.* New York: Atheneum Books, 1987.

Vickers, Michael J. *The Ancient Romans.* Oxford, England: Stamford Press Pte, 1992.

Warren, Mercy Otis. *History of the Rise, Progress and Termination of the American Revolution.* 2 volumes. Lester H. Cohen, ed. Indianapolis, IN: The Liberty Fund, 1994.

White, T. H. *The Once and Future King.* New York: G. P. Putnam's Sons, 1958.

Wilentz, Sean. *The Rise of American Democracy: Jefferson to Lincoln.* New York: W. W. Norton & Company, Inc., 2008.

Wood, Gordon S. *The Creation of the American Republic, 1776–1787.* Chapel Hill, NC: The University of North Carolina Press, 1969.

Primary Sources Consulted

American Political Writing During the Founding Era, 1760–1805. Charles S. Hyneman and Donald S. Lutz, eds. Indianapolis, IN: The Liberty Fund, 1983.

Antebellum American Culture: An Interpretive Anthology. David Brion Davis, ed. University Park, PA: Pennsylvania State University Press, 1979.

Aquinas, St. Thomas. *Selected Writings.* Ralph McInerny, ed. New York: Penguin Books, 1998.

Calhoun, John C. *A Disquisition on Government and Selections from the Discourse.* C. Gordon Post, ed. Indianapolis, IN: The Bobbs-Merrill Co., Inc., 1953.

Hayek, Friedrich. *The Road to Serfdom.* London, England: Routledge & Company, Ltd., 1944.

James Madison's "Advice to My Country". David B. Mattern, ed. Charlottesville, VA: University Press of Virginia, 1997.

Malone, Dumas. *The Correspondence Between Thomas Jefferson and Pierre Samuel du Pont de Nemours.* New York: De Capo Press, 1970.

Peters, John E., and Howard Deshong. *Out of Area or Out of Reach?: European Military Support for Operations in Southeast Asia.* RAND Corporation. Santa Monica, CA, 1995.

Stewart, Robert M. *Readings in Social and Political Philosophy.* New York: Oxford University Press, 1986.

Story, Joseph. *Commentaries on the Constitution of the United States.* Volume III. Boston: Hillard, Gray and Company, 1833.

The Letters of John Adams, Addressed to His Wife. Charles Francis Adams, ed. Boston: Charles C. Little and James Brown, 1841.

The Papers of James Madison: Presidential Documents and Diaries. Manuscripts Division. Library of Congress, Washington, DC.

The Papers of James Madison. Volume VII. David B. Mattern, J. C. A. Stagg, Jeanne K. Cross, and Susan Holbrook Perdue, eds. Charlotte, VA: University of Virginia Press, 1991.

The Webster-Hayne Debate on the Nature of the Union: Selected Documents. Herman Belz, ed. Indianapolis, IN: The Liberty Fund, 2000.

Secondary Sources Consulted

Abbott David W., and Edward Rogowsky. *Political Parties.* Chicago, IL: Rand McNally College Publishing Company, 1978.

Abraham, Henry J. *The Judicial Process: An Introductory Analysis of the Courts of the United States, England, and France.* 7th edition. New York: Oxford University Press, 1998.

Amar, Akhil Reed. *America's Constitution: A Biography.* New York: Random House Books, Inc., 2006.

Arnhart, Larry. *Political Questions: Political Philosophy from Plato to Rawls.* Prospect Heights, IL: Waveland Press, Inc., 1993.

Astley, Maurice. *The English Civil War.* 1990 reprint. Phoenix Mill, Stroud, England: Sutton Publishing, Ltd., 1974.

Bailyn, Bernard. *The Origin of American Politics*. New York: Vintage Books, 1970.
Beck, Paul Allen, and Frank J. Sorauf. *Party Politics in America.* 7th edition. New York: HarperCollins Publishers, Inc., 1992.
Bennett, Lerone, Jr. *Before the Mayflower: A History of Black America.* New York: Penguin Books, 1962.
Brodie, Fawn M. *Thomas Jefferson: An Intimate Portrait.* New York: W. W. Norton & Company, 1974.
Chambers, William Nisbet. *Political Parties in a New Nation: The American Experience 1776–1809.* New York: Oxford University Press, 1963.
Cicero. *Murder Trials*. Michael Grant, trans. New York: Penguin Books, 1975
Clark, Sir George. *The Illustrated History of Britain.* New York: Oxford University Press, 1971.
Collier, Christopher, and James Lincoln Collier. *Decision at Philadelphia: The Constitutional Convention of 1787.* New York: Random House, Inc., 1986.
Draper, Theodore. *A Struggle for Power: The American Revolution.* New York: Times Books, 1996.
Ellis, Joseph J. *Passionate Sage: The Character and Legacy of John Adams.* New York: W. W. Norton & Company, 1993.
———. *Founding Brothers: The Revolutionary Generation.* New York: Alfred A. Knopf, 2001.
———. *First Family: Abigail and John Adams.* New York: Vintage Books, 2010.
Franklin, John Hope, and Alfred A. Moss, Jr. *From Slavery to Freedom: A History of African-Americans.* 7th edition. New York: Alfred A. Knopf, 1994.
Fry, Michael Graham, Erik Goldstein, and Richard Langhorne. *Guide to International Relations and Diplomacy.* New York: Continuum International Publishing, 2002.
Hall, Kermit L. *The Magic Mirror: Law in American History.* New York: Oxford University Press, 1989.
Hibbert, Christopher. *Cavaliers and Roundheads: The British at War 1642–1649.* New York: HarperCollins Publishers, Inc., 1993.
———. *Redcoats and Rebels: The American Revolution Through British Eyes.* New York: Avon Books, 1990.
Hobson, Charles F. *The Great Chief Justice: John Marshall and the Rule of Law.* Lawrence, KS: The University Press of Kansas, 1996.
Hofstadter, Richard. *The Idea of a Party System: The Rise of Legitimate Opposition in the United States, 1780–1840.* Berkeley, CA: University of California Press, 1969.
Intellectual Origins of American National Thought: Pages From the Books Our Founding Fathers Read. Wilson Ober Clough, ed. New York: Corinth Books, 1964.
Kelly, Alfred H., and Winifred A. Harbison. *The American Constitution: Its Origins and Development.* New York: W. W. Norton & Company, Inc., 1948.
Knupfer, Peter B. *The Union As It Is: Constitutional Unionism and Sectional Compromise.* Chapel Hill, NC: University of North Carolina Press, 1991.
Kolchin, Peter. *American Slavery 1619–1877.* New York: Hill and Wang, 1993.
Leckie, Robert. *The Wars of America.* 2 volumes. New York: Harper-Collins Publishers, 1992.
Maier, Pauline. *From Resistance to Revolution: Colonial Radicals and the Development of American Opposition to Britain, 1765–1776.* New York: W. W. Norton and & Company, 1972.

McDonald, Forrest. *Ordo Seclorum: The Intellectual Origins of the Constitution.* Lawrence, KS: The University Press of Kansas, 1985.

———. *States' Rights and the Union: Imperium in Imperio, 1776–1876.* Lawrence, KS: The University Press of Kansas, 2000.

Oakes, James. *The Ruling Race: A History of American Slaveholders.* New York: W. W. Norton & Company, 1982.

———. *Slavery and Freedom: An Interpretation of the Old South.* New York: W. W. Norton & Company, 1990.

Quarrels That Have Shaped the Constitution. Revised Version. John Garraty, ed. New York: Harper Torch Books, 1988.

Rakove, Jack N. *Revolutionaries: A New History of the Invention of America.* New York: Mariner Books, 2011.

Ramsay, David. *The History of the American Revolution.* 2 volumes. Lester H. Cohen, ed. Indianapolis, IN: The Liberty Fund, 1990.

Randall, Willard Sterne. *Thomas Jefferson: A Life.* New York: Henry Holt and Company, Inc., 1993.

Sabine, George H., and Thomas L. Thorson. *A History of Political Theory.* 4th edition. Hinsdale, IL: Dryden Press, 1973.

Wedgewood, C. V. *The King's War 1641–1647.* 1983 reprint. New York: Penguin Books, 1958.

Whittemore, Robert C. *Makers of the American Mind: Three Centuries of American Thought and Thinkers.* New York: William Morrow and Company, 1964.

Wilson, Peter H. *The Thirty Years War: Europe's Tragedy.* Cambridge, MA: The Belknap Press of Harvard University Press, 2009.

Professional Journals, Magazines, and Newspapers

Adams, Walter, and William James Adams. "The Military-Industrial Complex: A Market Structure Analysis". *The American Economic Review.* Nashville, TN, 1 March 1972.

Alperovitz, Gar. "The War Was Won Before Hiroshima—And the Generals Who Dropped the Bomb Knew It: Seventy Years After the Bombing, will Americans Face the Brutal Truth?". *The Nation.* New York, 8 August 2015.

Anheim, John. "Quote…Misquote". *New York Times Magazine.* New York, 21 July 2008.

Bandow, Doug. "How Many Enemies, How Much Military Spending". *Huffington Post.* Washington, DC, 25 May 2011.

Chossudrovsky, Michel. "9/11 and America's 'War on Terrorism'". *The Center for Research on Globalization.* Montreal, Quebec, Canada, 13 September 2017.

"Editorial: 'Fairness' is Censorship". *The Washington Times,* 17 June 2008.

Friedman, Uri. "The Other 9/11: A CIA Agent Remembers the Chile Coup". *The Atlantic Monthly.* New York, 11 September 2014.

Frohlich, Thomas C., and Alexander Kent. "Countries Spending the Most on Military". *USA Today.* McLean, Virginia, 12 July 2014.

Gaines, Jim. "One-In-Four Americans Want Their State to Secede from the U.S., But Why?". *Reuters News Service.* New York, 19 September 2014.

Kaufman, Alexander C. "Hobby Lobby Still Covers Vasectomies and Viagra". *Huffington Post.* Washington, DC, 2 July 2014.

Kelley, Beverly. "In Politics, Perception is the Reality". *Los Angeles Times.* Los Angeles, CA, 17 January 1999.

Kellner, Simon. "Perception is Reality: The Facts Won't Matter in Next Year's General Election". *The Independent.* London, England, 30 October 2014.

Kifner, John. "4 Kent State Students Killed by Troops: 8 Hurt as Shooting Follows Reported Sniping at Rally". *New York Times.* New York, 5 May 1970.

"New Poll: Armed Revolution Could Be Necessary, 29 Percent of Voters Believe". *Huffington Post.* Washington, DC, 2 May 2013.

O'Hagan, Andrew. "The Joys of Propaganda". *New York Times Style Magazine.* New York, 22 February 2017.

Paltrow, Scot J. "Special Report: The Pentagon's Doctored Ledgers Conceal Epic Waste". *Reuters News Service.* New York, 18 November 2013.

Petras, James. "The Soaring Profits of the Military Industrial Complex, the Soaring Costs of Military Casualties". *Global Research.* Montreal, Quebec, Canada, 24 June 2014.

Plumer, Brad. "America's Staggering Defense Budget, in Charts". *Washington Post.* Washington, DC, 7 January 2013.

"Public Perception is Just Wrong About Key Obama Issues". *Bloomberg Political Report.* New York, 9 December 2014.

"Remembering Chile's 9/11: Democracy's Final Triumph over General Pinochet". *The Guardian.* London, England, 9 September 2003.

Rivkin, David W. "The Impact of International Arbitration on the Rule of Law". *Global Arbitration Review.* London, 2012.

Stewart, James B. "When Media Mergers Limit More Than Competition". *New York Times.* New York, 25 July 2014.

Turley, Jonathan. "Big Money Behind War: the Military-Industrial Complex". *Al Jezeera.* Doha, Quatar, 11 January 2014.

Uchitelle, Lewis. "The U.S. Still Leans on the Military-Industrial Complex". *New York Times.* New York, 22 September 2017.

Other Media Sources

Welles, Orson, Joseph Cotton, and Agnes Moorhead. *Citizen Kane.* Directed by Orson Welles. Hollywood, CA: R.K. O. Pictures, 1941.

Index

A

B

C

D

E

F

G

H

I

J

K

L

M

N

O

P

R

S

T

U

V

W

X

Y

Z

www.ingramcontent.com/pod-product-compliance
Ingram Content Group UK Ltd.
Pitfield, Milton Keynes, MK11 3LW, UK
UKHW020218290926
15470UKWH00001B/264

9 781433 158353